This is a sustained and sensitive attempt to define a genuinely African philosophy in relation to African cultural life. The author approaches this task through a detailed study of the conceptual scheme of the Akan. Most such studies of traditional concepts and ways of thinking have been conducted by Western anthropologists. Professor Gyekye, however, is able to draw on his own familiarity with Akan thought and background as a professional philosopher. From extensive research of a kind rarely systematically undertaken in the past, he offers a philosophical clarification and interpretation of Akan ontology, philosophical psychology, theology, and ethics. Such individual studies of traditional African modes of thought, he argues, are necessary for the emergence of a distinctively African philosophy, to criticize and develop African thought and cultural values in the modern world.

The issues raised are of great current concern among African thinkers, but they also have more general implications for the relationship of tradition to modernity and of philosophy to other elements of a culture. Anthropologists and comparative religionists as well as philosophers will find this a lucid, substantial, and deeply felt contribution to debates about the nature of African philosophy and the place philosophy can have in the life of a society.

An essay on African philosophical thought
The Akan conceptual scheme

An essay on African philosophical thought

The Akan conceptual scheme

KWAME GYEKYE
University of Ghana

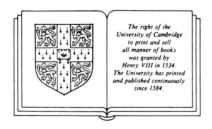

The right of the
University of Cambridge
to print and sell
all manner of books
was granted by
Henry VIII in 1534.
The University has printed
and published continuously
since 1584.

CAMBRIDGE UNIVERSITY PRESS
Cambridge
New York   New Rochelle   Melbourne   Sydney

B
5305
.G93
1987

Published by the Press Syndicate of the University of Cambridge
The Pitt Building, Trumpington Street, Cambridge CB2 1RP
32 East 57th Street, New York, NY 10022, USA
10 Stamford Road, Oakleigh, Melbourne 3166, Australia

© Cambridge University Press 1987

First published 1987

Printed in the United States of America

Library of Congress Cataloging-in-Publication Data
Gyekye, Kwame.
An essay on African philosophical thought.
Bibliography:p.
Includes indexes.
1. Philosophy, African.   2. Akans(African People)–
Intellectual life.   I. Title.
B5305.G93   1987   199′.6   87–6320

British Library Cataloguing-in-Publication Data
Gyekye, Kwame
An essay on African philosophical thought:
the Akan conceptual scheme.
1. Philosophy, African
I. Title
199′.6   B5305

ISBN 0–521–32525–0

For Dedo

Contents

vii

Contents

Preface

In recent years, with the growth in interest in the philosophical thought of African peoples, philosophers – both African and non-African – have begun to ask such questions as "Is there African philosophy?" and "What is African philosophy?" The questions clearly refer to the indigenous philosophical thought of African peoples and, given the dearth of written philosophical classics – of a doxographic tradition – in Africa's historical past generally, such questions can be regarded as apt and legitimate.

However, believing, as I do, that the lack of written philosophical literature does not by any means imply the absence of philosophical *thinking* or philosophical *ideas*, and that philosophy of some kind is behind or involved in the thought and action of every people, every culture, in my view, produces a philosophy. But as a result of the lack of writing in Africa's historical past, the indigenous philosophical output of African thinkers, in the traditional setting, has remained part of their oral traditions and has come to be expressed also in religious and sociopolitical beliefs and institutions. It has therefore seemed to me that the best and most seminal approach to dealing with the question of philosophy in African culture is by way of analytical elucidation and interpretation and critical evaluation of concepts and beliefs in traditional thought. Philosophical concepts, ideas, and propositions can be found embedded in African proverbs, linguistic expressions, myths and folktales, religious beliefs and rituals, customs and traditions of the people, in their art symbols, and in their sociopolitical institutions.

What the interested philosopher needs to do is to sort out in a more sophisticated and systematic way the philosophical elements of African thought on various fundamental questions about human life, conduct, and experience and to provide the necessary conceptual or theoretical trimming for those elements. This is what I have attempted to do in Part II, which analyzes the philosophical thought of the traditional thinkers among the Akan, the largest ethnic group in Ghana.

Let me say something from the outset about the term "African" in the title of this book. Despite the fact that the majority of this book is given to a discussion of concepts, beliefs, and propositions in *Akan* philosophical thought, I believe the appearance of the term there is justified. A basic position I have taken here is that philosophy is a cultural phenomenon, that philosophical thought is grounded in a cultural experience. It is the underlying cultural unity or identity of the various individual thinkers that justifies the reference to varieties of thought as wholes, such as Western or European or Oriental philosophy. That is, even though the individual thinkers who produced what is known as Western philosophy are from different European or Western nations, we nonetheless refer to such body of philosophical ideas as Western philosophy (in addition to, say, French, German, or British philosophy). The real reason for this is surely the common cultural experience and orientation of those individual thinkers.

I have been at pains to present facts and arguments, in Chapter 2 and in my concluding Chapter 12, to show that common features or underlying similarities are palpably discernible in the cultures and thought systems of African peoples. This underlying cultural identity, experience, and orientation should provide justification for referring to the philosophical ideas spawned by thinkers from various African nations or communities as African, *if only* the organizing concepts and categories of their philosophical investigations are extracted from the African cultural and historical experience. Yet to refer to the philosophical ideas of some African thinker as "African" does not mean at all that these ideas are necessarily held by all Africans, thinkers and nonthinkers. Thus, I do not intend the term "African" in the title of the book to mean that the philosophical ideas and doctrines of some Akan wise men examined here are necessarily held by all Africans (they are not even held by all Akans); neither do I intend it to mean that those ideas and doctrines are to be generalized for all Africans. However, I want to emphasize that for me a philosophical doctrine does not have to be shared by all Africans for it to be African; it need only be the product of the rational, reflective exertions of an African thinker, aimed at giving analytical attention or response to basic conceptual issues in African cultural experience.

Research for the publication of the book was begun some years ago - in fact a little over a decade ago. Drafts of about two-thirds of the chapters were written during the academic year of 1977–8, when I spent my sabbatical year at the University of Florida, Gainesville, as a Visiting Associate Professor of Philosophy. Before that, however, I had published some few papers on African philosophy which have found their way into this book:

1. "A Critical Review Article on John Mbiti's *African Religions and Philosophy*," *Second Order, An African Journal of Philosophy*, January 1975. A great part of this article appears in section 11.2, but in an expanded form.

2. "Philosophical Relevance of Akan Proverbs," *Second Order, An African Journal of Philosophy*, July 1975. The article is reproduced, with minor changes, in section 2.1.

3. "Akan Concept of a Person," *International Philosophical Quarterly*, September 1978. This article has greatly been expanded as Chapter 6.

4. "Akan Language and the Materialist Thesis: A Short Essay on the Relation Between Philosophy and Language," *Studies in Language*, International Journal Sponsored by the Foundations of Language, Vol. 1, No. 2, 1977. This article has been reproduced, with some changes, in section 11.1.

5. "An African Conception of Philosophy (Wisdom)," *Studia Africana*, Vol. 2, March 1978. A great part of the material of this article has been reproduced, but greatly expanded, as Chapter 4.

Chapter 12 is based on a paper I presented at a weekend symposium held at the University of Bristol in England in September 1978 under the auspices of the International Cultural Foundation of New York. Portions of this book have been presented in public lectures and seminars in some colleges and universities in the United States.

Acknowledgments

I would like, first of all, to express my gratitude to the University of Ghana's Research Committee, which granted me some financial assistance and thus enabled me to embark on the research for the publication of this book. I owe a great debt of gratitude also to the West African Aggrey Society (a Learned Society, itself originally funded by the Hazen Foundation of New Haven, Connecticut) for a huge financial grant I received for the research.

I must express my gratitude and appreciation to some individuals acknowledged in Akan communities in Ghana not only as wise men in their own right but also as the gurus of traditional wisdom. These individual wise men were most willing to put at my disposal, through interviews and discussions, not only their profound knowledge of Akan culture, lore, and tradition, but also their own thoughts and ideas. They readily and generously received me in their homes on all occasions, some of which were not, I know, very convenient for them. Among them I would like to make special mention of the following: the late Mr. J. A. Annobil of Cape Coast; Oheneba Kwabena Bekoe and Nana Boafo-Ansah, both of Akropong-Akuapem; Okyeame Akuffo Boafo ("State Linguist" during the first Republic of Ghana and for sometime Instructor in Akan Language and Culture at the University of Ghana); Mr. A. A. Opoku (formerly of the Ghana Broadcasting Corporation); the late Nana Ofori Atta III, Omanhene of Akim-Abuakwa; the late Opanin Twum Barima of Kibi, the late Nana Osei Bonsu of Kumasi, a well-known carver; and the late Okyeame Yaw Bireku of Akim-Achiasi (the author's hometown).

Acknowledgments

In bringing this book to its present form, I have benefited tremendously from the suggestions and comments of a few people who read it in draft. I thank my colleague, Professor Kwasi Wiredu, who read earlier versions of some of the chapters with great care and made elaborate comments from which I benefited a great deal. I wish to record my indebtedness to Dr. Richard A. Wright of the Department of Philosophy, University of Toledo, Ohio, who read Chapters 4–8 and whose suggestions and queries helped me a great deal to eliminate some errors and clarify my own position. Dr. Ellen S. Haring, then Chairperson of the Department of Philosophy, University of Florida, Gainesville, made helpful suggestions for improvement on Chapters 1 and 2. Sir Peter Strawson read Chapter 11, and I found his comments delightful. I salute the two anonymous referees selected by Cambridge University Press whose penetrating and trenchant comments, queries, and suggestions I found extremely helpful. I am deeply indebted to Mr. Jonathan Sinclair-Wilson, Philosophy Editor at the Press, from whose editorial assistance and skills the book has benefited immensely. I should record my gratitude and deep appreciation to my students in the University of Ghana and some colleges and universities in the United States to whom a number of chapters were presented in lectures and seminars and whose intelligent questions compelled me to clarify and amplify my own position. Any shortcomings and defects that might remain in this book, however, are the result of my own limitations.

My gratitude is extended also to Mr. Daniel Teye Korboe, an Administrative Assistant, and Mr. Emmanuel N. Okwei, Senior Administrative Assistant, both of the Department of Philosophy, who patiently produced the typescript.

Last, but not least, I should express my gratitude to my dear wife, Dedo, who most efficiently looked after the house and my three daughters – Maame, Asantewa, and Nana Abena Nyarkua – while I was away (and not infrequently) on research trips, and who accompanied me on a few of these trips. This book is gratefully dedicated to her.

Legon, Ghana   Kwame Gyekye

Guide to the pronunciation of Akan words

Since the book contains a number of Akan words, I consider it appropriate to provide the reader with a guide to their pronunciation. Even though Akan is my native language, in preparing this pronunciation guide on Akan words I consulted, on some technical matters, J. G. Christaller, *Dictionary of the Asante and Fante Language called Tshi (Twi)*, Second Edition (revised and enlarged), Basel, Basel Evangelical Missionary Society, 1933, pp. xvi–xix. Note that Asante and Fante are dialects of the Akan language.

Vowels

a as in **sat**
e as in **prey**
ē as in **let**
o as in **robe**
ō as in **rob**
u as in **flu**

The vowels ē and ō are open vowels and require the widest opening of the mouth.

The vowels are as a rule short; lengthening is indicated by doubling the letter, as in *daa* (everyday) and *afebōō* (eternally, forever).

Also as a rule, each vowel is pronounced *separately* even when it is joined to (or followed by) another vowel. Thus, there are no true (monosyllabic) diphthongs. For instance, *nkrabea* (destiny, fate) is pronounced in three syllables: *nkra·be·a*. Other instances of joined but separately pronounced vowels are *ae, ei, oi,* and *ui.*

Consonants

When they stand alone, consonants in Akan are generally pronounced as they are in English. However, unlike the Akan vowels, joined consonants are digraphic, that is, pronounced as *one* syllable. (Examples of English digraphs include *ph* in "*ph*one" and *gh* in "enou*gh*.")

ky as in **ch**ild or **ch**urch
gy softer than *ky* and close to the English *j*; my name, Gyekye, is thus pronounced **Je·**che
hy like the English *sh*; thus *hyebea* (destiny) is pronounced **she·**be·a
ny a palatalized *n*, as in O**ny**ame (God, Supreme Being)
kw It is difficult to find a suitably equivalent syllable in English for this diagraph: In pronouncing it the mouth is made to protrude (thus, **Kw**ame is pronounced as Qua·may) but the *u* after the Q is hardly sounded
nk like *ng* in si**ng**; thus in **nk**ra·be·a (destiny)

The diagraphs *tw, dw,* and *hw* are palatolabial sounds.

tw like *chw* pronounced simultaneously
dw like *dy* simultaneously pronounced with *w*, as in *dwen*, to think. In most cases *dw* passes into the English *j*; thus *Dwoda* (Monday) sounds like jo·da, and *Adwoa* (a female born on Monday) is pronounced A·jo·a (as it is in fact spelled by some Akan speakers)
hw In pronouncing this digraph the mouth is formed as for whistling.

I

The question of philosophy in African culture

1

On the denial of traditional thought *as* philosophy

Scholars, including philosophers, tend to squirm a little at the mention of African philosophy, though they do not do so at the mention of African art, music, history, anthropology, or religion. Whereas the latter cluster of disciplines has been – and is still being – cultivated or pursued by scholars, both African and non-African, in the various Centers or Institutes of African Studies around the world, African philosophy as such is relegated to limbo, and its existence doubted. Philosophy is thus assumed to be a special relish of the peoples of the West and the East.

There are, I think, two main reasons for the resilient skepticism regarding the existence of African philosophy. The first, which I shall examine in due course, is the lack of writing in Africa's historical past, which led in turn to the absence of a doxographic tradition, a tradition of recorded opinions. The second reason is that African traditional[1] thought is not always accepted as philosophy. Perhaps the best-known argument to that effect has been put forward by Robin Horton,[2] who has urged a distinction between philosophy and traditional (African) thought – a distinction that I regard as spurious because it implies that there is no philosophical component to traditional thought. Such a distinction stems, I believe, from the failure to see that "thought" is a generic or comprehensive concept under which religious, social, political, scientific, and philosophical thought, as well as other kinds, may be subsumed as species. Arguments are required to demonstrate that philosophy is not a species of thought in the case of African thought; but at the same time the confines of African thought must be delineated and reasons given for the inclusion of certain species

3

of thought in African thought. In an attempt to deny the existence of philosophy as a species of African thought, Horton asserts that the traditional cultures did not develop logic and epistemology, and "since Logic and Epistemology together make up the *core* of what we call Philosophy, we can say that the traditional cultures have never felt the need to develop Philosophy."[3] In a much earlier and well-known paper, Horton had defined philosophy thus: "And by Philosophy, I mean thinking directed to answering the question: 'On what ground can we ever claim to know anything about the world?' "[4] This definition is at best a definition of epistemology – a *branch* of philosophy – not of philosophy itself!

As Horton's characterization of philosophy in terms of epistemology is the peg on which he hangs his denial of the existence of the philosophical compcnent of traditional African thought, it deserves some consideration. In raising objections to Horton's definition and his view of what constitutes the core of philosophy, my hope is to find a more comprehensive, plausible, and attractive characterization of philosophy. The characterization I would endorse (stated in a number of places in this book) stems from a close examination of the nature and purpose of the intellectual activities of thinkers or sages from various cultures and societies of the world. That examination reveals, undoubtedly in my view, that philosophy is essentially a rational, critical, and systematic inquiry into the fundamental ideas underlying human thought, experience, and conduct – an inquiry whose subject matter *includes* epistemological concepts and categories, which Horton mistakenly singles out as constituting the main concerns of philosophy.

Several objections may be raised to Horton's thesis; but as a preliminary to my first objection, it may be asked whether he intends his assertion to be regarded as a statement of fact about the history of Western philosophy. If so, his thesis is highly disputable and should not have been presented as unqualifiedly true. On this matter one can contrast the views of several other philosophers. Abel concludes the introduction to his book with the words: "Let us begin our inquiry with the *traditional core* of philosophy, namely, *metaphysics*."[5] Sontag maintains that "Philosophy, insofar as it is the search for *first principles* or the basic assumptions implicit in any question, is metaphysics."[6] For this reason, "Every philosopher should be a metaphysician in that he should pay critical attention to his questions and to their assumed first principles. . . ."[7] In addition, Taylor asserts that "metaphysics is a foundation of philosophy, and

4

not its capstone. One's philosophical thinking, if long pursued, tends to resolve itself into basic problems of metaphysics."[8] Metaphysics, then, as fundamental to every other branch of philosophy, must constitute the core of (Western) philosophy.[9] Moreover, in a recent interview, Quine, whose works have mainly been in the fields of logic and epistemology, identified ontological problems as the main or most important questions of philosophy.[10]

Ontology (the theory of being or existence) is part of metaphysics, and it is metaphysics that, in my view, constitutes the core of Western philosophy. This conviction is suggested by the fact that what are often regarded as the perennial problems of philosophy are mostly metaphysical in character. This observation does not imply by any means that logic and epistemology are not important branches of philosophy. Metaphysics often involves epistemology, and no thinker would deny the vital importance of logic, though it is interesting to note that Aristotle, the founder of formal logic in the Western tradition, regarded it as an organon (instrument) of philosophy, not as part of it. Nevertheless, the place held now by logic in the Western tradition seems to date only from the middle of the nineteenth century.

Second, it is not clear whether Horton intends his assertion to be confined to European (or Western) philosophy, to the exclusion of Islamic, Indian, Chinese, and other kinds, or to be all-inclusive, embracing other non-Western philosophies as well. If the former, it is a mistaken view as I have just demonstrated; if the latter – that is, if he intends the reference of "what we call Philosophy" to include other, non-Western, philosophies – it is equally mistaken, for metaphysics (including mysticism) and ethics constitute the core of Islamic philosophy and of Oriental philosophies in general. "Indian Philosophy," wrote A. C. Ewing, "is traditionally more connected than English with the search for the good life in a religious sense. . . ."[11] All this means that what constitutes the core of one philosophical tradition does not necessarily constitute the core of another; how a particular subject (or set of subjects) becomes or turns out to be the core of a philosophical tradition is a complex question to unravel. Indeed, what philosophy is itself has been a bone of contention among philosophers.

Third, African traditional thought *did* develop some epistemology, at least of a rudimentary kind. Concepts such as "truth," "mode of reasoning," "skepticism," "explanation," and so on, appear in Akan thought,[12] and the linguistic expressions, proverbs,

5

and the general metaphysic of African peoples are replete with epistemological ideas and positions (see section 12.3.2). Paranormal cognition, for instance, is an important feature of African epistemology. (The fact that this mode of knowing does not occur, or occurs only marginally, in Western epistemology is irrelevant.) These African epistemological ideas and propositions, like other areas of African thought in general, were developed in a preliterate environment. As Busia noted: "The African has not offered learned and divergent disputations to the world in writing, but in his expression in conduct of awe, and reverence for nature, no less than in his use of natural resources, he demonstrates his own epistemology."[13]

I would concede, however, that there is not much evidence ("documented" in the proverbs, for instance) to demonstrate that epistemological ideas or proposals were developed to any high degree in African traditional thought comparable to that obtained in, say, post-Socratic Greek thought or post-Renaissance Western thought. The position is analogous to that of pre-Socratic Greek philosophical thought, which, of course, is known to have developed great metaphysical systems, but which appears to have paid inadequate attention to the analysis of epistemological concepts as such. Thus, writing on the history of epistemology in the Western tradition, D. W. Hamlyn observed: "The pre-Socratic philosophers, the first philosophers in the Western tradition, did not give any fundamental attention to this branch of philosophy, for they were primarily concerned with the nature and possibility of change. They took it for granted that knowledge of nature was possible. . . ." He added: "It was Plato, however, who can be said to be the real originator of epistemology, for he attempted to deal with the basic questions . . . ,"[14] that is, of epistemology.

As for the development of logic, by which Horton means formal logic, or as he puts it, "the general rules by which we can distinguish good arguments from bad ones,"[15] nothing much can be said in favor of African thought. A *formal* system of logic is hardly to be expected in a preliterate culture, even though beliefs in that culture can be accepted as rational and logical. However, the lack of the development of formal systems of logic in African thought – despite its "eminently rational and logical character," to quote Horton[16] – cannot be considered a sufficient reason for eliminating philosophy as a component of African thought, any more than the lack of formalized logic in ancient Greek philosophy *before* Aristotle

6

meant that philosophy did not exist in its completeness in ancient Greece. Pre-Socratic thought was, of course, rationally developed; so was African traditional thought. Horton in fact admits that African thought was eminently rational and logical. One important criterion of rationality is consistency, a notion that is evidenced in, for instance, the Akan proverb (referred to in section 2.1), "there are no crossroads in the ear" – meaning that one cannot accept truth and falsehood at the same time: a formulation of the principle of noncontradiction. A system of thought that is rational and focuses attention on fundamental questions about human life and experience can justifiably be considered philosophical, even though it may not have given adequate attention to the analysis of epistemological concepts.

It is pretty clear that epistemology and logic (in the sense of formal logic) did *not* constitute the core of pre-Socratic thought. And yet no one, to my knowledge, has ever denied the title of "philosophy" to pre-Socratic thought. On the contrary, pre-Socratic thought has become the foundation of the Western philosophical tradition. The obvious conclusion, then, is that to define the philosophical enterprise in terms principally of epistemology and formal logic, as Horton does, is to present it in overly narrow terms. Such narrow terms have, I have shown, no historical warrant even within the Western tradition itself, and ignore important facts in the philosophical traditions of other cultures.

When Wittgenstein and others say that the main task of philosophy is the analysis or elucidation of concepts, they refer to concepts of *all* kinds: concepts in metaphysics, ethics, epistemology, politics, aesthetics, economics, religion, science, and so on. Philosophers belonging to a given culture or era or tradition select those concepts or clusters of concepts that, for one reason or another, matter to them most and that therefore are brought to the fore in their analysis. The choice of concepts to be attended to may be determined by culture, history, intentions, hopes or fears, or by a combination of these factors. But what is clear is that the "chosen race" of concepts in time comes to make up the *core* of the philosophy of a particular group and, thus, of a particular philosophical tradition.

I have claimed that metaphysics is the core of (Western) philosophy. Metaphysics lies at the heart of African thought, for the sources do indicate that African peoples, like others, have given reflective attention to such fundamental matters as being, God, the nature of the person, destiny, evil, causality, free will, and so on (see Chapters 5 to 7 and section 12.3.1). Horton thought in fact that "most African traditional worldviews are logically developed to a high degree."[17]

The reflective impulse is also manifested in African religious thought. It is generally accepted that Africans are religious people, in the sense that they possess elaborate systems of religious beliefs and practices. Some of these are philosophical in that they deal with such fundamental questions as the meaning of life, the origins of all things, death, and related questions. In religion we seek answers to questions of ultimate existence; philosophy also is concerned with similar questions of ultimate existence.

To deny African peoples philosophical thought is to imply that they are unable to reflect on or conceptualize their experience, whereas the proverbs that, as I shall argue below, can be used with other materials as a source of African philosophical ideas are the undeniable results of reflection on their experience in the world. Philosophy proceeds from the facts of experience. In short, African thought, if it is thought at all, must encompass philosophy. It is this philosophy that must be distilled from the comprehensive thought of the community, and it is this philosophy that stands in need of elaboration, clarification, and interpretation. I cannot, therefore, accept the suggestion that the term "African philosophy" should be reserved for "that needful enterprise," the fashioning of "philosophies based upon contemporary experience with its many-sidedness." The author of this suggestion, Wiredu, thinks that African philosophy "is still in the making."[18] This view has been repeated by Bodunrin, who maintains that "an African philosophical tradition is yet in the making."[19] Yet Bodunrin at the same time admits that conscious philosophical reflection did take place in traditional Africa. "It is unlikely," he asserts, "that such conscious reflection did not take place in traditional Africa; it is however left to research to show to what extent it has. That it has cannot be denied *a priori*."[20]

The same position is taken also by Hountondji, who urges us to admit "that our African philosophy is *yet to come*." African philosophy, "like . . . African culture in general," he says "is before us, not behind us and must be created *today* by decisive action." But then he adds, curiously, that "this creation will not be effected *ex nihilo*, that it will necessarily embrace the heritage of the past and will

8

therefore rather be a *recreation*."[21] These statements are as bizarre and perplexing as they are incompatible. If African philosophy is "before us," if it is "yet to come," then we cannot *re*create it, for it makes no sense to speak of *re*creating that which is in the future. However, if we can in fact *re*create African philosophy – an action that cannot be "effected *ex nihilo*," then it follows surely that not all of it is before us or yet to come! Thus, Hountondji is forced by the logic of his own statements to affirm the reality of the African traditional philosophy that he denies because, according to him, it is a collective philosophy and therefore a myth.[22] Also, if by "heritage" Hountondji means African heritage, then he cannot talk of our heritage of the past and at the same time assert that "African culture in general is before us, not behind us." The culture of a people comprises the people's beliefs, values, mentalities, institutions, habits, ways of life, and so on. Are these constituents of African culture "before us" yet to be created? Of course not. If, on the other hand, he means the European heritage, then he is greatly mistaken, for we cannot create (or re-create) African philosophy – certainly not all aspects of it – out of the European heritage: If we could, it would not, to my mind, be African philosophy (see sections 2.4 and 12.4).

Further, the denial of the philosophical component of African thought cannot really be accepted. The reason is that philosophy, as an intellectual activity, is universal; it cannot be assumed to be confined to the peoples of the West and the East. Philosophy of some kind is involved in the thought and action of every people and constitutes the intellectual sheet anchor of their life in its totality. It is not given to humanity to make itself immortal; but it is certainly given to humanity to philosophize. We cannot but philosophize, that is, pose fundamental questions, and reflect on fundamental aspects, of human life, conduct, and experience (see section 2.4). In other words, although peoples of the world live in different cultural environments, there is nevertheless a common ground of shared human experiences, and hence there certainly are some basic questions relating to their existence on this planet that may commonly be asked by them, questions that are bound to exercise their minds *as* humans. Such questions, I believe, may be universal, transcending cultural and historical frontiers, even though the philosophical doctrines and propositions put forward in answer to them may in fact be very dissimilar and divergent.[23] Moreover, answers to philosophical questions provided by thinkers from different cultures may differ in quality, sophistication, and persuasiveness. For this reason, it should not surprise anyone to discover that a number of problems raised in philosophy elsewhere have been raised also in African thought, and that some of the doctrines found in Western philosophy, for instance, can be found also in African thought. As an example: Long before any Akan thinker read Plato, St. Augustine, or Descartes, and long before the Bible was introduced to the Akan people, some of the thinkers among them had, on my analytical interpretation of the sources, considered a person to be composed of two basic substances, a spiritual one that they called *ōkra* (soul) and a physical one that they called *nipadua* or *honam* (body, flesh) (see sections 6.1 and 6.2).

When I claim that philosophical activity is universal, I mean simply that thinkers from different cultures or philosophical traditions ask similar philosophical questions and think deeply about them. It is in terms of the philosophical attitude, of the propensity to raise questions relating to the fundamental principles underlying human experience and conduct, and not in terms of the uniformity of doctrinal positions, that philosophy can be said to be universal. This approach to certain fundamental questions about human experience is, in my view, the common denominator of all philosophical activities or doctrines.

It is therefore legitimate to make the assumption that every culture produces a philosophy, or, put differently, that there is a philosophical component to a culture's thought system. Because the philosophies of some cultures have been written down for centuries and as a result of the dissemination of the written word, it has been possible over time for those philosophies to be interpreted, elucidated, refined, and extensively developed both vertically and horizontally. The philosophies of some other cultures, notably those of Africa, have not met with such fortune, and have consequently remained part of the oral tradition.

Thus, in Africa philosophical ideas are not to be found in documents,[24] for traditional African philosophy is not a written philosophy, although this does not mean that it cannot be written down. Such ideas were embodied in proverbs, aphorisms, or fragments (as such pithy philosophical sayings are called in the context of pre-Socratic Greek philosophy). Yet this fact does not in any way imply the nonexistence of African philosophy. Socrates

10

did not write anything, although he inherited a written culture; but we know, thanks to Plato, that he *philosophized*. (This indicates that even as a discipline philosophy need not be a literary activity, despite all that can be said in favor of literacy.) In India, "the Upanishads, which are imbued with philosophy . . . were not written down for centuries."[25] An eminent Indian philosopher wrote: "The Vedas were handed down from mouth to mouth from a period of unknown antiquity . . . When the Vedas were composed, there was probably no system of writing prevalent in India."[26] (The Vedas constitute the religious and philosophical classics of India; the Upanishads form the concluding portions of the Vedas. Another Indian philosopher also wrote that written "Indian philosophy can be considered to be a series of footnotes to the Upanishads."[27]) Buddha "wrote no book, but taught orally."[28] Thus, traditional African philosophy is none the worse for the absence of written philosophical literature, for the absence of written philosophical literature does not in any way imply the absence of philosophical *thinking* or philosophical *ideas*.

Now, if the arguments so far advanced are valid, then it is indeed a mistake to maintain that the term "African philosophy" should be used to cover only the philosophy, that is, the written philosophy, that is being produced by contemporary African philosophers. For philosophy, whether in the sense of a worldview or in the sense of discipline – that is, in the sense of systematic critical thought about the problems covered in philosophy as worldview – is discoverable in African traditional thought. And my concern in Part II of this book, which is specifically on Akan thought, is to provide a systematic analysis and exposition of some aspects of that thought. I am *not* creating that thought as such; although an elaborate interpretation may – and sometimes must – involve the interpreter's own insight, this is not so far-reaching as to blur or tilt the essential orientations of that system. The difference between interpretative analysis of African thought and that of, say, Aristotle or al-Fārābī, lies mainly in the fact that whereas the sources of the former are unwritten, the sources of the latter are, of course, written. This fact makes it much easier to investigate the latter than the former. Nevertheless, both kinds of system are interpretable and analyzable. Thus, I conclude, with regard to African thought, that what is "still in the making," in my opinion, is *modern* African philosophy. Consequently, a distinction must be made between traditional African philosophy and modern African philosophy:

I. Question of philosophy in African culture

The latter, to be *African*, and have a basis in African culture and experience, must have a connection with the former, the traditional. The sources of traditional African philosophical ideas are the subject of the next chapter.

2

Philosophy and culture

2.1. Sources of African philosophical thought

African philosophical thought is expressed both in the oral ✗
literature and in the thoughts and actions of the people. Thus, a
great deal of philosophical material is embedded in the proverbs,
myths and folktales, folk songs, rituals, beliefs, customs, and
traditions of the people, in their art symbols and in their sociopolitical institutions and practices. In this connection, let me refer to the
views of several scholars, including philosophers, who have noted
some African cultural forms as expressive of philosophy. Wrote
Herskovits:

> In a culture as highly organized as that of Dahomey, . . . there
> was no lack of opportunity for the development of a complex
> philosophy of the Universe. The upper-class Dahomean does
> not need to restrict himself to describing concrete instances
> when discussing the larger concepts underlying his everyday
> religious practice, he is not at a loss when questions of the
> nature of the world as a whole, or abstract principles such as
> justice, or destiny, or accident are asked him.[1]

Parrinder wrote: "Art is a means of expressing a basic philosophy of
life. . . ."[2] Abraham observed that "As the Akans could not write,
they expressed their philosophicoreligious ideas through art. . . ."[3]
Fagg adverted to the religious and philosophical basis and content
of African art.[4] The philosophical content of African art emanates

13

from its well-known symbolic character. Also, art is one of the areas of African cultural tradition where the critical impulse of the African mind comes to the fore (see section 3.1).

Religious beliefs and practices in their complexities constitute an important source of African philosophical thought. Observed Idowu:

> The religion of the Yoruba . . . finds vehicles in myths, folktales, proverbs and sayings, and is the basis of philosophy. As there are no written records of the ancient past of the people, all that has been preserved of their myths, philosophy, liturgies, songs and sayings, has come to us by word of mouth from generation to generation.[5]

Mbiti's view was, "As with proverbs, the collection and study of religious songs is very scanty, and yet this is another rich area where one expects to find repositories of traditional beliefs, ideas, wisdom and feelings."[6] Busia wrote that "Akan drum language is full of riddles that conceal reflective thought and philosophy,"[7] and that "Funeral dirges philosophize on human life and death."[8] But philosophy in traditional Africa is also expressed or reflected in social values and has never confined itself to pure conceptualizations. For instance, the humanistic strand in Akan philosophic thought is expressed in the compassionate concern that people in an Akan community feel for their fellow man, in the social institution of the clan (*abusua*) with its web of kinship ties, and in other social relationships.

Africans, like other peoples, are endowed with mythopoeic imagination, and the continent abounds in myths and tales which, in the African setting, as certainly in others, are important as vehicles for abstract thought. Idowu observed that ". . . Odu myths enshrine the theological and philosophical thoughts of the Yoruba . . ."[9] The folktales, Rattray noted, "mirror more or less accurately the ideas of the people and their general outlook upon life, conduct and morals."[10] We can discern elements of speculative thought in the myths. One myth, briefly discussed in section 7.2.2, reveals or presents the position of the Akan thinkers on destiny, human choice, and free will. Another Akan myth conceives of the Supreme Being (Onyame: God) as withdrawing himself from human beings in consequence of the ungenerous act of an old woman who used to strike heaven (sky), the abode of the Supreme Being, with her pestle while preparing a meal. The Supreme Being

14

was, prior to her action, supposed to be very near to our physical world. The myth presents the notion of transcendence, a notion that entails the rejection of pantheism, which is the idea that equates God (Onyame) with the sum of all things.

To get at the full philosophical import of myths, however, requires detailed examination. The myths can be said to be imaginative representations of religious or philosophical (metaphysical) ideas or propositions; they presuppose conceptual analysis and conceal philosophical arguments or conclusions. Parmanides, Plato, and other philosophers have resorted to myths in order to present thought. Of Plato, Stewart wrote: "Myth. . .is an essential element of Plato's philosophical style and his philosophy cannot be understood apart from it."[11] A serious philosophical attention to African myths will, I believe, yield fruitful result. Such philosophical questions as the meaning and purpose of life, the origin of the world, God, human destiny, death, and other issues are the subject of myths.

Proverbs or aphorisms, like myths, can be utilized as a source of philosophical thought in Africa. "It is in proverbs," according to Mbiti, "that we find the remains of the oldest forms of African religious and philosophical wisdom."[12] I wish, however, to discuss the philosophical features of African proverbs as found in the Akan tradition. But my remarks may well apply to the proverbs as they feature in the traditions of other African peoples.

In 1879 J. G. Christaller, a German scholar and missionary who collected over three thousand Akan proverbs,[13] wrote in the preface of his work:

> May this collection [that is, of proverbs] give a new stimulus to the diligent gathering of folklore and to the increasing cultivation of native literature. May those Africans who are enjoying the benefit of a Christian education make the best of this privilege, but let them not despise the sparks of truth entrusted to and preserved by their own people and let them not forget that by entering into their way of thinking and by acknowledging what is good and expounding what is wrong they will gain the more access to the hearts and minds of their less favored countrymen.

R. S. Rattray, a British anthropologist in the employ of the colonial administration of the Gold Coast (now Ghana) in the early decades of this century, had this to say about the proverbs:

I. Question of philosophy in African culture

The few words [of the Author's Note] the present writer has felt it duty bound to say, lest the reader, astonished at the words of wisdom which are to follow, refuse to credit that a "savage" or "primitive" people could possibly have possessed the rude *philosophers, theologians, moralists, naturalists and even it will be seen philologists, which many of these proverbs prove them to have had among them.*[14]

In the recent literature on Akan – and for that matter African – proverbs, however, attention has generally been directed to the literary and the rhetorical aspects or roles of the proverbs.[15] Several writers[16] have also pointed out the significance of the proverbs for Akan axiology, that is, its system of values. But to my knowledge no serious attention has been given to explaining or pointing out the relevance of these proverbs to a general philosophy, although the rhetorical role of the proverb seems, I believe, to derive from some philosophical truth that may be embedded in it of which truth the maker or user of the proverb intends to persuade the listener(s). Nor has there been any real attempt to weave appropriate proverbs together in order to construct a coherent ethics or moral philosophy of the Akans. Of course, philosophers like Danquah[17] and Abraham[18] have made adroit philosophical use of Akan proverbs, and in doing so have already assumed the philosophical relevance of the proverbs. One fundamental task, however, must be accomplished: the delineation of the proverbs' philosophical features and explanation of why they can and ought to be utilized as a source of Akan philosophical ideas, alongside the myths, folktales, beliefs, and customs of the Akan people. I attempt that task in the paragraphs that follow.

Let us start by looking at the Akan word for proverb, *ebe* (pl. *mme*). The word, as I learned in the course of my field research, is linked etymologically with the word for palm tree, *abe* (pl. *mme*).[19] It turns out that there is an affinity between the characteristic features of the palm tree (*abe*) and those of the proverb (*ebe*). Products like palm oil, palm wine, broom, palm-kernel oil, and soap can be derived from the palm tree. The point to note is that these products all result from processes such as distillation. The palm-kernel oil or the palm wine is not immediately obvious to the eye as the juice of the orange is, for instance; they lie deep in the palm tree. In the same way, when someone says something that is not immediately understandable, the Akans say *wabu ebe*, "he has created or uttered a

16

proverb." In such a case one must go deeply into the statement in order to get at its meaning. The meaning of a proverb is thus not obvious or direct; it is profound, not superficial, the distillate of the reflective process. A Socratic philosophic statement such as "Virtue is knowledge" or "No one willingly does wrong" is certainly the result of an elaborate, perhaps also complex, reflective process. [Incidentally, I should make it clear that I am not concerned with establishing general criteria for distinguishing between those terse or pithy sayings in the language that are regarded as proverbs and those that are not so regarded. It must suffice that there are some pithy sayings in the Akan language that are regarded by the users of the language as proverbs (*mmɛ̄*).]

Some writers have described African proverbs as "situational." Mbiti says: "[But] proverbs in particular deserve a separate treatment since their philosophical content is mainly *situational*."[20] William Bascom says: "Proverbs, which are the most important type of aphorism in Africa, have a deeper meaning than is stated literally, a meaning which can be understood only through the analysis of the social *situations* to which they are appropriate."[21] And Ruth Finnegan writes: "A knowledge of the *situations* in which proverbs are cited may also be an essential part of understanding their implications."[22] These writers suggest that the meaning of African proverbs cannot be properly grasped except by reference to certain social situations from which the proverbs arose. This may be true for four reasons. First, some of the things referred to in the proverbs may be local and so may be the characteristics that are attributed to them. For instance, regarding the proverb *obi ntōn ne akokobere kwa* ("One does not sell his hen without reason"), one might ask what is so important about the hen. Second, some of the proverbs are the conclusions of some local folktales. For instance, the proverb *woamma wo yōnko antwa nkron a, wo nso wonntwa du* ("If you do not let your neighbor have nine, you will not have ten") is the conclusion of a folktale in which the egoistic behavior of Ananse (the Spider) brings him to a miserable state. This proverb, and others like it, is a repudiation of ethical egoism, the doctrine that everyone ought to pursue his own interests to the total disregard of those of others. Third, some of the proverbs derive from the customs and beliefs of the people and from certain events in their history. Fourth, one needs to know the rhetorical context in which a proverb is used in order to work out its meaning. Proverbs are, in this respect, like metaphors.

I. Question of philosophy in African culture

The characterization of the proverb as "situational" has an important implication for the nature of Akan philosophy. That implication is embodied in the Akan proverb *asem mmae a abebu mma* ("If the occasion has not arisen, the proverb does not come"), or its positive equivalent *asem ba a na abebu ba* ("When the occasion arises, it calls for a proverb"). The key word here is the ambiguous *asem*. In these proverbs it may be rendered as "situation," "occasion," "circumstance," "event," "happening," "experience." On this showing, proverbs must have arisen out of the experiences of the people. They must be the result of reflection on their experiences in the world, telescoped for us in language. The terseness of the proverb indicates that it is a summary of complex ideas that are condensed so that they are memorable in an environment that knew no writing.

But if the proverbs are distilled from experience and in turn form one of the sources of Akan philosophical ideas, then the Akan philosophical system may be characterized at least partly as empiricist, not rationalist. Abraham's view that "Because morality was [so] based on metaphysical beliefs, the ethics of the Akan was rationalistic"[23] is implausible. If by "rationalistic" he meant that for the Akan thinkers moral ideas and ideals derive from reason or mind independently of experience, then he is mistaken. Morality for the Akan originates from society and its experiences; it is the result of a social awareness and need; morality for them is essentially a social phenomenon (see Chapter 8). The experiential nature of the proverbs is the important implication in the description of the proverbs as "situational," although this point may not have loomed large in the minds of the writers who used the words "situational" or "situation" in connection with the proverbs.

Elliptical and enthymematic in expression, these pithy sayings are pregnant with philosophical significance. Their character may in fact be likened to the Socratic maxims – which were given elaborate rational discussions and justification in the writings of Plato and Aristotle. An Akan proverb like *nkrabea nyinaa nsē* ("Each destiny is unlike any other") or *obi nnyē yiye nnya bōne* ("The pursuit of beneficence brings no evil on him who pursues it"), in its cryptic character is as analogous to the Socratic maxim "No one willingly does wrong" or "Virtue is knowledge," as it is to any of the sayings of the Chinese philosopher Confucius (551–479 B.C.):

18

2. Philosophy and culture

> If you set your mind on humanity, you will be free
> from evil.
> If one's acts are motivated by profit, he will have
> many enemies.
> He who learns but does not think is lost, he who
> thinks but does not learn is in danger.
> A good man does not worry about not being
> known by others but rather worries about not
> knowing them.[24]

These examples indicate that a philosophical claim or doctrine can be stated in as few words as the author thinks fit, knowing that amplification and clarification may always be supplied later. Therefore, it would be inconsistent to regard as philosophical the statement "every event has a cause" found in, say, Aristotle or Leibniz and refuse to regard as philosophical the Akan proverb "everything has its 'because of'" (i.e., every action or event has a reason or cause), or to take the statement "what is was to be" to be philosophical and not the Akan saying "what is fated to prosper or succeed cannot be otherwise."

One essential difference, however, between the Socratic (or the Confucian) and the Akan case is that whereas we usually know the author of the former type of maxim, we do not know who in an Akan community created a particular proverb. Lacking a tradition of recorded opinions, we cannot generally trace the individual origin of a particular proverb.[25] Nevertheless, a proverb must have been originated by someone. On the other hand, however, the proverbs, like the maxims, can be explained rationally by the *anyansafo* (sages, philosophers) of the Akan community who, in fact, were the originators of the proverbs because it is they who engage in reflective thinking.

The proverbs are about God, the world, the nature and destiny of man, social and political life, moral principals, pleasure, happiness, and so on. Thus, they are not only about Akan values but touch the various branches of philosophy. Let me now illustrate this briefly.

The proverbs *nsēm nyinaa ne Nyame* [translated by Danquah as "God is the justification (end cause) of all things"] and *asase teré na Onyame ne panyin* ("The earth is wide but God is the chief") perhaps indicate the ontological principle that God is the ultimate being. From the proverb *nnipa nyinaa ye Onyame mma, obi nnyē asase ba* ("All men are children of God, no one is a child of the earth"), we

19

infer the Akan conception of humans as theomorphic beings, having in their nature an aspect of God; this is what they call *ōkra*, soul. This proverb has moral overtones, for there must be something intrinsically valuable in God for everyone to claim to be His child. Man, being a child of God, would also be intrinsically valuable, and as such he is an end in himself and must not be used as a means to an end – a sidelight into Akan humanism. The latter doctrine is attested also in the proverb *onipa ne asēm: mefrē sika a, sika annye so, mefrē ntama a, ntama annye so, onipa ne asēm*, that is, "It is man that counts: I call upon gold, it answers not; I call upon drapery, it answers not. It is man that counts."

The following cluster of proverbs *onipa nnyē abē na ne ho ahyia ne ho* ["Man is not a palm tree that he should be complete (or self-sufficient)"]; *onipa na ōma onipa yē yie* ["The prosperity (well-being) of man depends upon man"]; and *wo nsa nifa hohorow benkum, na benkum nso hohorow nifa* ("The right arm washes the left arm, and the left arm also washes the right arm") – all of these indicate the social character of Akan ethics and the view that the good of all determines the good of each. Seek the good of the community and you seek your own good. Seek your own good and you seek your own destruction. Mutual aid, interdependence, is a moral obligation.

As mentioned earlier in passing, the ethical doctrine of egoism is repudiated in Akan moral philosophy, as attested also in the proverbs *wutiatia obi de so hwehwē wo de a wunhu* ("Trampling on another's right to seek your own, ends in disappointment") and *Obiako di ewo a ētoa ne yam* ("If one eats the honey alone, it plagues one's stomach").

Akan notions of fatalism and predestination are expressed in such proverbs as *Onyame nkrabea nni kwatibea* ("There is no bypass to God's destiny"); *Onyankopon nkum wo na ōdasani kum wo a wunwu da* ("Unless you die of God, let living man kill you, and you will not perish"); *asēm a Onyame de asie no, ōteasefo nnan no* ("The order God has settled, living man cannot subvert"); and *yēkra wo tuo a wunnwu agyan ano* ("If you were destined to die by the gun, you would not die by the arrow").

Finally, the proverb *aso mu nni nkwanta* ("There are no crossroads in the ear") indicates that one cannot accept truth and falsehood at the same time – a formulation of the principle of noncontradiction, which asserts that no statement can be both true and false. Examples might be multiplied.

2. Philosophy and culture

Concepts like God, human nature, fate (destiny), egoism, the social contract, and others that are referred to in Akan proverbs of course figure prominently in Western, and perhaps also in Oriental, philosophy. One need not suppose, however, that the philosophical ideas expressed or implied in the proverbs were not original to the Akan thinkers, for the Akan thinkers, not being literate in European languages, could hardly have borrowed those ideas from European sources.

If Akan proverbs were of philosophical interest only if they could be used to produce a philosophical system different from that of the West or the East, one might ask, Why should the Akan philosophical system be necessarily different from any other? If my remarks regarding the possibility of doctrinal affinities in world philosophies are reasonable, then we cannot maintain that the philosophical system of one people must necessarily be different in all respects from that of another people. From the Akan proverbs already cited and the philosophical ideas that they embody, on some philosophical questions the answers of the Akan thinkers may well be similar to those of thinkers of the West or the East, but on others they may be different. It may be concluded, then, that if one found in the Akan philosophical system analogues of, say, Western philosophical problems and doctrines, and one then jumped to the conclusion that Western conceptual schemes have been imposed on the Akans, or that certain inarticulate and "woolly" African thoughts have been forced into Western or foreign conceptual pigeonholes in order to win them some "respectability," one would be mistaken.

Akan proverbs are the wise sayings of individuals with acute speculative intellects. They become philosophically interesting when one sees them as attempts to raise and answer questions relating to the assumptions underlying commonly held beliefs and to make a synthetic interpretation of human experience. As already noted, Akan proverbs, like other African proverbs, generally do not have identifiable authors, though this fact does not detract from the value of the ideas they contain. In the history of Western philosophy, for instance, not all the authors of philosophical ideas are known; some have remained anonymous.[26] In some cases, the authenticity of the authorship of particular philosophical treatises has been challenged by scholars.[27] The authenticity of some of the fragments themselves (which, as a source of knowledge of early Greek philosophy are, I believe, analogous to African proverbs) has been questioned.[28] Some scholars have argued that the *Categories*

21

was not the authentic work of Aristotle but that of a pupil.[29] Whoever the author, there is no denying that the ontological doctrine adumbrated in this treatise has been very influential and has been the point of departure in many subsequent explorations. In Islamic philosophy, also, we come across the same phenomena: anonymous authorship, false attributions, controversies over authorships.[30] The author of a philosophical treatise known as *Theology of Aristotle*, which was in fact a modified version of the *Enneads of Plotinus* and had a significant influence on Islamic thought, was unknown. The authorship of a very important philosophical Arabic treatise known as *Fusus al-Hikma* ("Bezels of Wisdom") has been in dispute. The treatise was long believed to be the work of al-Fārābī (d. A.D. 950). Georr,[31] however, argued that it was composed by a pupil of al-Fārābī, whereas[32] Pines argued that it was the work of Avicenna (d. A.D. 1037). The significance of the treatise lies in the fact that it enunciated the distinction between essence and existence for the first time in the history of philosophy. Gilson describes the distinction as an "epoch-making distinction . . . it marks a date in the history of metaphysics."[33] All this indicates that attention is to be rightly given more to *ideas* than to their authors, who themselves must have been subject to various diffuse influences. In the African or Akan case, therefore, attention must be paid to the ideas embodied in the proverbs, myths, and fables, the anonymity of their authors notwithstanding.

Two concluding observations: There was a period of proverbs or aphorisms in the history of Indian philosophy. We learn that the first attempts at systematic thinking in India "were presented in the form of aphorisms, which are pithy and often incomplete sentences, easy to remember at a time when writing was not in vogue and knowledge was transmitted orally from father to son and from teacher to pupil."[34] The difference between the African and the Indian cases is that whereas, with the introduction of writing into Indian culture, the aphorisms were explicated, this did not happen with the introduction of writing into African culture. Regarding the Indian aphorisms, Raju observed: "But the aphorisms, being pithy and incomplete, themselves required an explanation. And this was furnished in the form of commentaries in which different commentators introduced their own ideas and doctrines to supply missing links in thought."[35] The writing of philosophical commentaries on the proverbs not only enlarged the meaning and understanding of the proverbs, but also led to the emergence of identifiable individuals to whom specific philosophical propositions or doctrines could be attributed.

My second observation is this: The primary sources of knowledge and study of the philosophical thought of the early thinkers in ancient Greece are "fragments." These fragments, some of which are disjointed, are the words of the early Greek philosophers themselves that have survived in citations or quotations. "By a fragment," wrote G.S. Kirk, who has done much work on pre-Socratic philosophy, "is meant an authentic quotation of an author's own words."[36] With regard to the fragments of Heraclitus (fl. 500 B.C.), Kirk observed:

> It is possible that Heraclitus wrote no book, in our sense of the word. The fragments, or many of them, have the appearance of being *isolated statements*. . . . In or perhaps shortly after Heraclitus' lifetime a *collection of these sayings* was made, conceivably by a pupil . . . Originally Heraclitus' utterances had been *oral and so were put into an easily memorable form*.[37]

Some of the sayings attributed to Heraclitus are, according to Guthrie, "a random collection."[38] On the nature of the fragments, another scholar has observed: "Since the fragments that survive . . . consist mostly of *single sentences*, we have little or no direct evidence as to how the *various ideas* in it were assembled, but their pithiness and profundity are still unmistakable."[39] The fragments were, thus, a collection of sayings (Greek: *gnomai*, sayings, aphorisms, maxims) and, because of their philosophical content or relevance, surviving fragments were utilized by later thinkers engaged in the reconstruction and resurrection of early Greek philosophy.

Here are some examples of the fragments attributed to Heraclitus:[40]

Much learning does not teach understanding.

Unless you expect the unexpectable you will never find truth, for it is hard to discover and hard to attain.

Everything flows and nothing abides.

You cannot step twice into the same river, for other waters are continually following on.

Thus many of the surviving fragments are cryptic, elliptical, and pithy, not unlike African proverbs and maxims. The use of proverbs, aphorisms, or sayings to formulate a philosophical proposition or doctrine was therefore not a method peculiar to African thinkers in the past. That method, as we have seen, was employed by the forebears of Western and Indian philosophy. It would be inconsistent, therefore, to recognize the fragments as embodying our earliest intimations of Greek philosophy, and then to refuse to accept (some) African proverbs and sayings as *a* source of knowledge of African traditional philosophy.

2.2. Collective and individual thought

African traditional philosophical thought has been described by several scholars as "collective," either because it is supposed to be the production of all or most of the members of the community, or because it is supposed to be accepted by the whole community; whereas when we talk of Greek philosophy we usually mean the philosophical ideas of individual thinkers, and the same goes for German philosophy, British philosophy, Islamic philosophy, and all other kinds. In Africa's historical past, there has been an absence of the latter kind of philosophers, that is, *known* and *identifiable* individual thinkers who stand out and can claim to have originated specific philosophical doctrines and to whom we can trace such doctrines. But surely it was individual wise men who created African "collective" philosophy. A *particular thought or idea* is, as regards its genesis, the product of *an individual mind*. And although it is logically possible for two or more individuals to think the same thought or to have the same idea at the same time, nevertheless the production of the thought as such is the work of the mind of each of the individuals concerned. It is always an individual's idea or thought or proposition that is accepted and gains currency among other people; at this stage, however, it is erroneously assumed to be the "collective" thought of the people. "Collective" thought, then, is a misnomer. There is, strictly speaking, no such thing as "collective" thought, if this means that ideas result from the intellectual production of a whole collectivity. What has come to be described as "collective" thought is nothing but the ideas of individual wise people; individual ideas that, due to the lack of doxographic tradition in Africa, became part of the pool of communal thought, resulting in the obliteration of the differences among these ideas, and in the impression that traditional thought was a monolithic system that does not allow for divergent ideas. Yet, as productions of individual intellects, we can reasonably conceive these ideas (or some of them) to be varied and divergent.

2. Philosophy and culture

In the light of the foregoing, I completely reject Hountondji's characterization of African traditional philosophy as a myth simply because, as he sees it, it is a collective philosophy,[41] which he takes to mean a philosophy that is "common to all Africans," that to which "all Africans are supposed to adhere."[42] He vehemently opposes such labels as "Yoruba philosophy," "Dogon philosophy," and "Akan philosophy,"[43] as well as the "Yoruba concept of a person" and the "Negro–African philosophy of existence,"[44] because it is implicitly assumed – wrongly, he would say – that all the people of a community or a nation adhere to those conceptions. Such an assumption, according to Hountondji, is a myth, "the myth of unanimity," the myth of "consensus."[45] But Hountondji is unwarranted in asserting that the phrase "Akan concept of a person" means implicitly or explicitly that all Akans accept or agree with the concept. In Chapter 3.1, I argue the meaningfulness and appropriateness of such phrases, which Hountondji finds so repugnant.

Some people, like Hountondji, wish to denigrate, if not ignore, the relevance and impact of the culture on the reflections of the individual thinker. Believing, as they do, that philosophizing is a wholly individualistic affair, they fail to recognize that the thinker perforce operates on the diffuse and inchoate ideas of the cultural milieu. We obviously cannot divorce the philosophy of an individual thinker from the ideas current among the people, for the philosophy of the individual thinker is rooted in the beliefs and assumptions of the culture. It is precisely because a philosophy has – and must have – its roots or basis in the culture of a people that we are justified in referring to the philosophical ideas of Socrates, Plato, and Aristotle as Greek philosophy; of Locke, Berkeley, and Hume as British philosophy; of some unnamable individual wise men in Akan society as Akan philosophy; and so on. How can we possibly refer to the ideas of the above-mentioned philosophers as Greek or British if those ideas did not have a basis in the culture, traditions, and mentalities of the societies that nurtured them, or if those ideas were palpably antithetical to the Greek or British cultural ethos? These questions are important, and I intend to examine them more closely. The relationship between philosophy and culture is the pivot on which my thesis regarding the nature of African philosophy turns.

I believe that philosophy is the product of a culture. It would certainly be instructive and rewarding to examine the philosophical doctrines of individual thinkers in the West and East against their cultural background. Given the limitations of space, a couple of cases, must suffice. We begin with Thales, an acknowledged forerunner in the Western philosophical tradition. Thales (fl. 585 B.C.) was one of the Ionian (Greek) philosophers who have been credited with making a breakthrough in Western man's conception of natural phenomena, which hitherto was given to explaining them in mythological and supernatural terms. The three Western philosophical forebears (Thales, Anaximander, and Anaximenes) are known to have explained natural phenomena in rational and scientific terms. They are, thus, said to have succeeded in effecting a transition from *mythos* to *logos*. Their main concern, however, was to look for the ultimate principle (*arche*) of all things. Thales, it is said, found this principle in water: All things originated from water. We learn from Aristotle that the notion of the origin of all things from water was common in the mythological traditions of the Greeks and the peoples with whom they came in contact. In Greek mythology Ocean was the father of all things.[46] Similarly, the Ionian notions that the universe is animated (*empsychon*) and that the cosmic processes somehow parallel the vital activity of which men are conscious in their own living have a long background in prehistory.[47] Cornford, a great scholar of ancient Greek philosophy, was of the opinion that "the minds of the Ionian philosophers were not pure intelligences, absolutely vacant and presenting to the external world the placard 'To be let unfurnished.' "[48] (That is, stated positively, the minds of the Ionian philosophers were already furnished with the ideas, beliefs, thoughts of their society.) After adverting to Anaximander's concept of the unlimited (*apeiron*), Cornford added that he did not think that the concept was originated by Anaximander. He consequently observed: "It may mean that the image, or concept, or belief is *part of our social tradition*, which we have been taught and remember. The authoritative character is due to the sanction of the collective mind of our group. This applies to our moral ideas and beliefs."[49] In his inaugural lecture in Cambridge University in 1931, Cornford observed that philosophical discussion in any given epoch is determined by a set of tacit assumptions, which are *"that groundwork of current conceptions shared by all men of any given culture and never mentioned because it is taken for granted as obvious."*[50] Russell intended, in his history of philosophy, "to exhibit each philosopher, as far as truth permits, as an outcome of his *milieu*, a man in whom were crystallized and

2. Philosophy and culture

concentrated thoughts and feelings which in a vague and diffused form, were *common* to the community of which he was a part."[51] In the preface of another edition of this same book he wrote: "My purpose is to exhibit philosophy as an integral part of social and political life: *not as the isolated speculations of remarkable individuals.*"[52] Consequently, he was led to observe that "Aristotle's opinions on moral questions are always such as were conventional in his day."[53] Aristotle in his ethical investigations takes as his starting point the current views about happiness or virtue: "It is enough if we take the most common opinions and those that seem reasonable."[54]

In his theorizing about the nature of the soul, Aristotle begins by maintaining the indivisible unity of the soul and body, and so appears to be setting himself against the mainstream of Greek psychology, which saw the soul and the body as distinct entities. But realizing that the logic of his position implies the mortality of the soul on the disintegration of the body – a position that flies in the face of Greek traditional views – he introduces a concept called the Active Intellect [*nous poeitikos*], which is part of the soul and which he says is eternal and immortal[55] – a position that was consonant with tradition. Indeed, the identity between goodness and happiness in Greek moral thought dates from the times of Homer. Thus, a scholar of Aristotle's ethics, Hardie, remarked that "Aristotle in the EN [the *Nicomachean Ethics*] is at least in part an interpreter of Greek experience . . ." as well as "an acute and wise commentator on the human situation."[56] In sum, then, one may observe that Greek philosophy grew out of the minds of the people and was in fact a component of Hellenic culture.

In modern philosophy how can we explain the persistence of rationalism among continental philosophers on the one hand, and of empiricism among British philosophers on the other hand, if not by reference, respectively, to "the European mind" and "the British mind?" How can we explain the preponderance and the resilience of the spiritual (religious) element in Oriental philosophies if not by reference to "the Oriental mind" and traditions? In such contexts "mind" refers to the characteristic mentalities, the habits and tendencies of thought produced by actions, and the impressions resulting from experience. So understood, "mind" is the product of certain unconscious social or cultural influences and experiences that to a great extent determine, or at least influence, the intellectual bent of an individual thinker.

All this means that we cannot completely and absolutely separate the philosophy of an individual thinker from that of the people and the age. On the contrary, there is an intimate, perhaps organic, relationship between an individual thinker and the general beliefs and thoughts of the community. So-called folk ideas and beliefs constitute the warp and woof of the intellectual fabric of the individual philosopher, whose importance lies in an ability to make coherent, through criticism, the diffuse ideas, beliefs, and feelings of the community. Individual thinkers are heirs to a whole apparatus of concepts and categories within which they work out their thought. They inherit the very language they use to express their ideas, and thus from the outset the bent of their thought is influenced. This conceptual scheme may be modified over time through the critical activities of individual thinkers. But these critical efforts are themselves engendered and made possible by a given conceptual scheme. Such critical efforts are generally aimed at refining or trimming a conceptual system, not at subverting that system root and branch. Thus, although Aristotle set out to demolish Plato's Theory of Forms – the hub of Plato's philosophical system – and therefore to deal a blow at Greek rationalism, he came in the end to establish a system that was to all intents and purposes analogous to the Platonic.

I shall now suggest an answer to a question that bothers some scholars who, seeking a uniformity or universality in approaches to philosophizing, are skeptical about proverbs as a source of African philosophical thought because they do not find parallels in other philosophical traditions. (The roles of the proverbs in the history of Indian philosophy and the fragments of early Greek philosophy to which I have already referred, are closed books to them.) Okere, for instance, has asked the question (to which he anticipates a negative answer), "Do European proverbs qualify too as European philosophy?"[57] This question can easily be resolved within the context of the relationship between the general ideas of the people in a community and the philosophy of an individual thinker who shares a cultural and traditional background with them. If it is true that there is a close relationship between the ideas of a given culture and the philosophy of an individual thinker who belongs to that culture, then the proverbs, insofar as they contain some of the ideas of the people, surely form part of the philosophical heritage of that people, be they Africans, Europeans, Indians, or what have you. Inasmuch as European proverbs, as I demonstrated earlier, constitute one of the sources of the European community's stock of *ideas*, which the individual thinker uses and shapes, they may be said to be embodied in European philosophies – even though one cannot *now* lay his finger on a particular proverb and show how it was philosophically used by a Locke, a Hume, or a Hegel.

One of the conclusions of the foregoing discussion is that we can legitimately and intelligibly speak of Akan or Yoruba philosophy. Such a philosophy was, to be sure, the production of *individual* wise people in the Akan or Yoruba community, whose thoughts were influenced by the ideas and beliefs of the community. What the modern African philosopher can, and ought to, do is to explicate, interpret, and sort out in a sophisticated way the conceptions of such individual wise persons, with a view to making those conceptions more presentable to the contemporary philosophical palate. The general ideas, some of which may be inchoate, that should form the basis of an analytical interpretation, already exist, as do the languages that are vestibules to the conceptual world.

2.3. Language and philosophical thought

A number of philosophers have come to the realization that language, as a vehicle of concepts, not only embodies a philosophical point of view, but also influences philosophical thought. This observation implies that the lines of thought of a thinker are, at least to some extent, determined by the structure and other characteristics of his or her language, such as the grammatical categories and vocabulary. Thus, it is admitted by students of Aristotle's philosophy that though his doctrine of the categories was ontological and logical and not linguistic, it derived from a consideration of linguistic facts.[58] Thus, it has been suggested that "If Aristotle had spoken Chinese or Dacotan, he would have had to adopt an entirely different logic or at any rate an entirely different theory of categories."[59] Sandman has observed:

> It is more than probable that certain basic features of Aristotle's logic were suggested to him by grammatical distinctions, and it is doubtful whether the "substance-accidence" relation would have been given the place of honor in logical theory by a philosopher speaking a language for which the contrast between the noun and the verb was less significant than in Greek.[60]

29

I. Question of philosophy in African culture

Perhaps one of the areas of philosophy in which one can most clearly discern the influence of language is ontology. In the *Republic* (596ᵃ), Plato says: "Whenever a number of individuals have a common *name*, we assume them to have also a corresponding Idea (or Form)." His point here is that the fact that we are able to apply one predicate expression to a number of different individuals implies that there *is* (or *exists*) an entity, that is, a common property, named by the predicate expression in which each of the individuals participates (to use Platonic terminology): If *x* is red and *y* is red and *z* is red, then there must be something, "redness," which they all have or participate in. We find Aristotle also arguing as follows:

> And so one might even raise the question whether the words "to walk," "to be healthy," "to sit" imply that each of these things is existent, and similarly in any other case of this sort; for none of them is either self-subsistent or capable of being separated from substance, but rather, if anything, it is that which walks or sits or is healthy that *is* an existent thing. Now these are seen to be more real because there is something definite which underlies them which is implied in such a predicate; for we never use the word "good" or "sitting" without implying this.⁶¹

Aristotle is saying that because in our normal linguistic activities, which are based on grammatical structures, we say "Kwame is walking," "Kwame is healthy," "Kwame is sitting," and so on, therefore there must be some entity, Kwame, who is the doer of all these actions or in whom qualities like "health" and "goodness" inhere, and without whom the actions and qualities (that is, objects designated by predicate expressions) would not be. From this Aristotle concludes that entities designated by singular subject expressions, such as Kwame, have an independent sort of existence, whereas the referents of predicate expressions depend for their existence on their subjects (or substances, to use Aristotelian terminology). Substances then are more basic ontologically than the designata of predicate expressions.

Scholars of Greek ethics point out that Greek moral thought is essentially teleological, rather than deontological. That is to say, that an action is considered morally good and commendable insofar as it is conducive to the attainment of some purpose or end (Greek: *telos*) and that the notion of "duty for duty's sake" or of "rightness" as an intrinsic characteristic of a particular action is alien to Greek

30

moral thought. The teleological thrust of Greek moral thought has been found to be connected with Greek moral *language*. "For in the Greek language there is really no word that means 'ought' or 'right' in the sense in which we (that is, English language speakers) use them to imply the idea of moral obligation. The chief moral term upon which they would naturally start their investigations is the word Agathos, which we translate as 'good.' "[62] But the Greek word *agathos* – good – as applied to a person means that the person performs that which fulfills or attains his end or purpose success-fully;[63] not one who is generous, kind, compassionate, considerate of the needs of others, and so on, as the notion is conceived in other moral philosophies.

J. L. Austin observed that "when we examine what we should use in what situations, we are looking again not merely at words . . . but also at the *realities we use the words to talk about*: we are using a sharpened awareness of words to sharpen our perception of, though not as the final arbiter of, the phenomena."[64] In Africa Alexis Kagamé, who has examined the concept of being among the Rwanda–Burundis, has shown that Bantu metaphysical categories are based on grammatical categories of the Bantu language.[65] Mbiti informs us that in the East African languages there are no concrete expressions to convey the idea of a distant future. From this he infers a two-dimensional conception of time, with a long past and a present.[66] (An examination of the Akan language of time, however, leads to a different conclusion: see section 11.2.) Thus, it is pretty clear that linguistic structures and characteristics influence – and may in fact determine – the construction of moral and metaphysical doctrines. It may therefore be said that language does not merely suggest, but may also embody, philosophical perspectives. For it seems that every language implies or suggests a vision of the world. Consequently, in Part II of this book, which is devoted specifically to the analyses of concepts in Akan thought, I have made extensive use of the Akan language and its linguistic structure.

If ontologies or philosophies are thus influenced by the structures and characteristics of languages, then they must be relativistic. Some philosophers think that philosophical problems or theses are language-oriented and depend on language for their plausibility or validity. This means that philosophical theses are strongly influenced by the characteristics of the languages in which they are formulated, and that no meaningful and profound analysis or comprehension of the theses can be achieved without adequate attention to the structures and characteristics of those languages. I do, however, argue in section 11.1 that, whereas language may embody a philosophical insight, the question of whether or not a particular philosophical problem or thesis is language-oriented cannot be determined on a priori grounds, antecedent to the actual examination of that problem or thesis formulated in one language within the context of the characteristics of another language.

Logic, the most exact branch of philosophy, may even be influenced or determined by language. The problem that has exercised the minds of philosophers and logicians is: Do logical laws derive from language rules or are they language-neutral and therefore independent of the particular language in which they are formulated? What is the relationship between logic and the grammatical rules of a language?

This problem, which is still being discussed by philosophers of logic, engaged medieval Islamic philosophers and logicians as well. Some of them held that the Greek logic that had come to them in translation was established on the basis of the Greek language and its grammatical rules. Inasmuch as these rules are different from those of the Arabic language, Greek logic therefore could not be "imposed" upon the Arabic-speaking peoples.[67] An opportunity exists for the African philosophical logician and philosophical linguist to investigate the grammatical structure of an African language in order to see what light it can throw on logical theories.

2.4. On defining African philosophy: some proposals

In Chapter 1, I responded to Wiredu's assertion that African Philosophy "is still in the making" by saying that what is still in the making is *modern* African philosophy, which is to be distinguished from traditional African philosophy. I consider Part II of this book as subsumed under traditional African philosophical thought, the indigenous philosophical thought of the Akan people that has been handed down from generation to generation. By modern African philosophy, I refer to the philosophy that is being produced by contemporary African philosophers, but which *reflects*, or has a *basis* in African experience, thought categories, and cultural values. This being so, the distinction between traditional and modern African philosophy cannot be hard and fast. For some of the elements or categories of traditional thought, because of their outstanding

2. *Philosophy and culture*

qualities, their persistent influence, or their inseparability from the cultural life and thought of the people, will naturally find their way into the modern African philosophical syllabus.

At the second Congress of Negro Writers and Artists held in Rome in 1959, the Commission on Philosophy passed the following resolution:

> Considering the dominant part played by philosophic reflection in the elaboration of culture, considering that until now the West has claimed a monopoly of philosophic reflection, so that philosophic enterprise no longer seems conceivable outside the framework of the categories forged by the West, considering that the philosophic effort of traditional Africa has always been reflected in vital attitudes and has never had purely conceptual aims, the Commission declares:
> (1) *that for the African philosopher, philosophy can never consist of reducing the African reality to Western systems*;
> (2) that the African philosopher must base his inquiries upon the fundamental certainty that the Western philosophic approach is not the only possible one; and therefore,
> (a) urges that the African philosopher should *learn from the traditions, tales, myths and proverbs of his people*, so as to draw from them the laws of a true African wisdom complementary to the other forms of human wisdom and to *bring out the specific categories of African thought.*
> (b) calls upon the African philosopher, faced by the totalitarian or egocentric philosophers of the West, *to divest himself of a possible inferiority complex*, which might prevent him from starting from his African being to judge the foreign contribution. . . .[68]

I consider this resolution to be significant. It underlines the idea that modern African philosophers must base themselves in the cultural life and experience of the community. While reflecting modern circumstances, such philosophical activity may commit itself to refining aspects of traditional thought in the light of modern knowledge and experience.

The cultural or social basis (or relevance) of the philosophical enterprise seems to indicate that if a philosophy produced by a modern African has no basis in the culture and experience of African peoples, then it cannot appropriately claim to be an *African* philosophy, even though it was created by an African philosopher.

33

I. Question of philosophy in African culture

Thus, the philosophical works of the eminent Ghanaian thinker Anton Wilhelm Amo,[69] who distinguished himself by his philosophical acumen in Germany in the eighteenth century, cannot be regarded as *African* philosophy. It is obviously an oddity that the thought of an African philosopher cannot count as African philosophy. Yet, given the reality or relevance of the cultural element involved in philosophizing, this oddity cannot be dispelled, but stares us in the face. Wiredu has argued that African thought, which is traditional – an expression that, for Wiredu, means (as far as Africa is concerned) "pre-scientific" and "non-scientific" – should not be compared with Western thought, which is scientific.[70] It should instead be compared with Western folk thought. But Wiredu allows a comparison between Western philosophy and "the philosophy that Africans are producing today."[71] But it is indisputably true that a *very* great part of the philosophy being produced by African philosophers today is based on Western categories, concepts, mentalities, and experience, and is therefore most appropriately regarded as a *contribution* to the study and understanding of Western philosophy.

According to Wiredu, because the ancestors of the modern African philosopher "left him no heritage of philosophical writings," therefore the modern African philosopher "must of necessity study the written philosophies of other lands. . . . *In this way* it can be hoped that a tradition of philosophy as a discursive discipline will eventually come to be established in Africa which future Africans and others too can utilize."[72] Thus, Wiredu advocates that, because of the lack of philosophical writings in Africa's historical past, Western or other foreign concepts and categories should be made the points of departure for (modern) African philosophy. Having immersed themselves in Western and other philosophies, African thinkers would then be in the position to establish in Africa a tradition of philosophy as a discipline. But Western philosophy was itself brewed in a cultural soup whose ingredients were the mentalities, experiences, and the folk thought and folkways of Western peoples. Toward the end of his paper referred to in the preceding paragraph, however, Wiredu, surprisingly, urges the African philosopher to "pay more attention" to "his own background of folk thought."[73] It is not clear what role, in Wiredu's scheme, the examination of African folk thought can play in the building up of a tradition of philosophy that is to be based on the categories of Western philosophy.

34

2. Philosophy and culture

Even though Bodunrin sees the desirability of African philosophers setting their works in an African context, he says that this need not be so. Consequently, he asserts: "Thus, if African philosophers were to engage in debates on Plato's epistemology . . . their works would qualify as African philosophy."[74] This position Bodunrin presents as that of a school of philosophy in Africa.[75] The position, I take it, is generally that African philosophy of the "professional" type "which is only just beginning"[76] can develop through participation in controversies on the philosophical works of individual Western philosophers. I disagree, for two main reasons. First, such participation would merely serve to enlarge our understanding of the work of those Western philosophers; they would be contributions – perhaps excellent ones – to the appreciation of those philosophies, and cannot properly claim to be part of an African philosophy. It is well known, for example, that some American philosophers study – and thus contribute to the development of – Indian or Chinese philosophy, but they do not consider such contributions as part of American or Western philosophy. American students of philosophy would be surprised if Confucianism and the Upanishads were presented to them as part of the American philosophical heritage, even though this does not detract from the fact that non-American (non-Western) philosophies could enrich American or Western philosophical outlook or experience.

Second, Bodunrin's position on the nature and content of African philosophy is a case, in my opinion, of putting the cart before the horse. In attempting to establish an African philosophical tradition one should rather start one's investigations from the beliefs, thought, and linguistic categories of African peoples. It is interesting to note that in adverting to the philosophical approaches of Socrates and the beginnings of Greek philosophy in general, Bodunrin sees that Greek philosophy was born through "*a criticism of traditional cultural beliefs*,"[77] that is, the cultural beliefs of the Greeks. Why cannot an authentic (modern) African philosophy be born in the same way, that is, through the analysis and critical evaluation of African cultural beliefs and experiences?

I now turn briefly to the prescriptions of Hountondji for the nature of African philosophy, which I find even more misguided because, unlike Wiredu and Bodunrin, Hountondji states them without qualification. Having discounted African traditional philosophy as philosophy on the grounds that it is a collective activity – wrongly assumed to be common to all the people – whereas

35

philosophy is an individual enterprise, Hountondji then presents what he calls "a new concept of African philosophy."[78] This "new concept" must be made to "include all the research into Western philosophy carried out by Africans."[79] He opines that "the African philosophers who think in terms of Plato or Marx and confidently take over the theoretical heritage of Western philosophy, assimilating and transcending it, are producing authentic African work."[80] He describes this as "a radically new definition of African philosophy, the criterion now being the *geographical origin of the authors* rather than an alleged specificity of content."[81]

This to me is a tissue of errors, to which much of my criticism of Wiredu and Bodunrin also applies. The so-called new concept of African philosophy may be "radically new," but it is equally radically false and radically unacceptable. If a philosopher geographically located in Africa spends his or her lifetime studying and researching into Western philosophy, that work, according to Hountondji, will count as authentic African philosophy. This geographical criterion will not do. An American or British philosopher, geographically located in the United States or Great Britain, who spends a lifetime studying and researching into Chinese or Indian philosophy would never imagine that he or she is producing an authentic American or British work. So far as he or she is concerned, the contribution is being made to Chinese or Indian philosophy, not directly to American or British philosophy. The reason is not that Chinese or Indian philosophy is inferior to British or American philosophy, but that the categories, assumptions, values, and mentalities upon which the former is based are different (at least in some respects) from those of the latter. Again, if a British philosopher teaching a course on ancient Greek philosophy in London assigns *my* published articles on Plato and Aristotle to students, he or she would not be assigning articles on African philosophy, even though the articles were written by an African geographically located in Africa. The reason the British philosopher would assign my articles for a course in Greek philosophy is that he or she believes them to help in the understanding of issues in *Greek* philosophy, that they make some *contribution* to the knowledge of *Greek* philosophy.

In sum, then, much of what Hountondji is urging modern African philosophers to do is, in my view, merely to *contribute* to the study of Western philosophy, forgetting the history and the constituents (elements) of this philosophy. Yet the philosophy of a

36

2. Philosophy and culture

people is invariably a tradition. But a tradition requires that its elements (or most of them) be intimately related to the mentalities and cultural ethos of the people who possess the tradition, that these elements be related among themselves in a meaningful way, that they endure and be sustained, and that they be the subject of continuous pruning and refinement. (Note that I do not rule out the possibility of alien elements enriching a tradition, but such a tradition must already be standing on its own feet, as it were.)

Now, how can a tradition of *African* philosophy be established when modern African philosophers are immersed in contributing to Western philosophy? Is the African tradition in philosophy to be built by employing the concepts and categories of Western thought as the subject matter of African philosophical debates? And for all time? I submit that a respectable tradition of philosophy in Africa will be established only when modern African philosophers engage on the field, primarily, of African conceptual schemes, only when African philosophical arguments are presented with concepts and categories derived from African thought and experience as the elements of philosophical activity. This prescription is suggested by a knowledge of the history of philosophy in other cultures of the world. Acquaintance with that history shows the difficulty of basing African philosophy purely on the Western tradition of philosophy.

Islamic culture might perhaps be offered as an example in which the origins of philosophy were related to the philosophical writings of other lands. It is not, however, a satisfactory example if considered closely.

Philosophical thought in Islam is sometimes considered as having been based on foreign – in this case Greek–Hellenistic – concepts and categories.[82] The Arabs, having received Greek philosophy and science in translation in and after the ninth century A.D., studied them thoroughly and made commentaries on them. In time, Islamic philosophy emerged, whose categories and concepts, according to the story, were wholly, or almost wholly Greek (or better, Greek–Hellenistic). But this account of the beginnings of philosophy in Islam is not accurate. For, before A.D. 800, after which date translations of the Greek–Hellenistic scientific and philosophical works into Arabic began to be made, some philosophical thinking had been going on among the Muslim philosophical theologians (*Mutakallimūn*) through their reflections on the doctrines of the Koran. The Koran, like other scriptures, contains some doctrines

37

that appear to be inconsistent and therefore puzzling to the philosophically inclined mind. For instance, although asserting the
absolute unity of God, it also speaks of divine attributes without
making clear the logical relation between God and those attributes;
although affirming divine causality and creation, it also speaks of
human free will, and so on.[83] Such conflicting or puzzling doctrines
produced both philosophical and theological debates.

The first group of scholars to raise philosophical issues arising
out of Koranic doctrines were the Mutazilites, who were the first
Muslim rationalists, for they considered reason as the criterion of
knowledge. The earliest form of philosophical speculation in Islam
was thus occasioned by an attempt to make the religious doctrines
of the Koran internally coherent, an attempt that did not wait upon
translations of the Greek philosophical works into Arabic. A rider
that must be added here, however, is that Greek philosophical
doctrines and debates were certainly of great relevance and assistance in the formulation and discussion of the philosophical problems that arose in Islam. Greek logic in particular was consciously
and consistently pursued by Muslim scholars, who generally regarded logic as an organon (Arabic: *āla*) to be used against the
onslaughts of unorthodox thinkers. Logic was also found to be
valuable in technical controversy.[84]

Now Western scholars of the history of philosophy in Islam
allege that Islamic philosophy declined after the twelfth century
A.D., that is, after the death of Averroes (d. 1198). This claim is far
from the truth. What really happened was that after that time
Greek–Hellenistic philosophy began to peter out. That is to say, it
was the purely Greek–Hellenistic philosophical elements in the
Islamic philosophical enterprise (except for logic) that began to
decline after the twelfth century. Thenceforth Islamic philosophy
took a more metaphysical and mystical turn, an orientation that
was congruent with the ethos of Eastern cultures. It was the
concepts, categories, and mental outlooks rooted in Islamic culture
and tradition that guided the pursuit and cultivation of Greek–
Hellenistic philosophy. The elements or doctrines of the ancient
Greek thinkers that endured in Islamic philosophy after the medieval period were those consonant with an Oriental *Weltanschauung*.

The reference to Islamic experience indicates that philosophy, if it
is to endure, must have a basis in the culture, experiences, and
mentalities of the people who produce it. That is, philosophical
reflection should start from such elements; its organizing principles

and categories must be extracted from them. Given the dynamic nature of culture and experience, however, philosophy cannot afford to ossify. For this reason, and in view of the relevance of philosophy to the affairs of men and society, it must be considered as a *conceptual response* to basic human problems at different epochs. However, it does not mean that because philosophy must grapple with fundamental human problems posed by new situations, earlier philosophical doctrines and answers must necessarily be rejected. Their continuity and endurance will depend on a number of factors: the fundamental nature of such doctrines and the values embodied in them, the extent to which they harmonize with the ethos of a culture in a given era, the strength of the hold they exercise on the life of the people. With this as a background, let us now turn to a dicussion of the content of an African philosophy.

The philosophical enterprise is connected ultimately with the search for the wisdom needed to form the basis for a satisfactory way of life. We know the historical role of philosophy in human affairs: Philosophy responds at the conceptual level to the fundamental problems posed at any given epoch. African societies in the past half century have certainly been grappling with a variety of problems, most of which are the results of colonialism, imperialism, and industrialism. Solving such problems and reconstructing African societies in the postcolonial era will certainly require profound investigation into fundamental ideas and general principles. This is where philosophy becomes of immense relevance. It is the task of modern African philosophers not only to deal with the consequences of colonialism on African society and culture, but also to face squarely the challenges of industrialization and modernization. In doing so, they might take their cue from the philosophical activities of nineteenth-century European philosophers like Marx, Hegel, and Saint-Simon, and from their responses to the consequences of the French Revolution. I am not referring to the specific doctrines and solutions such philosophers put forward, but to the *way* they responded to the circumstances of their societies. They philosophized with the contemporary situation in mind; they gave conceptual interpretation to contemporary experience. Scholars of Plato's thought would acknowledge that the *Republic* was a commentary on contemporary Athenian sociopolitical experience, just as Aristotle's *Nicomachean Ethics* was at least in part an interpretation of Greek experience. It has been said of the American philosopher John Dewey that

"many of his own writings were attempts to apply *critical intelligence to the moral and cultural issues of his day*."[85]
In like manner modern African philosophers must try to provide conceptual responses to the problems confronting contemporary African societies; their philosophical output or a great part of it – if it is to be African – must reflect the contemporary African situation. They could operate with immediate profit and practical relevance in social, moral, legal, and political philosophy. For instance, the past two decades have seen a great deal of political instability in a number of African countries, leading to military takeovers of the reins of government. It is appropriate for African philosophers to investigate the fundamental questions relating to African political life and institutions, such as: How can the legitimacy of military governments be established? Can the one–party system of government be justified on the basis of fundamental moral or political principles? What ideology should Africa evolve or adopt as a basis for socioeconomic development, and what is the philosophical basis for such an ideology? Is there any moral justification for political violence, revolution, and guerilla war? What moral problems are generated by development and modernization, and by the transfer of technology? What connection, if any, exists between moral standards and economic conditions? These are some of the questions that must engage the attention of the modern African political and moral philosopher. Similarly, fundamental questions about the structure and objectives of the African systems of law and education should be examined by the African legal and educational philosopher. Of course questions such as these are, and can be, asked by philosophers of other, non–African societies. But I believe that the proposals put forward by African philosophers in answer to them may in fact be different from those of non–African philosophers. The important thing is that African philosophers would be responding conceptually to a contemporary situation of their societies. By means of their ideas and arguments, African philosophers engaged in such relevant investigations can influence the general climate of opinion and, consequently, public policy.

But modern African philosophers cannot afford to neglect the concepts and values in traditional African life and thought, which after all constitute the background of the modern African cultural experience. They should therefore critically examine such concepts and values as humanism, communalism, altruism, consensus, and others as they function in African sociopolitical life and thought. Other subjects for investigation are the language of African morals, the relation between logic and language (using African languages), and such epistemological concepts as truth, knowing, and paranormal cognition. The reason for urging examination of concepts in traditional African thought is not only that very little, if any, work has been done in this area, but also that this is the only way to avoid a wholesale and indiscriminate condemnation of African values. Wiredu, for instance, has said that ". . . traditional conceptions of things just cannot provide an adequate basis for contemporary philosophy."[86] This kind of judgment, even if it may contain some truth, is, in my view, too sweeping and premature. For the "traditional conceptions" of things have not been given adequate philosophical formulation, articulation, and analysis by modern African philosophers, and therefore we do not know to what extent they can and cannot be accommodated by the ethos of contemporary culture, and to what extent and how they should be modified. Only when this task of analysis and elucidation has been carried out shall we discover which aspects of the "traditional conceptions" – and there are surely some of them – should be salvaged and which should be jettisoned.

In my opinion the social, nonindividualistic character of traditional African ethics, the traditional African conceptions of the value of man and the relationships between people in a society, and the sense of community and solidarity, mutual social responsibility – these are in harmony with the contemporary cultural ethos and can provide an adequate basis for a contemporary social and moral philosophy. Wiredu in fact admires the nonreligious, nonsupernaturalistic conceptions of African morality "from which the modern Westerner may well have something to learn."[87] "I believe," he wrote, "that this freedom from supernaturalism in our traditional ethic is an aspect of our culture which we *ought to cherish and protect* from countervailing influences from abroad."[88] Further, he considers the nature of consensus as conceived in Akan traditional thought to be a political virtue:

> A much commended trait of our traditional culture is its infinite capacity for the pursuit of consensus and reconciliation. An urgent task facing us today is to find ways of translating this virtue into institutional forms in our national life. In view of the changes and chances of our recent past, this

I. Question of philosophy in African culture

is a task to which all of us should address ourselves. *Our culture may yet save us.*[89]

If our (African) culture may yet save us, then it must readily be admitted that it can, at least in some ways, provide an adequate basis for a contemporary philosophy.

My conclusion is that modern African philosophy must not – and cannot – dispense with a full-fledged inquiry into concepts in African traditional philosophy. Such an inquiry would provide an adequate basis for making judgments about African cultural values and their relevance for the contemporary world. Moreover, I believe most of the traditional concepts and values have, generally speaking, not relaxed their grip on modern African life and thought. Thus, a modern African philosophy would comprise the conceptual responses to the problems and circumstances of modern African societies as well as interpretation, criticism, and clarification of concepts in African traditional thought. The latter is necessary in order to provide continuity in philosophical orientation, at any rate in respect of some core philosophical concepts and values.

In thus delineating the content of a modern African philosophy, I am not by any means suggesting that the modern African philosopher should not pay attention to the philosophies produced by non-African cultures. I have already observed that there are universal human experiences, ideas, values, sentiments, ideals. It therefore makes sense to study and know the philosophical output of other cultures, for such study may help deepen the understanding of our own. But the fact still remains that the forms of such (alien) philosophies were hammered out on the anvil of the cultural and historical experience of other peoples. I suggest therefore that *the starting points, the organizing concepts and categories of modern African philosophy be extracted from the cultural, linguistic, and historical background of African peoples*, if that philosophy is to have relevance and meaning for the people, if it is to enrich their lives.[90]

In this connection the history of philosophy in Islam is relevant. I pointed out that it was the Greek–Hellenistic elements in Islamic philosophy that really declined after the twelfth century A.D. Thereafter the metaphysical and religious ethos of Near Eastern culture reasserted itself and determined the direction of philosophical development. The significance of the new orientation of Islamic philosophy for our present purposes is that unless a philosophy interacts with the mentalities and core values of a people, it will not endure but will sooner or later atrophy. After attending the Indian Congress of Philosophy in 1951, A. C. Ewing made the following noteworthy remarks:

> . . . Indian philosophy is traditionally more connected than English *with the search for the good life in a religious sense.* . . . India remains a great stronghold of metaphysical idealism, based on epistemology, mystical experience, and the idea that a study of the nature of the self discloses that it is identical with the supreme principle of reality. . . .
>
> It is a commonplace that *the Indians are a very religious people*, and the connection between philosophy and religion fostered by Hinduism and the fact that *Indian philosophers are on the whole much more interested in the problems raised by the philosophy of religion* than in those raised by the philosophy of science helps to account for their *immunity* to naturalism and positivism.[91]

Thus, in spite of India's long contact with Westernism in all its facets, the core values – the religious values – of Indian life and thought were still in the ascendant among the factors influencing the direction of Indian philosophical reflection. In the case of Africa, any abiding philosophy will have to take cognizance of core values such as, in my view, humanism and communalism.

I end this section by asserting that philosophy is essentially a cultural phenomenon; it is part of the cultural experience and tradition of a people. And it will pay African philosophers, although latecomers, to examine closely how the philosophical enterprise began and was developed elsewhere. I hope that I have not left the impression that African philosophy will be a unique system or a windowless monad, only that it will have some characteristics of its own.

3

Methodological problems

3.1. False impressions about the unwritten character of African traditional philosophy

There exists a number of false impressions of African traditional philosophy created by, or resulting from, the lack of writing in Africa's historical past. First and foremost is of course the denial, by some scholars, of the existence of philosophy in African culture on account of the lack of written philosophical material. Thus, a few years ago when I suggested to a colleague that some study should be made of African traditional philosophy, he immediately asked, "Does it exist? Where are the philosophical texts?" When I asked him, "Is philosophy to be found only in written texts?" he answered in the negative.

Second, the lack of written records has led most scholars to believe that African traditional thought is rigidly monolithic, offering no divergent positions and therefore no alternative metaphysics. Horton, for instance, says: "To me the most important thing about the traditional cultures is that, in each, there is a single, over-arching world-view which reigns without competition; which has, as it were, a monopoly of people's cognitive preoccupations."[1] He supposes that traditional cultures lack "the multiplicity of world-views competing for man's cognitive allegiance."[2] His perception of the distinction between traditional and scientifically oriented cultures leads him, thus, to describe the former as "closed" and the latter as "open."[3] Recently Derek Gjertsen objected to

3. Methodological problems

Horton's characterization of the distinction between traditional and scientifically oriented cultures. Gjertsen denied that traditional thought lacked the awareness of alternatives and that the theoretical tenets of traditional society are accepted absolutely and unquestioningly.[4] Three decades ago the anthropologist Daryll Forde observed:

> It is *not* to be assumed that the views and attitudes of a people concerning the duties of men among themselves and their relations to the universe are necessarily *all of one piece*. Anthropological studies of many cultures have shown that even in small and comparatively isolated societies, where differences of wealth, rank and power are small, *there need be no complete integration of belief and doctrine, still less the domination of conduct in all spheres by a single system of beliefs or basic ideas.*[5]

That is, Forde completely rejects the characterization of African thought as collective – a characterization endorsed by Horton and Hountondji, among others – to which every person in African society adhered.

In his most recent article already referred to, Horton appears to stick to his guns with regard to what he had earlier considered as the lack of awareness of alternative theoretical frameworks among the thinkers of the traditional society. He now reexpresses this earlier view as the "lack of inter-theoretic competition in the traditional setting."[6] However, the two expressions – "lack of inter-theoretic competition" and "lack of awareness of theoretical alternatives" (or "alternative theoretical frameworks") – are by no means equivalent and cannot logically be substituted for one another. Neither does the new phrasing make his position clearer and more plausible. Implicit in it is, in fact, a rejection of the earlier one, for the new formulation constitutes a *recognition* of the existence and awareness of theoretical alternatives in the traditional thought system, notwithstanding the qualification that those alternatives were (allegedly) not competing among themselves. Horton thus appears to have shifted the emphasis from the existence or nonexistence of alternative theoretical frameworks to the competition, or the lack of it, among (some existing) alternatives. One must acknowledge the existence of alternatives before deciding whether or not they were competing. From my point of view, the fact of the existence of alternatives (which Horton now recognizes implicitly or explicitly) is extremely important. Given the plurality of theoretical or doctrinal frameworks, it is hardly conceivable that inter-theoretic competition of some kind never occurred.

The belief about the monolithic character of African traditional thought undoubtedly stems from its characterization as collective. This characterization, which is implausible and erroneous, in turn arises from the lack of doxographic tradition in past African culture. But, as I have already remarked, thought, wherever it is produced, is always the production of an individual, not of a group. This is inherent in the notion of thought itself. Given this fact, I wonder how some scholars ever concluded that African thought was collective. Was it because a number of people were supposed to believe in the same idea, or because only one particular idea was supposed to have filtered through to us from the diffuse and indistinct unwritten traditional sources? Those who assert that African thought is collective fail to indicate how it was ever produced or could have been produced. Its existence appears to be assumed: A communal society can produce only communal (collective) thought. Because the communal society, it is alleged, does many (if not all) things together, it must therefore also "think" together and think the same thought. This kind of reasoning assumes that individuality is completely absorbed in the communal apparatus – a position I argue against later in this book. To put it bluntly, it is as if decades or centuries ago, most (if not all) the people in an African society met together to deliberate on their conception of, say, the soul.

It is obvious that scholars like Horton and Hountondji see a logical parallel between collective thought on the one hand and collective decision making on the other hand. But no such parallel exists. The reason is that although every member of a group, council, or cabinet participates in making a collective decision (and agrees to be bound by it), or shares in the exercise of a collective power, it is not the case that every member of a society participates in the creation of *thought*, for thought is the creation of individuals, identifiable in some cultures, unidentifiable in others. Yet, despite their individual origins, there is justification for considering such individual thoughts as, for instance, Greek or Akan without assuming that every Greek or Akan necessarily and unquestioningly adhered to it.

The justification is provided by the relationship that exists between the thought of an individual thinker and his or her culture. Given this relationship, it makes sense, contrary to Hountondji's

views, to speak of Dogon or Akan or Yoruba or African philosophy. And, on this showing, the phrase "Yoruba concept of the
person" is as legitimate and sensible as the phrase "Ionian concept
of *arche*." The former should not be taken to imply that there is (or
was) only *one* conception of a person held in Yoruba philosophy, or
that the concept has one and the same designatum for all. It merely
means, in the African case, that the author is interpreting and
elucidating a conception of a person produced or put forward
originally by an individual Yoruba thinker on the basis of ideas that
have survived in proverbs and other sources of Yoruba philosophy.
That same conception of a person may have been held, perhaps
independently, by other Yoruba thinkers. I say "perhaps independently" to allow for the possibility that these others may only have
been persuaded by the originator of the idea. But this does not
foreclose the possibility of another modern thinker giving a different analytical interpretation of the same concept on the basis of
ideas based on the same kind of sources. Thus, using a set of ideas
from Akan traditional sources, Kwasi Wiredu sees the Akan as
holding a conception of the person that is not as rigidly dualistic as
it appears in my analysis (in Chapter 6) and that borders on some
form of materialism.[7]

Different, sometimes incompatible, ideas surely coexist in African thought systems. This has been noted by some earlier research-
ers (mainly anthropologists and sociologists). Nevertheless almost
all of them presented the thought of the ethnic group they were
studying as a unity. In this they considered only one set of ideas and
beliefs that *in their view* were probably held by the "majority" of the
people they used as "informants," thus ignoring other ideas as "out
of the ordinary." Even so, there is evidence to indicate the existence
of a degree of plurality of thought and of intellectual disagreement
in the traditional setting.

In Akan thought, for instance, Rattray noted different ideas of the
sunsum ("spirit") of a person with some of his informants saying
that the *sunsum* and the *ōkra* (soul) are the same, and others
disagreeing. He noted the "sometimes contradictory" nature of
"all these quotations,"[8] referring to the statements of his informants.
Meyerowitz, too, remarked different "versions" of the *sunsum*.[9] In
the course of my own field research I have encountered varying
views on the nature of the *sunsum* and its relation to the *ōkra* (soul)
(see section 6.3). I admit that all these different notions may be
regarded as forms of a single basic idea – that there is an immaterial

aspect of the human being, and therefore that they do not illustrate Horton's criterion or conception of "alternative world-views" – of the person, in this case. But the position of Nana Boafo-Ansah, a traditional elder, on the nature of a person and the existence of spiritual entities sets him apart from others. For in a discussion we[10] had with him he denied the existence of *ɔkra* (soul) and the *sunsum* ("spirit"), and showed himself no mean materialist in a metaphysical environment that is apparently charged with spiritualism. Nana Boafo-Ansah thought that Onyame (Supreme Being, God), the ancestors, and the *abosom* (lesser spirits) were all "figments of the imagination," *onipa n'adwen* (that is man's mind, mental construct), as he put it. He thus denied the entitative interpretation of the *sunsum* in an expression such as "his *sunsum* is weighty," which is one Akan way of saying that a person "has a strong personality." For him the word *sunsum* merely denotes qualities such as dynamism, commanding presence, etc. Nana Boafo-Ansah's denial of the existence of spiritual entities would be taken as an isolated case by one who wants to insist on the alleged monolithic character of traditional thought. On the contrary, however, his position may be shared by others if only one had spent more time in the field and had talked with more of the traditional elders.

Different interpretations of the concept of destiny (*nkrabea*) probably reflect different conceptions of destiny held by Akan thinkers (see sections 7.2.1 and 7.2.2). There is a conception of single destiny as well as one of double destiny. Some believe that destiny can be changed; others hold that it is unalterable. People disagree about the source of a person's destiny, with one claiming that destiny is divinely imposed, another that it is self-determined. And so it goes.

The evidence I have adduced here to show the plurality of world views in Akan thought is limited and therefore inadequate. Nevertheless, it does indicate the existence of a variety of conceptions in Akan traditional thought, if not the existence of philosophical schools or sects as such. It does suggest, however, that Horton's view of the "single over-arching world-view" as the important characteristic of traditional thought may be false.

Let me pose a question about some doctrines in the history of Western philosophy: How fundamentally different were the views on the soul (or person) held in Greek philosophy in particular and Western philosophy generally up to the seventeenth century A.D.? The conception of man and the world held by the pre-Socratics

3. *Methodological problems*

through Plato, Middle Platonism, through Plotinus and Neoplatonism, St. Augustine and the Church Fathers, St. Thomas Aquinas and the Scholastics and through Descartes, was basically a single conception: dualism. There were isolated cases of antidualism, but generally dualism reigned supreme. Greek ethics was of a single kind: teleology. Yet no one has pointed out that Western metaphysical thought during that period lacked a really alternative metaphysics.

The third impression about African traditional thought is that it is not critical. According to the *Oxford English Dictionary*, critical means "being given to passing judgment upon something with respect to its merits or faults; fault-finding; involving or exercising careful judgment or observation." Critical thinking, thus, involves judgment of something's value and truth. It is of course possible to think critically without noting one's thoughts in writing. Thus, even though Socrates wrote nothing, we know or believe, thanks to Plato, that he engaged in critical thinking. But without Plato this fact – that Socrates' thought was critical – would not have come down to us: Instead, we would have bald, isolated, and perhaps philosophically profound and interesting statements. In spite of Plato, we do not know whether we have Socrates' own words and how he actually argued. In the Akan, or the African case in general, there were no Platos to write down the various arguments surrounding (or, leading to) a particular proverb or conclusion, let alone provide a rational discussion of it in writing. Consequently, there would be no such knowledge of the criticism that took place in the evolution of traditional thought, such as can be found in written discourse.

The critical attitude or element in African traditional thought is demonstrable in some of the sources of African philosophical thought discussed in the previous chapter. The critical element is manifested clearly as well in African art. "Among the Akan," wrote Warren and Andrews, "there are *individuals* who, owing to their artistic knowledge and experience, are consulted to *evaluate* art pieces and to make aesthetic *judgments* about them. Some of these *critics* are elected to formal positions; others enjoy informal recognition by virtue of their wisdom and long experience."[11] Criteria for evaluation become established. Thompson remarks: "There exists in Subsaharan Africa, locked in the minds of kings, priests and commoners, a reservoir of artistic *criticism*. Whenever tapped, this source lends clarity to our understanding of the arts of tropical Africa." He observed that "Yoruba art *critics* are experts of strong mind and articulate voice who measure in words the quality of works of art."[12] Thus, judging and evaluating, essential to the critical attitude, were consciously pursued in African arts and aesthetics. On what grounds can one reasonably say that these manifestations of the critical attitude were absent from other areas of the African thought?

The oft-quoted Akan proverb,

> Wisdom is not in the head of one person,
> *(nyansa nni onipa baako ti mu)*

means (1) that other individuals may be equally wise and capable of spawning equally good, if not better, ideas; (2) that one should not, or cannot, regard one's intellectual position as final or beyond criticism, but expect it to be evaluated by others; and (3) that, in consequence of (2), one should be prepared to abandon one's position in the face of another person's superior ideas or arguments, or in the event of one's own ideas or arguments being judged unacceptable or implausible by others. Such an attitude to the wisdom, ideas, or thoughts of others can hardly fail to be critical. The fact that differences are evident in, for instance, Akan conceptions of person, destiny, spiritual entities, etc, implies that the ideas or propositions of some persons must have been found unacceptable by others. Mrs. Eva Meyerowitz, who undertook elaborate research among some sections of the Akan people in the 1940s and 1950s, asserted that "the concept of the Kra (soul) [was] evolved by generations of thinkers."[13] The question, then is: Is it possible for the critical element to be completely absent in the *evolution* of a concept?

One other point: Horton, who denies African traditional thought the name of philosophy because it did not develop formal logic and epistemology, admits that African thought was eminently rational and logical, and that traditional world views were "logically elaborated to a high degree." But such rational and logical thinking would have been impossible had it not been based on "rules," perhaps not formally elaborated but nevertheless present in their consciousness. Now, "to be logical" is not identical with "to be critical." Nevertheless, logic is an important part of critical thinking. Thus, traditional thought could not have been logical without bearing at least some of the marks of critical thinking: a worldview that is "logically elaborated to a high degree" must in some ways be critical.

50

Finally, the critical attitude is certainly not unique or exclusive to philosophy for it is exhibited in any field of intellectual activity: in history, art, literature, law, politics, etc. A philosophical discourse must be *critical*, but it does not mean that any critical discourse is philosophical. Thus, while a critical attitude is essential to philosophical activity, that alone does *not* suffice to distinguish it from other intellectual activities. What essentially distinguishes philosophical activity from other intellectual activity is, as most philosophers will agree, the *fundamental* nature of its inquiry and of its subject matter. The crucial concern of philosophy is to reflect upon the fundamental ideas that shape and influence the life of humanity. But such fundamental inquiry can hardly be pursued with success, nor its results fully comprehended, without the presupposition of the critical attitude. So that, if in fact African thinkers did pay philosophical attention to fundamental aspects of the life, conduct and experience of man – which we know they did – then the presence of the critical attitude can be assumed.

In sum, then, the complete denial by some scholars of philosophy among African peoples, the assumed monolithic nature of African traditional thought, the alleged nonindividualistic (collective) and uncritical nature of that thought – these are some of the mistaken impressions about African traditional philosophical thought. There are two principal reasons for the currency of these impressions. The first relates of course to the lack of literate culture in Africa's history, which has wrought untold, irretrievable damage not only to African philosophy but to other aspects of the African life, such as its history. The second reason is that some scholars have come to their conclusions on the basis of incomplete and superficial research and analysis.

3.2. Difficulties besetting the study of African traditional philosophy

The most obvious and the greatest difficulty in studying or researching into African traditional philosophy stems from the fact that it is an unwritten, an undocumented philosophy. The question then becomes how one can succeed in resurrecting the philosophical doctrines and arguments of African thinkers. In Chapter 2 I argued that in Africa philosophy can be found in the myths, proverbs, folk tales, and beliefs of the people. There are, however, enormous difficulties in understanding and interpreting them. The possibility of misunderstanding and misinterpretation is real; the possibility of wrongly attributing views is always there. One may undertake interviews and discussions with living traditional wise people in an attempt to overcome this difficulty, but one can never be sure that the conceptions or interpretations of the traditional elders are themselves not colored by ideas and doctrines of Christianity or Islam with which some of them are acquainted.

Although some philosophical ideas can certainly be distilled from such sources as I have mentioned and from discussions with traditional thinkers, a further difficulty arises in connecting isolated and sometimes unrelated ideas into a coherent system, even assuming the compatibility of those ideas. The scholar of African philosophy must pay attention to the logic of ideas, that is, the logical relations between them, draw inferences, and suggest explanations that introduce some order into the fragmentary and chaotic mass of discrete ideas. This exercise in logic, conceptual ordering, and theorizing is not easy. It requires a great deal of experience in scholarship and textual analysis; it requires painstaking care; it presupposes a great deal of sustained interest and enthusiasm on the part of the scholar. Unless one's analytical interpretation is marked by such intellectual and dispositional virtues, one may not make much of it.

The scholar of African traditional philosophy, who almost invariably was trained in a Western philosophical environment and who perhaps cannot completely and immediately divorce him- or herself from that philosophical background, faces another difficulty: namely, the possibility of introducing foreign ideas into the analyses, and thus understanding African philosophy through foreign eyes. (This is not to rule out references to non-African philosophies by way of comparison and in an attempt to make explanations clearer.) This danger becomes more real when one considers that the scholar probably will be using a foreign language in interpreting and analyzing African thought, a (foreign) language that is both structurally different from the African language (in which the concepts originally occur) and that is rooted in the life of a rather different culture.

The analysis in one language of concepts originally expressed in another language naturally involves translation. But, as we know, in translation we are dealing not just with words but with concepts as well. It is the translation of concepts that gives rise to serious problems. How can we know that our translations are perfect, and that word W_1 used to render another (supposedly equivalent) word W in a different language corresponds to the original in all aspects of its use? On what grounds, can we say that W_1 is a perfect translation of W? If in language L, W is used to designate the concept C, can W_1 (supposed to be a translation of W) in language L_1 also be said to designate the same concept C? Although it is generally easy to find equivalent expressions in different languages, the concepts associated with the words of one language are not necessarily the same as those associated with the words of the language into which one is translating. For this reason the problem of translation is a real one for philosophers engaged in the study and analysis of African thought using the media of alien languages. How can one be certain, for instance, that the Akan word ōkra correctly translates the English word "soul"?

A further difficulty: How does one deal with the diverse and sometimes incompatible views that emerge from interviews and discussions with traditional thinkers and from proverbs and other sources?

These difficulties are not insurmountable nor are they peculiar to the study of an unwritten philosophy. The serious scholar should be able to study and present doctrines in African traditional philosophy as clearly and accurately as possible.

Regarding the difficulty of getting at indigenous ideas in the light of Africa's historical contact with Christianity and Islam, I wish to say that in Akan, as indeed in every African community, there are certain individuals who are steeped in the traditional lore. These individuals are regarded as wise persons in their own right. They stand out in their own communities and command the respect and esteem of their townsfolk. A researcher who goes to any Akan town or village would invariably be directed to such individuals; they are generally tradition-bound in their intellectual and general outlooks. Some of them have had no formal education at all; others have had some formal (Western) education, mostly through elementary school. While some may be Christians or churchgoers and so have some acquaintance with Christianity, all of them, in discussions, are able intellectually to distinguish between traditional conceptions and those of Christianity and of Islam as well, although its influence in Akanland has been marginal.

As regards the impact of Islam, Parrinder observed: "One would have thought that Islam would have produced a greater effect on pagan African beliefs than is apparent. Strangely enough, this effect seems to have been remarkably small. . . . Muhammadan ideas of the soul have varied, and do not appear to have affected African beliefs; rather the reverse has not infrequently happened."[14] As regards Christianity, it became clear to me in the course of my field research that sometimes the formulation of an indigenous thought may appear to be influenced by biblical language, but it is enough, for the purposes of the researcher, if there is sufficient evidence that the thought wrapped in biblical language was original. For instance, in a discourse on Onyame (Supreme Being) one traditional discussant stated that "no one knows His beginning and His end" (*obi nnim n'ahyēase ne n'awiei*), and another that "everything is from Onyame and ends up in Onyame" (*biribiara fi Onyame na ewie 'Nyame*). The language of these propositions rings a biblical bell, and appears to be the kind that could be used by the Christian missionary. Nevertheless, there is evidence that the language expresses a conception of the Supreme Being (God) that can be said to be held originally by most Akan people (see n.10 of Chapter 5). Christianity neither introduced nor fashioned Akan words and proverbs that express the concept of an infinite God, for instance. However, it is not my intention to make the claim – which would be extravagant – that Christianity has not permeated the religious life and thought of the Akan. It has, undoubtedly, although there is evidence that at certain traumatic moments in the life of the Akan the influence of Christianity may be seen as a thin veneer. (It is a well-known fact that, in times of personal crises, misfortunes, failures, and fears, a number of Akan Christians do consult the traditional fetish-priests or the so-called witch-doctors.) The minimum claim I am making is this: that despite the diffusion of Christian ideas, the basic or mainstream religious thought of the Akan can be stripped of the incrustations of alien religious doctrines and that therefore it can be reached through research and analysis.

Now, as regards the difficulty of piecing together the philosophy of the Akan people from the welter of diverse and sometimes incompatible statements that emerge both from discussions with traditional wise people[15] and from proverbs and other sources, I must emphasize that the attempt here is *not* to get at *the* philosophy of the Akan people as a unitary body of philosophical ideas. Such an attempt will be doomed to failure in the light of the diverse nature of the sources. Instead I shall attempt here to resurrect, through analytical interpretation, the philosophical ideas held by *some* individual Akan thinkers, ideas that in part have survived in proverbs and other sources of Akan philosophy. It is such individual thinkers and their ideas that I have in mind when I use such expressions as "Akan thinkers," "Akan conceptions," "Akan thought," "Akan philosophy." I must not be taken to imply that I am presenting a set of philosophical ideas held by all Akan people, thinkers and nonthinkers alike. In my reconstruction of Akan philosophical thought, I have selected (perhaps arbitrarily), from the traditional sources, some statements and ideas by some individual thinkers that I have found important in my analytical exegesis and evaluation. I have focused on the logic of such ideas and statements in terms of their relations and implications. But I admit the possibility that another modern philosopher might obtain statements and ideas from the same traditional sources (at least some of which may differ from those I used) and produce a different synthesis based on those sources.

On the problem of translation, I take the view that it is not so severe as to obstruct our apprehension of ideas or thoughts expressed in different languages.[16] Even though it is logically true that our ideas or thoughts, as part of our mental furniture, are private, it does not follow from this that the ideas expressed by a speaker of one language bear no relation to those expressed by a speaker of another language in terms of their designata. It is certainly possible for two persons, speaking different languages, to have the same ideas and for those ideas, as it were, to converge on the same object. This is the case not only logically but also in reality. It is indeed this reality that is the basis for the obvious fact of translingual and interpersonal communication and understanding.

Thus, it is possible, through translation, for a scientist speaking one language to grasp the results of scientific research developed and produced in a different language. I think we can say that given two sentences S_1 and S_2 in two different languages, S_1 correctly translates S_2 if both say the same thing and therefore express the same thought; sameness of thought presupposes sameness of meaning. Suppose a number of physicians drawn from several countries of the world attend a conference in Kumasi (Ghana). The king of Asante (the Asantehene), who had earlier delivered the keynote address of the conference, becomes ill not long after the opening ceremony. When some of the visiting physicians arrive at the hospital to visit the king, someone meets them and says, "The king is dead!" On returning from the hospital, the physicians announce to the assembled world press, each in his or her native language (having thus translated the sentence originally made in English), the death of the king. The English physician says, "The king is dead," the German "Der König ist tot," the Arab "māta al-malik," the French "Le roi est mort," and the Akan "Ohene no awu." Do the physicians not mean the same thing, namely, the-death-of-the-king, despite the fact that they use different languages in making their statements?

I believe that the ideas of one conceptual system can be explicated in the language of another system. In explicating and analyzing African concepts in a foreign language, a number of things need to be done. These include profound inquiry into the nature of the concept in both the African language and the language which is to be used for translation; where a word has diverse or complex meanings, the necessary qualifications must be made; it may be necessary sometimes both to give reasons why a particular word is being used to translate another word, and to show one's awareness of the difficulties in translating a particular word. Even though these operations may not necessarily achieve complete success, they should ensure a high degree of correctness in our translation and thus our understanding. Thus, even though Akan thought may in some respects be different in its concepts and doctrines from Western philosophy, the differences are such as can be captured by the resources of a Western language like English. The problem of translation therefore is not unsurmountable.

On the question of understanding and interpretation, the scholar should try to get at the inner meaning of the material in question. Even if one speaks the language of the thinkers whose philosophical ideas he is studying, one should pay particular attention to the philology and semantics of that language. On points of interpretation one should frequently consult not only with those known to be well versed in the nuances of the language, but also with the traditional thinkers about concepts expressed in the language and the designata of those concepts. How a thinker handles a concept expressed in the original language is an essential part of any attempt to interpret and appreciate that thought. The attempt to analyze, interpret, and present philosophical ideas unavoidably requires one to engage in supplying, within limits, "the missing links in thought," to use Raju's words.[17] This is so even in studying written philosophical discourse; much more is it true in studying and presenting unwritten philosophical thought. So it is that I have attempted to supply the missing links in Akan thought, links that are either implicit in, or required by, the logic of the elliptical and allusive statements in the sources, or derive from my own (fallible) understanding of the issues involved – issues that must be explored primarily within the Akan cultural, linguistic, and intellectual framework in particular and the African cultural framework in general. In this regard, it must be admitted that in any exegetical work the input of the exegete, although kept to a minimum, is inevitable.

Finally, the scholar should be constantly on guard against reading preconceived notions into a study of African thought. Consciousness of this pitfall will do much to ward off the temptation to analyze the ideas of African philosophy within a foreign conceptual framework.

These, then, are some methods that may be adopted to overcome the difficulties that confront the scholar of African traditional philosophy.

II

The Akan conceptual scheme

4

The Akan conception of philosophy

My intention in this chapter is to examine the Akan conception of wisdom or philosophy. The difference between wisdom and philosophy in Akan conceptions is slight, and there is only one word used for both.

In the Akan language there is no word for "philosophy," in the sense of "love of wisdom." Despite this fact, some linguists try to force some seemingly appropriate word into the Akan language. For example, Christaller and Berry[1] give *nyansapē* as a translation of "philosophy." This word is an etymological translation of "philosophy," and means "love of wisdom" or "quest for wisdom," and similarly "philosopher" is rendered by *onyansapēfo*, "lover of wisdom." Although these two expressions, *nyansapē* and *onyansapēfo*, are correct etymological translations of their Greek equivalents, they are dubious from the point of view both of the vocabulary and usage of the Akan language and the Akan conception of philosophy (to be explained below). My researches indicate that these two expressions were not indigenous to the Akan language, nor have they been accepted or incorporated into the current vocabulary and usage. Consequently, there is in reality no such expression as *onyansapēfo*, "lover of wisdom." And the reason for this, it seems to me, is that in Akan conceptions one is conceived of at once as a *wise person (onyansafo)*, not a lover of wisdom. It is such a wise person who in fact does or would have the ability, flair, and disposition to ask certain types of questions and make certain types of inquiries. And the Akan thinkers in fact hold that *nyansa* (or, *adwen*, its possible equivalent), understood as the capacity for philosophical thinking, is a mental faculty that is inborn; it is not acquired.

61

However, where *nyansa* means skill, practical knowledge, it can – and has to – be acquired.

The basis of the assertion that *nyansa* is inborn is the Akan belief that it is the spirit (*sunsum*) of a person that makes *nyansa* possible (*sunsum no na ema nyansa*), and that thinking is in fact a function of the spirit (*adwen no wo sunsum no mu*).[2] According to the Akan conception of the person (see Chapter 6) *sunsum* (spirit) is an innate faculty possessed by a person at birth. It is thus clear why the word *nyansapē*, seeking wisdom, would not occur.[3] The wise person is not one who seeks or searches for wisdom. He or she would not be wise *if* he were to search for wisdom, where wisdom refers to an activity rather than a body of knowledge. What we search for is a body of knowledge or truths.

The position of the Akan thinkers, as just interpreted, may be contrasted with that of Pythagoras (c. 532 B.C.). When he, according to the familiar anecdote, was referred to as a wise man, he said that his wisdom consisted in knowing that he was ignorant, and that he should therefore not be called "wise" but a "lover of wisdom." It seems to me, however, that Pythagoras was merely being modest in refusing to be called *sophos* (wise man), and preferring to be called *philosophos* (lover of wisdom), for surely it is a *sophos* who can ask the type of questions and adopt certain approaches to problems that would be regarded as philosophical. That is to say, being a *philosophos* is already evidenced in the nature of the intellectual activities of the *sophos*. Hence there must be an obvious link between the *sophos* and the *philosophos* in terms of their methods and concerns. On this showing, even if the Akans do not actually have a word for "philosophy" ("love of wisdom") as such, we may conclude from the intellectual activities of the *onyansafo* (wise man) that he or she must be considered a philosopher in the sense of a thinker (*odwendwenfo, obadwenfo*). Consequently, the Akan expression *nyansa* must be rendered by both "wisdom" and "philosophy,"[4] among others to be mentioned below. A word that may be used interchangeably with *nyansa* (wisdom) is *adwen*, which means "thinking," hence *odwendwenfo, obadwenfo*, thinker. Thus the wise person (*onyansafo*) is a thinker.

That wisdom or philosophy is an activity may be inferred from the fact that according to the Akan thinkers *nyansa* (wisdom) is seen in what a person says (*nyansa wo kasa mu*)[5] and how he or she says it; that is, it is through discussion and discourse that a person shows that he or she is wise. In a gathering in the traditional court of the king or in any public place, for instance, the person who is able to provide an intellectual analysis of the subject matter under discussion, the person who is able to argue and convince others, the person who is able to bring together all the relevant facts in order to point up an underlying reason or meaning – it is such a person who in an Akan community is considered wise and a philosopher (*onyansafo*).

The reference to a gathering in the royal palace that is normally attended only by the elders (*mpanyinfo*) of the community may give the impression that it is only among the elderly that wise people are to be found. Such an impression would be false, for a young adult also may be considered wise if he or she can display the intellectual characteristics already mentioned. One reason why the elders are traditionally acknowledged as repositories of wisdom is that, in an environment in which writing was nonexistent, they possess the cumulated philosophical reflections of many thinkers. Another reason was that because Akan philosophy is based principally on experience, it was natural to credit the elderly person with wisdom because he or she had gained experience in life, although it surely does not follow that every elderly person had the intellectual ability to make philosophical sense of his or her experiences.

That wisdom is not confined to the elders follows from the fact that the Akan hold that thinking is an activity of the *sunsum* (spirit), a mental capacity, and that every human being has *sunsum*. This implies that anyone has the potential to be wise. Although mental capacity does not exist in the same degree in everyone, it is, as already pointed out, held to be developable. This means that it is theoretically possible for someone to develop mentally, though not necessarily to the point of becoming wise (a philosopher). For not just any kind of thinking makes a person wise. In this connection, we are reminded of the Akan proverb,

> Speech (talk) is one thing, wisdom another.
> (*asɛm nko, nyansa nko*)

Words do not constitute wisdom; the good speaker is not necessarily wise. To be wise, that is, a philosopher, requires a certain type of intellectual effort, activity, and approach. The one whose thoughts are profound (*obi a n'adwen mu dɔ*) is considered a philosopher, for it is such a person who is considered to have the ability and disposition for creating proverbs that contain philosophical speculations and constitute an important source of Akan ideas.

II. The Akan conceptual scheme

The *onyansafo* reflects, imagines, intuits, and then condenses these reflections, imaginings, and intuitions in proverbs. The *onyansafo* is able to speculate about human experience. Probing aspects of human experience and the external world, he or she may pose questions about the fundamental principles that underlie human life. The aim is to make a synthetic and coherent picture of human experience and the world, inferring from that experience that which is ultimately real and true. The thoughts of such a person are distilled in proverbs, although by this I do not mean that proverbs are the only manifestation of intellectual activity. The Akan philosopher aims at comprehensive understanding of the world and human life and conduct. He or she attempts a description of not only how things are, but also how human beings ought to live and what their values ought to be – hence the existence of many proverbs relative to morality. The wise person of the Akan community is essentially a speculative philosopher.

There are, however, two kinds of wise person in the Akan community. The wisdom of the first kind is oriented or restricted to personal relations and to success in personal life. Such a person is not really a philosopher. The other sort is the person who is interested in the principles underlying human life. It is the second type who, in my view, can appropriately be described as a philosopher.

The wise person's creativity – evidenced, for instance, in the ability to originate philosophical proverbs – and possession of a profound and inquiring mind constitute the background of the proverb,

> The wise man is spoken to in proverbs, not in
> speeches (or, words).
> (*onyansafo wobu no bē na wōnka no asēm*)

The ambiguous word, *asēm*, here means speech, talk, lecture, discourse. The proverb asserts that since the wise person has the intellectual ability to grasp the profound meanings of proverbs immediately, he or she should be spoken to in proverbs; one need not deliver a lecture or long speech before succeeding in conveying one's idea. The wise person sees for him- or herself the conclusions or implications of such pithy sayings. The proverbs, which are, as it were, capsules of ideas, can be "broken down" or "broken into" (*mpaepaemu*: "analysis") by the wise person.

But the Akan wise person analyzes not only proverbs or, for that matter, propositions but also concepts or ideas (*adwene*). In the course of my field research I would ask such questions as, "What is *nkrabea* (fate, destiny)?" or "What is the Akan conception of *nkrabea*? (*adwene bēn na Akanfo wɔ wɔ nkrabea ho*?)" My discussant would proceed to explicate or clarify the meaning (*aseē*) of the concept. But – and here is the point to note – while elucidating the concept he or she would refer to relevant proverbs. This means that in the view of the Akan wise person, analysis of propositions or concepts cannot dispense with experience. (In this connection generalizations and even principles would be considered as having some basis in experience.) If it could, it would be reduced to mere linguistic analysis, and in the Akan conception of philosophy, as I interpret it, with its practical orientation, linguistic analysis as such would have little, if any, place. For if philosophy is conceived in terms of linguistic analysis, it can do nothing to help solve human problems in the world. Such a philosophy would be arid, idle, and vacuous, and would be described by the Akan thinkers as *nyansa hunu*, useless philosophy, or impractical (inoperative) philosophy (*nyansa a wɔmfa nnyē adwuma*[6]), wisdom that is not put to good purposes.

The wise person in the Akan conception is one who can "analyze" (*mpaepaemu, mpensempensemu*) the problems of people and society with a view to suggesting answers. An Akan proverb has it that

> Wisdom is not like money, to be tied up and
> hidden away.
> (*nyansa nnyē sika na wɔakyekyere asie*)

The wise person should apply wisdom to daily life. That wisdom or philosophy should be used in solving practical problems is expressed also in the proverb, literally translated as

> If a problem lasts for a long time, wisdom comes to
> it.
> (*asem kyē a, nyansa ba ho*)

That is, it is the wise person who, after grappling with a problem for a long time, succeeds in disentangling it. The proverb also implies that philosophizing is a long intellectual process; it takes time. But the more time it takes the more seasoned it becomes, and the more able it is to solve problems. In sum, then, the "analytical" activity of the Akan philosopher consists in intellectually disentangling human problems, and his or her reflections on those problems (some of which are embodied in proverbs) would therefore become a philosophy of life, offering rational guidance on questions of individual action and social policy. Philosophy thus provides people with a fundamental system of beliefs to live by.

That philosophy is essentially oriented toward action and practical affairs is reflected in other meanings of *nyansa*. In addition to wisdom, *nyansa* also means skill, dexterity, art, artfulness, learning, knowledge.[7] Thus, the practical dimension of Akan philosophy is already embedded in the original meaning of the word *nyansa*. The Greek *sophia* is also translated, in addition to wisdom, as skill, intelligence, practical wisdom, learning.[8] But the practical character or orientation of Akan philosophical thought appears to have succeeded more in moving on an even keel: "A fact about philosophy in a traditional society," observes Wiredu, "particularly worthy of emphasis, is that it is alive in day-to-day experience. When philosophy becomes academic and highly technical, it can easily lose this quality."[9] Although in the West philosophy is generally becoming more and more dry, abstract, and technical and thus out of touch with practical wisdom, the highly technical nature of philosophical discourse is principally a conscious effort on the part of its practitioners at making the intentions of that discourse articulate, acute, and comprehensible. Only when the technicality of the discourse involves or results in its breaking loose from the practical problems of life may it generate doubts about its relevance. There is not sufficient evidence for the conclusion that the technical nature of philosophical discourse in the West has deflected the attention of philosophical thinking from human problems and concerns. And it is appropriate, in my opinion, that such deflection not take place.

The *ultimate* goal of philosophizing ought to be the concern for the nature of the good in mankind or society – for human value, and not for abstract matters for their own sake. (The word "ultimate" here is important and is used advisedly: It indicates that concern for abstractions should somehow conduce eventually to the determination of the nature of human values.) Every branch of philosophy is, and ought to be, concerned directly or indirectly with the problems of human value. The practical orientation of Akan philosophy appears, therefore, to be worthwhile.

Our investigations into the Akan conception of philosophy indicate that Akan philosophy is oriented toward action and practical affairs. For the traditional Akan thinker there is an intimate relationship between philosophy and life. Philosophy is the articulation of a concrete way of life, not just a tissue of well-laundered concepts. Akan philosophy may thus be characterized as a philosophy of living experience, as evidenced, for instance, in the proverbs, and expressed in real and vital attitudes. Such a conception of philosophy undoubtedly is of great relevance to the contemporary circumstances of Ghanaian or, for that matter, African societies.

5

Concepts of being and causality

5.1. God and the other categories of being

Quite often the impulse of philosophical reflection finds its first expression in religious life and thought. A philosophical idea may be found concealed in a religious perspective or expressed in religious language. This is the case with Akan ontology, that is, the doctrine of being. For the religious language, attitude, and practices of the Akans provide a great deal of insight into their conception of reality, that is, the sorts of entities considered to be real or to exist. It is the reality of an entity or object that in fact constitutes the ground of its being worshiped; the object of worship must be presumed to exist.

The language of the religious rite of libation immediately reveals the entities that are considered real in Akan metaphysics. A typical prayer of libation runs as follows:

Supreme God, who is alone great, upon whom men lean and do not fall, receive this wine and drink. Earth goddess, whose day of worship is Thursday, receive this wine and drink. Spirits of our ancestors, receive this wine and drink . . .[1]

These words from the prelude of the libation prayer attest to the existence of a Supreme Being (Onyame, Onyankopōn), deities (*abosom*: lesser spirits[2]), and ancestors (that is, ancestral spirits: *nsamanfo*), in descending order. Next after these entities are humans and the physical world of natural objects and phenomena. Thus the hierarchical character of Akan ontology is clear: the Supreme Being at the apex, and our phenomenal world at the bottom of this hierarchy. The Supreme Being, the deities, and the ancestors are spiritual entities. They are considered invisible and unperceivable to the naked eye: This is in fact the definition of the word "spiritual," for the Akans use the word *sunsum* ("spirit") generally to refer to the mystical, the unempirical, the nonphysical. Given the belief of most Akans that at least part of nature or the physical world is animated, and that man too is partly spiritual, we have to conclude that Akan ontology is essentially or primarily spiritual (see Chapter 6); the Akan universe is a spiritual universe, one in which supernatural beings play significant roles in the thought and action of the people. What is primarily real is spiritual.

It must be noted, however, that the world of natural phenomena is also real, even though in ultimate terms the nonperceivable, purely spiritual world is more real, for upon it the perceivable, phenomenal world depends for sustenance. There is no distinction between the sensible (perceivable) world and the nonsensible (nonperceivable) world in the sense of the latter being real and the former being unreal, as in other metaphysical systems. The distinction lies entirely in the perceivability of one and the unperceivability of the other. But the perceivability of the one – namely, the world of nature – does not in any way detract from its reality. From this perspective, it would seem that reality in Akan conceptions is one and homogeneous. But this in fact is not the case. For the characteristics of the physical world are different from those of the spiritual world. The Akan metaphysical world is thus a dual world, notwithstanding the fact that the activities of the inhabitants of the spiritual world extend to, and are "felt" in, the physical world.

As already noted, Akan ontology is clearly pluralistic. Yet it is equally clear, from the religious language of libation, the attributes ascribed to Onyame (the Supreme Being), and the general religious attitude and behavior of the Akan people, that within this broad, comprehensive ontological pluralism, there are categorial distinctions, and that all these entities are not on the same level of being – a fact that follows from the hierarchical character of Akan ontology. From the several attributes or descriptions of Onyame,[3] it would undoubtedly appear that he is the ultimate ground of being.

The Akan conception of God, Onyame (or Nyame), may be reached by first examining the names or epithets that are given to him. He is known as

II. The Akan conceptual scheme

1. *Onyankopōn*: Alone, the Great One, the Supreme Being.
2. *Bōrebōre*: Creator, Excavator, Hewer, Carver, Architect, Originator, Inventor.[4]
3. *Obōadeē*: Creator.
4. *Odomankoma*: Infinite, Boundless, Absolute, Eternal.[5]
5. *Obiannyēw*: Uncreated.
6. *Tetekwaframua*: He who endures from ancient times and forever.[6]
7. *Tweaduampōn*: The Dependable One.
8. *Brekyirihunuade*: All-Knowing, Omniscient.[7]
9. *Enyiasombea*:[8] Omnipresent.
10. *Otumfo*: The Powerful One, Omnipotent.
11. *Atoapem*: Ultimate, Final (literally: Unsurpassable).[9]

These descriptive titles give us some insight into the conception of Onyame originally[10] held by the Akan people regarding his nature and position in relation to the other denizens in their ontology.

Onyame is the Absolute Reality, the origin of all things, the absolute ground, the sole and whole explanation of the universe, the source of all existence. Absolute Reality is beyond and independent of the categories of time, space, and cause. As *tetekwaframua* and *ōdomankoma*, Onyame transcends time and is thus free from the limitations of time, an eternity without beginning, without an end. The fact that Onyame dwells in an infinite time gives the lie to the supposition, made by Mbiti, that Africans do not have a concept of a long or infinite future, for surely a concept of an eternal, infinite being implies a concept of an infinite time (see section 11.2). If there were no concept of an infinite time the infinite being would be limited by time, and he would no longer be infinite. But *ex hypothesi* he is infinite; therefore, he must dwell in an infinite time. While containing space, Onyame is not held to be spatial. He is not bound or limited to any particular region of space. He is omnipresent (*enyiasombea*), all-pervading. The fact that Onyame is not confined to any particular locality is the basis of the proverb: "If you want to say something to Onyame, say it to the wind" (*wopē asēm aka akyerē Onyame a, ka kyerē mframa*). The Akans often draw an analogy between God, or for that matter any spiritual being, and the wind. Just as the wind is invisible and intangible – yet its effects are seen everywhere – so is Onyame invisible, intangible, and omnipresent. The analogy, however, is obviously incomplete, for the wind can be physically felt whereas Onyame cannot.

5. Being and causality

As the ultimate source of being, Onyame created the whole universe, including the deities or lesser spirits, out of nothing. He is the *ōbōadeē*, "the creator of the thing," the *bōrebōre*, originator. At some point in the distant past, Onyame created the world, and having brought the world into existence, he sustains it with his infinite power (*otumfo*). All things end up in him (*atoapem*), that is, into him all things are dissolved. Thus, a discussant stated: "Everything is from Onyame and ends up in Onyame."[11] Onyame himself is uncaused (*ōdomankoma*). The Akan view here follows from the notion of infinity. Causality operates and is applicable in all matters of change in the world. But Onyame, being infinite and eternal, is not subject to change and *a fortiori* to causality.

The names ascribed to Onyame and their significations indicate that Onyame is the ultimate or absolute reality, an attribution that is found in proverbs such as "All things are dependent upon Onyame" (*nsēm nyinaa ne 'Nyame*), and "The earth is wide but Onyame is the elder" (*asase terew na Onyame ne panyin*), that is, Onyame is the progenitor, the primordial ancestor. Further evidence regarding the ultimacy of the reality of Onyame vis-à-vis the reality of the other entities in the Akan ontological universe may be gathered from the religious attitudes and behavior of the Akan people. Here are some of the short prayers and the constant references and invocations made to Onyame by the Akan people at certain times and occasions:[12]

1. At the start of any undertaking the Akan would say: "Onyame, help me!" (*Onyame boa me*).
2. The expression "If it is the will of Onyame" (*sē Onyame pē a*) is constantly on people's lips at the start, or in the course, of a pursuit.
3. If one inquired about another's health, the latter would almost invariably say, "By the grace of Onyame, I am all right" (*Onyame adom me ho yē*).
4. Salutations and words of farewell are couched in the form of prayer to Onyame. For instance, "May you go in the company of Onyame" (*wo ne 'Nyame nkō*); "I leave you in the hands of Onyame" (*me de 'Nyame gya wo*).
5. If one narrowly escapes a disaster one would say, "If Onyame had not intervened . . ." (*se Onyame ampata a . . .*); "Onyame alone" (*Onyame nko ara*).
6. The priest at the shrine of a deity, when consulted in case of

71

illness, would always say: "If Onyame permits, I shall cure you."

Such sayings, as I understand them, are not clichés but genuine religious expressions used by those who have confidence in the ultimate power of Onyame. These spontaneous religious references or invocations are made *only* to Onyame and never to the deities that generally are the direct objects of worship.

The well-known artistic symbol "Except God" (*Gye 'Nyame*) expresses the idea of the omipotent, eternity, uniqueness, supremacy of Onyame. Kofi Antubam, the late Ghanaian (Akan) artist, was given an elaborate interpretation of the symbol by an informant: "This great panorama of creation originated from the unknown past: No one lives who saw its beginning. No one lives who will see its end, Except God."[13] The meaning of the symbol is simply that only Onyame is omnipotent, supreme, eternal.

Now it is evident from the names of Onyame, the Supreme Being, from the religious attitudes and expressions of the Akan people including their ejaculatory prayers, and from the ideas about Onyame contained in Akan proverbs and art that, although there are several categories of being, Onyame is in fact the ultimate reality. As the Uncreated and First Cause, he is independent of all the other categories of being. Other entities are real because, being rooted in Onyame, they partake of, or participate in, his reality. Their reality is, therefore, derivative and adventitious. Thus, while Onyame is the Absolute Reality, other entities, being dependent categories, are only dependently real. Deities, ancestral spirits, humans and the physical world cannot therefore be said to be absolutely or ultimately real. Parrinder was, therefore, wrong, at least as far as the Akan concept of Onyame is concerned, when he thought that the Supreme Being, God, was conceived to be "sometimes first among equals."[14] How can Onyame, who is conceived as "Alone the Great One" (*Onyankopōn*), have an equal when he constitutes the highest category of being? The concept of equality implies a relation and a relation implies the existence of at least two things. But since Onyame is the only member of a class, the concept of equality is inapplicable here.

The Akan universe, essentially spiritual, is endowed or charged with varying degrees of force or power. This force or power is *sunsum*, usually translated as "spirit," which, as noted, is commonly used to refer to the mystical and nonempirical, as in *sunsum yare*

5. Being and causality

(spiritual disease). In this metaphysic all created things, that is, natural objects, have or contain *sunsum*; every deity (*ōbosom*) is a *sunsum*, but not vice versa. This *sunsum* derives ultimately from Onyame who, as the Supreme Being, is the Highest Spirit or Highest Power. *Sunsum*, then, appears, on my interpretation, to be a generic concept; it appears to be a universal spirit, manifesting itself differently in the various beings and objects in the natural world. At the same time, the word *sunsum* is used in two different but related senses.

First, it is used to refer to any self-conscious subject whose activities are initiated self-consciously. In this sense, Onyame, the deities, and the ancestors are said to be spirits, that is, spiritual beings with intelligence and will. Second, it is used to refer to the mystical powers believed to exist in the world. These powers are held to constitute the inner essences or intrinsic properties of natural objects, and are believed to be contained in those objects. Thus, *sunsum* is used in both a specific sense, to refer to the essence of a particular deity or man, and a general sense, to refer to all beings and powers unperceived by man.

There are two ways in which the two senses of *sunsum* are related. The first is that the mystical powers in the world and in natural objects are categorially related to the deities, although they derive ultimately from Onyame. The second is that the deities are supposed to reside in natural objects such as trees, plants, rocks, mountains and hills, rivers and brooks. Notwithstanding the relatedness of the two senses or uses of *sunsum* some scholars make a distinction between spirits (which, according to my analysis, include Onyame, the deities, the ancestors, etc.) and what they call supernatural powers or forces. Mbiti, for instance, writing about religious or metaphysical concepts of Africa in general, said: "African people know that the universe has a power, force or whatever else one may call it, in addition to the items in the ontological categories which we discussed in Chapter Three."[15] Busia wrote: "To the Ashanti the universe is full of spirits. There is the Great Spirit, the Supreme Being, who created all things, and who manifests his power through a pantheon of gods; below these are lesser spirits which animate trees, animals or charms."[16] [Since Busia distinguishes the gods (deities) it is correct, I think, to take his expression "lesser spirits" as a reference to the supernatural or magical forces or powers.] Parrinder also made a similar distinction.[17]

73

What is not clear to me, however, is whether these supernatural or magical forces (for example, those operative in witchcraft, charms, and amulets) belong to a category of being distinct from that of the deities (*abosom*) or whether they are categorially linked to the deities. The statements of Mbiti, Busia, and Parrinder suggest the former. Rattray also seems to distinguish the magical powers (*suman*, pl. *asuman*) from the deities, regarding the former as "among the lowest grades of superhuman powers,"[18] "lower graded spiritual power."[19] Elsewhere, in a more elaborate discussion of *suman*, Rattray observed: "Although *suman* may form part of an *obosom* (god), *suman* and *ōbosom* are in themselves distinct, and are so regarded by the Ashanti."[20] In saying that the two are distinct in themselves Rattray means most probably that in terms of the actual exercise of power *suman* and *ōbosom* are distinct, but that they are not distinct in terms of their nature, the former forming part of the latter. It seems to me that the magical or supernatural powers are in fact part of the manifestation or operation of the characteristic activities and powers of the deities (*abosom*), that they are a specific extension of the powers of the *abosom*. The *asuman* (which include charms, amulets, and talismans) are in Akan communities actually *prepared* by priests and priestesses, who serve the deities and thereby appropriate the powers of the deities. There is evidence to support this view, namely, that the magical powers are not categorially distinct from the deities. Kwaku Mframa, an Akan medium-priest of many years experience who submitted to a long series of interviews, stated repeatedly that much of the power of the medium-priest rests upon the help provided by the good witches attached to his shrine.[21] Helaine Minkus reported that two of her "informants went further and denied that the gods have any power at all, declaring that the effects produced are due solely to a group of witches who combine their power."[22] The views of the medium-priest and the "informants" of Ms. Minkus indicate a real relationship between the mystical powers and the deities. It appears certain therefore that what are called supernatural or magical powers do not constitute a distinct, autonomous category of being additional to the categories discussed earlier in this chapter, but that they are a subcategory of the deities (*abosom*).

It may be mentioned, parenthetically, that the fact that all created things are held to be *sunsum* or to contain *sunsum* may give the impression that the Akan world view is pantheistic. Such an impression, however, would be erroneous, for Akan thinkers do not maintain that Onyame (God) is identifiable with the sum of all things. They do not identify the creator with the creature, the author with his work. Indeed, the concept of transcendence[23] held by them implies a rejection of pantheism. A more appropriate description of the Akan system might be *panpsychism*: Everything is or contains *sunsum* (spirit). In saying that natural objects contain *sunsum* or power Akan thinkers mean to attribute to them an intrinsic property, namely, the property of activity or an activating principle. If this interpretation of the Akan position is correct, then it rejects by implication the view, held by the Cartesians and others in Western philosophy and also in Islamic philosophy,[24] that matter is essentially passive or inert and that a creative divine being must therefore activate it. According to Akan thinkers, then, activity is a property intrinsic to matter, that is, natural objects; it is the essence of natural objects to be active, to possess power.

As noted before, the Akan universe is conceived as a hierarchy of beings with Onyame at the apex, then the deities, ancestors, humans, and the world of natural objects and phenomena, in that order. Parrinder, in my view, was wrong, at least as far as the Akan conception goes, in using the pyramid or triangle as an analogy to explain the relationships between the various categories of being in Akan ontology. He wrote: "... a pyramid or triangle was apt illustration of the order of the spiritual forces. At the apex was the supreme God, on one side of the triangle were the nature gods, and on the other side the ancestors, while at the base were the lower magical powers."[25] This analogy places the deities (what he calls "nature gods") and the ancestors on the same footing, whereas the religious practices and attitudes of the Akans indicate that the deities are considered more powerful than the ancestors, who are considered to be "nearer" to man – for they were once human, whereas the deities were never human. A vertical line, therefore, would be a more appropriate figure to use in displaying the ordered relations between the different entities in Akan ontology.

In the web of interaction between the various entities in this hierarchy, an entity can destroy or affect any other *below* it. Thus, Onyame can destroy the deities (hence the obeisance made to him by the priest who serves a deity) as well as the other spiritual beings, humans, and the whole world; thus, a witch can kill a human being, for although the witch is also a human being he or she is believed to have a power which is extraordinary and greater than that possessed by the "ordinary" person. It follows that entities with the same degree of potency cannot destroy or affect one another. Thus, an Akan proverb has it that "unless you die of God let living *man* kill you, and you will not perish" (*Onyankopōn ankum wo na ōdasani kum wo a, wunwu da*). The proverb means that entities with equal potency, like men, cannot really affect one another, but that Onyame, with an unequaled or incomparable potency, can destroy man. On the other hand, the hierarchical conception implies that a lower entity cannot subvert a higher entity; hence the proverb, "the order Onyame has established, living *man* cannot subvert"[26] (*ade a Onyame ahyehyē onipa ntumi nsēe no*). Furthermore, such an ordered conception belies the description by anthropologists and others of Akan religion as "idolatry," "fetishism," "nature worship," and the like, meaning that the Akans worshiped man-made objects as well as objects of nature. Now, according to the Akan hierarchical order, natural objects are below man; man therefore cannot make obeisance to such lower entities. Thus, any worshipful attitude shown toward natural objects, such as trees and rivers, is in fact directed to deities that are believed to inhabit them. The worshipful attitude toward "objects of nature" is therefore a mere recognition on the part of the Akan people of the existence of a category of spiritual beings higher than man. Here one sees something that anthropologists and other writers on Akan religion failed to see, namely, the influence of a metaphysical system on the religious perspective or behavior of a people.

Akan ontology, essentially spiritualistic, is, on my interpretation, neither wholly pluralistic nor wholly monistic; it is both pluralistic and monistic. It admits several entities as real, but it recognizes only one of them, namely Onyame, as the ultimate reality, the absolutely real. The entities of this ontology are hierarchically ordered, a higher entity having the power to destroy a lower entity. This latter fact partly explains the Akan conception of causality.

5.2. Causality

One might begin by asking why a discussion of causality should be appended to a discussion of a theory of being. The answer is a simple one: It is because the Akan conception of causality is closely tied to their conception of the world, to their theory of being. Consequently, section 5.1 on the Akan theory of being provides the background and the framework for explicating their concept of causality.

76

5. Being and causality

Akan thinkers maintain a doctrine of universal causation: Everything has a cause (*asẽm biara wõ ne farebae*). Hence, the proverbs, "Whenever the palm tree tilts it is because of what the earth has told it" (*se abẽ bõ ne mu ase a, na ẽwõ nea asase ase no*);[27] "If Birebire had not come, there would have been no calamity" (*Birebire amma a, amene mma*).[28] Nothing happens without a cause.

In our discussion of the Akan theory of causality we shall pay particular attention to events that are considered by them as unexpected or extraordinary; events that in their view do not occur according to the course of nature. It is such occurrences for which they have characteristic causal explanations. They have not concerned themselves much with finding explanations for ordinary or regular occurrences in nature, such as the flooding of a river after a heavy rainfall, the drying up of rivers in times of drought, poor harvests due to the lack of sufficient rains, catching few fish at certain times of the year, the growth of plants, a pregnancy that lasts nine months, the fatality of certain diseases, and so on. Such events are held by them to be part of the order of nature established by the omnipotent creator, Onyame; they are part of Onyame's arrangement (*Onyame nhyehyẽe*), and, as a previously quoted proverb has it, "The order Onyame has established, no living man can alter." Thus, they seem to say that there is a "necessary" causal connection between such events. Since it has long been observed that whenever it rains heavily and for a long time the river floods, and whenever it does not rain for a long time poor harvests and famine follow, they are not specially interested in looking for causal explanations for such expected occurrences. Answers to questions such as "*What* caused the flooding of the river?" or "*Why* is this year's harvest so poor?" or "*How* did the bushfire in the farm occur?" are provided within the framework of their empirical knowledge of natural events: "The uninterrupted rainfall of the past four days caused the flooding of the river"; "This year's harvest is so poor because of the lack of sufficient rainfall"; "The burning of a large forest for charcoal, not far away, spread to the cocoa farm, causing the bushfire." Causal explanations for such natural occurrences are thus empirical, scientific, and nonsupernaturalistic. Different attitudes, however, are adopted with respect to another kind of what other cultures would regard as natural occurrences.

The occurrences that engage their attention and for which different explanations are given are those that they regard as "extraordinary" or "contingent," occurrences that are held to fall outside the course of nature and so are taken to be exceptions to the laws of nature. These occurrences do not fit into their conception of the normal order of things, for they imply a disruption of the preestablished order of Onyame. Some examples might be: an unusually long period of drought, a tree falling and killing a farmer on his way to his farm, a pregnancy that extends much beyond a period of nine months, a person dying from a snakebite, a person being afflicted with a certain kind of disease, a person being accidentally shot to death by a hunter, and so on. Such occurrences have certain characteristics: They are infrequent and hence are considered "abnormal"; they are discrete and isolated; they appear to be puzzling, bizarre, and incomprehensible; they are not considered subsumable under any immediately known law of nature. It is not that the Akans do not know that a falling tree can kill a person or that certain diseases can be fatal. In such situations the question the Akan poses is not "Why did the falling tree kill him?" but "Why did *that* tree fall at *that* particular time and kill *that* particular person?" Putting this type of question suggests that, for them, events like the falling of a tree and the biting of a snake cannot be ultimate causes; they can only be regarded as immediate or secondary causes. Those events by themselves are deemed insufficient or unsatisfactory to explain their effects. It is and can only be an ultimate cause that caused *that* tree at *that* time to kill *that* man. Note that the "ultimate" cause here is not necessarily the Supreme Being; it could be any of the lesser spirits or ancestral spirits.[29]

In two respects events that are considered in the Akan philosophy of causation as extraordinary bear some resemblance to happenings that are regarded as accidents (*asiane*). First, both direct their attention to the situation of the individual person *qua* the consequence or victim of an occurrence. Second, both have causes ("accident" to the Akan thinker is not an uncaused event). But they differ in that extraordinary events include both "impersonal" occurrences, such as an unusually long period of drought and an uninterrupted rainfall for over four weeks, and "personal" occurrences, that is, occurrences which directly affect a person such as dying from snakebite or being killed by a falling tree. By contrast, accidents (*asiane*) are restricted to personal misfortunes. Thus, accidents and extraordinary events are not the same.

A preliminary objection may be raised against the viability of the Akan idea of the extraordinary event and the classification of natural occurrences into ordinary and extraordinary, normal and abnormal, "necessary" and "contingent." One might well argue that any type of event, however irregularly or infrequently it occurs, must be considered as part of the course of nature, and that such an event may thus not, after all, be as extraordinary as it is supposed to be. Such an argument may be allowed. But to the Akan an extraordinary event must be a peculiar one indeed. An event considered extraordinary by Akan thinkers is one that has traumatic consequences. The falling of a tree, which is perfectly ordinary, leaves no one spellbound or confounded. Of the greatest interest is why a particular man should be there just at that moment and be trapped. It is that aspect of the event that is considered "extraordinary." But such a concept of the extraordinary event can hardly be considered intelligible and adequate. For events considered extraordinary are not so unique, isolated, and discrete as to be completely inexplicable by a natural or scientific law. If they had paid greater attention to their own experience, the thinkers would probably have had a different view of the character of the so-called extraordinary events; they would have convinced themselves that it was, after all, not impossible, as it were, to compound those atomic events into molecular ones.

Yet it is generally for events considered extraordinary that the Akan thinkers have serious and well-meaning causal explanations. So let us turn to how they conceive of causal relations in such events.

The Akan doctrine of being provides the metaphysical framework for analyzing and understanding the Akan concept of cause. The world is, according to them, a world of action. This concept of action is developed into a metaphysics of potency. The concept of action itself derives from their view that the world is primarily spiritual; what exists is spirit, and the world teems with spirits or spiritual beings. These spiritual beings are powers, or endowed with powers, of varying capabilities. Since a higher being has the power to destroy a lower being, humans and the world of natural objects and phenomena can easily be controlled by such spiritual powers. These powers or spirits, then, are causes of action and change in the world. And inasmuch as every causal situation involves action and change – for there cannot be an effect without something being changed – causal reference is often made to powers or spirits. In this connection, some information we have from Busia is instructive and apposite.

II. The Akan conceptual scheme

In 1946 the Akwamuhene of Ankaasi, a village near Kumasi, died. Forty days before, he had given evidence at court in a case in which another man had been accused of murdering the Akwamuhene's own father. The accused person was acquitted chiefly on the evidence of the Akwamuhene, who a few days later fell ill. On the twenty-eighth day of his illness he confessed to a friend that he believed his father's ghost was punishing him because he had given false evidence at the trial. He did not recover from his illness, and died. No other *explanation* was required, for it was the general belief that his father had punished him for his conduct.

Another death also occurred recently (1946) at Wenchi. In 1940 an elderly man died there. His funeral rites were curtailed because some of the members of the lineage were away. It was decided that the full rites should be performed later. This was not done for six years. Then another member of the lineage, a nephew of the elderly man, fell ill and died. A native physician declared that the death had been caused by the spirit of the elderly man because the lineage had not performed his funeral rites. This was generally held to be a *sufficient explanation* for the death.[30]

In an Akan community, if a falling tree kills a man, or if a man dies in a car accident or from a snakebite, the cause of the death would generally be thought to be a spirit. A purely scientific or naturalistic explanation would not suffice, because a snakebite or car accident does not always result in death. For the Akan, then, a purely scientific or naturalistic explanation of natural events presupposes an *absolute* regularity or uniformity in nature. But such an absolute uniformity is subverted by the existence of irregular, abnormal occurrences.

Akan thinkers provide causal explanations for those events that do not, in their view, form themselves into a regular pattern. The irregularity of such events immediately gives rise to the question "Why?" Here I wish to make a distinction between two kinds of why-questions. The first relates to situations considered normal, ordinary, and easily comprehensible. In these, explanations would be given in empirical and naturalistic terms. An example of such a why-question is: "Why is this year's harvest so poor?" raised by an Akan farmer. Poor harvest might be ascribed to lack of sufficient rainfall, for instance. Such a why-question, eliciting a purely empirical explanation, I refer to as why$_1$-question. The second kind of why-question comes up in situations where particular persons happen to be the victims. Such situations are regarded by the Akan as abnormal, extraordinary, and incomprehensible, and they invariably elicit nonempirical, supernaturalistic explanations. An example of such a personalized why-question is: "Why did *that* tree fall and kill *that* particular person?" The death of that person would be ascribed to some supernatural being or power. I refer to this second kind of why-question as a why$_2$-question. The two kinds should be noted, as most scholars ignore why$_1$-questions in African causal explanations and fasten on why$_2$-questions.[31]

Let me say a bit more about why$_2$-questions. The question "why$_2$" comes up when, for instance, a person dies from a snakebite or from a disease because the effect (death) appears mysterious to them. In their experience such an effect did not always occur. In the event of a man dying from some disease, they would, to quote Busia writing about the treatment of the sick in Akan culture, ask: "*Why* did a disease that had on many occasions responded to the traditional healer's treatment fail to respond in a particular case? Many others had had the same disease and had been successfully treated with the same remedies. *Why* did this particular patient die when the others had recovered?"[32] The causal explanation for this type of event would be made in supernaturalistic terms.

In considering such so-called abnormal or extraordinary events, Akan thinkers obviously fail to consider other factors that may be relevant. The quantity of poison injected by the snake, the physical constitution of the person, the speed with which he was brought to the healer, etc. – these are some of the factors that may have contributed to the death of a person bitten by a snake. Such factors may also account for the opposite effect in cases that did not result in death. Thus, in their causal explanations, Akan thinkers turn too quickly from the what-, how-, and why$_1$-questions to why$_2$-questions. Instead of asking, What brought this about? or How did this happen?, they insist on asking, Why$_2$ did it happen? The reason, however, is that even though they know of the what- or how-questions, they maintain that the answers to those kinds of questions do not go far enough to be satisfactory, for there is or may be something that is unclear and ought to be clarified or known. For them, the way to clarify or know is to ask other kinds of questions than the what- or how-questions. Hence, why$_2$-questions are considered deeper kinds of questions, leading to different kinds of explanations. One may also conclude, however, that why$_2$-questions actually constitute an admission of their inability to give adequate explanations to certain events.

One way to avoid the why$_2$-questions where the answers to the what- or how-questions are unknown or unsatisfactory is to introduce the concepts of chance and luck. But explanations of unexpected natural events in terms of chance or luck are repugnant to determinist Akan thinkers, who hold that "nothing just (or, merely) happens" (*biribiara nsi kwa*),[33] and that "everything has its 'because of,' " that is, reason, cause (*biribiara wɔ ne sɛ nti*). Their conception of an orderly universe completely rules out the possibility of an unqualifiedly random event, and therefore chance, defined as an uncaused event, can have no place in their explanations of the causes of natural events. The Akans do have concepts of accident (*asiane*) and luck or fortune (*akrade*). But for Akan thinkers an accident is not simply a chance event, an event that just happens to take place; it *has* a cause. To them an event may be considered an accident insofar as it may, for some reason, be thought not to be part, or an inevitable consequence, of a man's destiny (*nkrabea*).[34] Thus, accident (*asiane*) and luck (or fortune: *akrade*) are believed to operate solely on the level of human nature[35] and purpose, not on the level of the order of nature. That is to say, in nature there are no chances or accidents. For them, as for Aristotle, a chance event as such would in fact be an event whose cause is unknown, not one lacking a cause. When a European explains an unpredictable or unexpected natural event by reference to chance, coincidence, luck, or fortune, from the point of view of Akan thinkers that is the same as saying that the cause is unknown. But the Akan thinker would here retort that ignorance of the cause of an event does not imply the nonexistence of a cause.

Although supernatural factors play important roles in Akan causal explanations, recognition is given also to the causal roles of physical objects. Causal explanations in terms of supernatural factors are generally made when human beings feel the immediate or direct effects or are the victims of natural events. Thus, a tree falling and killing a *man* on his way to his farm would almost invariably be explained in supernatural terms. But if on his way to the farm the farmer comes upon a big tree that had fallen across the path and he then remembers the previous night's rainstorm, he would certainly attribute the cause of the fall of the tree to the rainstorm. Similarly, he would causally explain poor harvests in natural terms: either the destructive action of insects or the lack of adequate rainfall or the infertility of that piece of land. Cause, for this type of event, is conceived in terms of physical agency or efficiency.

The acknowledgment of physical (nonsupernatural) causality indicates a conception of dual causality, the physical being invoked in consequence of ordinary or regular sequence of events, the regularity making the situation comprehensible; the spiritual being invoked in cases regarded as extraordinary or abnormal events. This concept of dual causality follows from the concept of dual reality discussed earlier in this chapter. Furthermore, whereas spiritual causality is vertical – the causal direction going only from a higher being to a lower one – physical causality is horizontal.

The Akan theory of causality, as discussed here, is in some ways a consequence of the hierarchically ordered Akan ontology. In this ontology any higher being can have causal power or control over a lower being, but the causal relation of a higher being to a lower being is asymmetric; thus a lower being can have no causal power over a higher being. The world of natural objects and phenomena is at the bottom of this hierarchy; it is the lowest kind of being and can therefore be causally controlled by the other beings. Causal relations must therefore be explained or understood within the framework of Akan psychophysical metaphysics. Thus, in cases where human beings are the victims of events, the ultimate cause is regarded as a supernatural being. In such cases natural laws, which consider the relations only between material objects, are incapable of offering adequate causal explanations. Natural laws describe but do not explain; real explanations must make reference to spirits. Why$_2$-questions, which figure prominently in Akan thinking about causality, purport to elicit deeper explanations of natural events. It is when such explanations are not forthcoming that some European thinkers, for want of something better, resort to chance, a concept that is rejected in determinist Akan philosophy. Nevertheless, in Akan explanations, recognition is appropriately given to the causal roles of physical (material) objects. That is to say, physical laws are also considered causally relevant and operative, even though limited to relations between physical phenomena. Akan thought, however, appears emphatic in its position that in our complex and bizarre world, physical laws, which are the creation of human intellects, cannot claim to exhaust all possible explanations of events and behavior. One final point: In my view, the Akan thinkers' insistence on regularity, uniformity, or repetition of a certain kind of event, implicit in their ideas about causation, is appropriate, as without such an assumption no reliable scientific predictions can be made and no inference from the observed to the unobserved can be drawn.

6

The concept of a person

What is a person? Is a person just the bag of flesh and bones that we see with our eyes, or is there something additional to the body that we do not see? A conception[1] of the nature of a human being in Akan philosophy is the subject of this chapter.

6.1. Ōkra (soul)

We are given to understand from a number of often quoted, though mistaken, anthropological accounts that the Akan people consider a human being to be constituted of three elements: ōkra, sunsum, and honam (or nipadua: body).

The ōkra is said to be that which constitutes the innermost self, the essence, of the individual person. Ōkra is the individual's life, for which reason it is usually referred to as ōkrateasefo, that is, the living soul, a seeming tautology that yet is significant. The expression is intended to emphasize that ōkra is identical with life. The ōkra is the embodiment and transmitter of the individual's destiny (fate: nkrabea). It is explained as a spark of the Supreme Being (Onyame) in man. It is thus described as divine and as having an antemundane existence with the Supreme Being. The presence of this divine essence in a human being may have been the basis of the Akan proverb, "All men are the children of God; no one is a child of the earth" (nnipa nyinaa yē Onyame mma, obiara nnyē asase ba). So conceived, the ōkra can be considered as the equivalent of the concept of the soul in other metaphysical systems. Hence, it is correct to translate ōkra into English as soul.

II. The Akan conceptual scheme

Wiredu, however, thinks that this translation "is quite definitely wrong."[2] He, for his part, would translate the ōkra as "*that whose presence in the body means life and whose absence means death* and which also receives the individual's destiny from God."[3] Surely the (here) italicized part of the quotation accurately captures the Akan conception of the soul – ōkrateasefo, the living soul – whose departure means death. This is indeed the primary definition of the soul in practically all metaphysical systems. I do not think, however, that the concept of destiny is an essential feature of the Akan definition of the soul, even though the concept of the soul is an essential feature of the Akan conception of destiny (see Chapter 7).

Wiredu's reason for thinking that it is wrong to translate ōkra as soul is mainly that whereas "the soul is supposed in Western philosophy to be a purely immaterial entity that somehow inhabits the body, the ōkra, by contrast, is quasi-physical."[4] He adds, however, that "It is not of course supposed to be straightforwardly physical as it is believed not to be fully subject to spatial constraints. Nor is it perceivable to the naked eye. Nevertheless, in some ways it seems to be credited with paraphysical properties."[5] Wiredu's characterizations of the ōkra as "quasi-physical" and having "para-physical" properties are completely wrong. He acknowledges that "highly developed medicine men" or people with extrasensory (or medicinally heightened) perception in Akan communities are said to be capable of seeing and communicating with the ōkra. It must be noted, however, that these phenomena do not take place in the ordinary spatial world; otherwise anyone would be able to see or communicate with the ōkra (soul). This must mean that what those with special abilities see or communicate with is something non-spatial. Thus, the fact that the ōkra can be seen by such people does not make it physical or quasi-physical (whatever that expression means), since this act or mode of seeing is not at the physical or spatial level.

I understand the term "quasi-physical" to mean "seemingly physical," "almost physical." Such description of the ōkra (soul) in Akan thought runs counter to the belief of most Akan people in disembodied survival or life after death. For a crucial aspect of Akan metaphysics is the existence of the world of spirits (*asamando*), a world inhabited by the departed souls of the ancestors. The conception or interpretation of the ōkra as a quasi-physical object having paraphysical properties would mean the total or "near total" (whatever that might mean) extinction of the ōkra (soul) upon the death of the person. And if this were the case, it would be senseless to talk of departed souls continuing to exist in the world of spirits (*asamando*).

In attempting further to distinguish the Akan *ōkra* from the Western soul, Wiredu writes:

> The *ōkra* is postulated in Akan thought to account for the fact of life and of destiny *but not of thought*. The soul, on the other hand, seems in much Western philosophy to be intended to account, not just for life *but also for thought*. Indeed, in Cartesian philosophy, the sole purpose of introducing the soul is to account for the phenomenon of *thinking*.[6]

Wiredu, I believe, is here taking "thought" in the ratiocinative or cognitive sense, its normal meaning in English. But his position is undercut by his reference to the concept of *thought* in Cartesian philosophy. For it is agreed by scholars of Descartes that by *thought* (or thinking: *cogitatio*) Descartes means much more than what is normally connoted by the English word. Thus, Bernard Williams writes:

> It is an important point that in Descartes' usage the Latin verb *cogitare* and the French verb *penser* and the related nouns *cogitatio* and *pensée*, have a wider significance than the English *think* and *thought*. In English such terms are specially connected with ratiocinative or *cognitive* processes. For Descartes, however, *cogitatio* or *pensée* is any sort of conscious state or activity whatsoever; it can as well be a sensation (at least, in its purely psychological aspect) or an act of will, as judgment or belief or intellectual questioning.[7]

Thus, what Descartes means by mind or thought is *consciousness*. Despite his reference to Descartes, I think Wiredu uses "thought" in the narrow sense, that is, of ratiocination or cognition. "Thought" in the narrow sense is of course a function or an act of consciousness. Any living human being must have consciousness. This being the case, consciousness, which is equivalent to the soul or mind in Descartes, can be a translation of *ōkra*. On this showing, it cannot be true, as Wiredu thinks, that "when we come to Descartes, the difference between the *ōkra* and the soul becomes radical and complete."[8] My analysis, if correct, implies the opposite. I argue below (section 6.3) that thought (*adwen*) in the narrow sense is in Akan philosophy an activity of the *sunsum*, which I interpret as a part of the soul (*ōkra*). Having raised some objections to Wiredu's interpretation of what he calls the Akan concept of mind, I return to my own analysis of the Akan concept of the person.

The conception of the ōkra as constituting the individual's life, the life force, is linked very closely with another concept, honhom. Honhom means "breath"; it is the noun form of home, to breathe. When a person is dead, it is said "His breath is gone" (ne honhom kō) or "His soul has withdrawn from his body" (ne 'kra afi ne ho). These two sentences, one with honhom as subject and the other with ōkra, do, in fact, say the same thing; they express the same thought, the death-of-the-person. The departure of the soul from the body means the death of the person, and so does the cessation of breath. Yet this does not mean that the honhom (breath) is identical with the ōkra (soul). It is the ōkra that "causes" the breathing. Thus, the honhom is the tangible manifestation or evidence of the presence of the ōkra. [In some dialects of the Akan language, however, honhom has come to be used interchangeably with sunsum ("spirit"), so that the phrase honhom bōne has come to mean the same thing as sunsum bōne, that is, evil spirit. The identification of the honhom with the sunsum seems to me to be a recent idea, and may have resulted from the translation of the Bible into the various Akan dialects; honhom must have been used to translate the Greek pneuma (breath, spirit).] The clarification of the concepts of ōkra, honhom, sunsum and others bearing on the Akan conception of the nature of a person is the concern of this chapter.

6.2. Sunsum (spirit)

Sunsum is another of the constituent elements of the person. It has usually been rendered in English as "spirit." It has already been observed that sunsum is used both generically to refer to all unperceivable, mystical beings and forces in Akan ontology, and specifically to refer to the activating principle in the person. It appears from the anthropological accounts that even when it is used specifically, "spirit" (sunsum) is not identical with soul (ōkra), as they do not refer to the same thing. However, the anthropological accounts of the sunsum involve some conceptual blunders, as I shall show. As for the mind – when it is not identified with the soul – it may be rendered also by sunsum, judging from the functions that are attributed by the Akan thinkers to the latter.

On the surface it might appear that "spirit" is not an appropriate rendition for sunsum, but after clearing away misconceptions engendered by some anthropological writings, I shall show that it is appropriate but that it requires clarification. Anthropologists and sociologists have held (1) that the *sunsum* derives from the father,[9] (2) that it is not divine,[10] and (3) that it perishes with the disintegration of the *honam*,[11] that is, the material component of a person. It seems to me, however, that all these characterizations of the *sunsum* are incorrect.[12]

Let us first take up the third characterization, namely, as something that perishes with the body. Now, if the *sunsum* perishes along with the body, a physical object, then it follows that the *sunsum* also is something physical or material. Danquah's philosophical analysis concludes that "*sunsum* is, in fact, the matter or the physical basis of the ultimate ideal of which ōkra (soul) is the form and the spiritual or mental basis."[13] Elsewhere he speaks of an "interaction of the material mechanism (*sunsum*) with the soul," and assimilates the *sunsum* to the "sensible form" of Aristotle's metaphysics of substance and the ōkra to the "intelligible form."[14] One might conclude from these statements that Danquah also conceived the *sunsum* as material, although some of his other statements would seem to contradict this conclusion. The relation between the *honam* (body) and the *sunsum* (supposedly bodily), however, is left unexplained. Thus, philosophical, sociological, and anthropological accounts of the nature of the person give the impression of a tripartite conception of a human being in Akan philosophy:

Ōkra (soul)	immaterial
Sunsum ("spirit")	material (?)
Honam (body)	material

As we shall see, however, this account or analysis of a person, particularly the characterization of the *sunsum* ("spirit") as something material, is not satisfactory. I must admit, however, that the real nature of the *sunsum* presents perhaps the greatest difficulty in the Akan metaphysics of a person and has been a source of confusion for many. The difficulty, however, is not insoluble.

The functions or activities attributed to the *sunsum* indicate that it is neither material nor mortal nor derived from the father. Busia says that the *sunsum* "is what moulds the child's personality and disposition. It is that which determines his character and individuality."[15] Danquah says: "But we now know the notion which corresponds to the Akan '*sunsum*' namely, not 'spirit' as such, but personality which covers the relation of the 'body' to the 'soul'

II. The Akan conceptual scheme

(Ōkra).''[16] That the *sunsum* constitutes or rather determines the personality and character of a person is stated by Danquah several times.[17] Rattray observed that the *sunsum* is the basis of character and personality.[18] Eva Meyerowitz also considered the *sunsum* as personality.[19] My own researches indicate that the views of Busia and Danquah regarding the connection between *sunsum* and personality are correct, but that they failed to see the logical implications of their views. There are indeed sentences in the Akan language in which *sunsum* refers to a person's personality and traits. Thus, for "He has a strong personality" the Akans would say, "His *sunsum* is 'heavy' or 'weighty' " *(ne sunsum yē duru)*. When a man is generous they would say that he has a good *sunsum (ōwō sunsum pa)*. When a man has an impressive or imposing personality they would say that he has an overshadowing *sunsum (ne sunsum hyē me so)*. In fact sometimes in describing a dignified person they would simply say, "He has *spirit*" *(ōwō sunsum)*, that is, he has a commanding presence. And a man may be said to have a "gentle" *sunsum*, a "forceful" *sunsum*, a "submissive" or "weak" *sunsum*. Thus, the concept of the *sunsum* corresponds in many ways to what is meant by personality, as was observed by earlier investigators.

It is now clear that in Akan conceptions the *sunsum* ("spirit") is the basis of a man's personality, and, in the words of Busia, "his ego."[20] Personality, of course, is a word that has been variously defined by psychologists. But I believe that whatever else that concept may mean, it certainly involves the idea of a set of characteristics as evidenced in a person's behavior – thoughts, feelings, actions, etc. (The sentences given above demonstrate that it refers to more than a person's physical appearance.) Thus, if the *sunsum* is that which constitutes the basis of an individual's personality, it cannot be a physical thing, for qualities like courage, jealousy, gentleness, forcefulness, and dignity are psychological, not sensible or physical. The conception of personality as the function of the *sunsum* makes a material conception of the latter logically impossible. (Some Western philosophers and theologians in fact identify personality with the soul.[21]) On the basis of the characteristics of *sunsum*, Parrinder describes it as the "personality-soul," perhaps using the term for the first time.[22]

As noted, certain statements of Danquah suggest a physicalistic interpretation of the *sunsum*. On the other hand, he also maintains that "it is the *sunsum* that 'experiences,' "[23] and that it is through the *sunsum* that "the ōkra or soul manifests itself in the world of experience."[24] Elsewhere he says of the *sunsum*: "It is the bearer of conscious experience, the unconscious or subliminal self remaining over as the *ōkra* or soul."[25] It is not clear what Danquah means by the "bearer" of experience. Perhaps what he means is that the *sunsum* is the subject of experience – that which experiences. Experience is the awareness of something. Since a purely material thing, such as wood or a dead body, cannot experience anything, it follows that the *sunsum*, *qua* subject of experience, cannot be material. If, as Danquah thought,[26] it is the *sunsum* that makes it possible for the destiny (*nkrabea*) of the soul to be "realized" or "carried out" on earth, then, like the *ōkra* (soul), an aspect of whose functions it performs, the *sunsum* also must be spiritual and immaterial. Danquah's position on the concept of the *sunsum*, then, is ambivalent, as is Busia's. Busia says that one part of a person is "the personality that comes indirectly from the Supreme Being."[27] By "personality" Busia must, on his own showing,[28] be referring to the *sunsum*, which must, according to my analysis, derive directly from the Supreme Being, and not from the father. (What derives from the father is the *ntoro*, to be explained directly.) It must, therefore, be divine and immortal, contrary to what he and others thought. That *sunsum* cannot derive from the child's father is proved also by the fact that trees, plants, and other natural objects also contain *sunsum*, as we saw in the previous chapter.

The explanation given by most Akans of the phenomenon of dreaming also indicates, it seems to me, that *sunsum* must be immaterial. In Akan thought, as in Freud's, dreams are not somatic but psychical phenomena. It is held that in a dream it is the person's *sunsum* that is the "actor." As an informant told Rattray decades ago, "When you sleep your *'Kra* (soul) does not leave you, as your *sunsum* may."[29] In sleep the *sunsum* is said to be released from the fetters of the body. As it were, it fashions for itself a new world of forms with the materials of its waking experience. Thus, although one is deeply asleep, yet one may "see" oneself standing atop a mountain or driving a car or fighting with someone or pursuing a desire like sexual intercourse; also, during sleep (that is, in dreams) a person's *sunsum* may talk with other *sunsum*. The actor in any of these "actions" is thought to be the *sunsum*, which thus can leave the body and return to it. The idea of the psychical part of a person leaving the body in sleep appears to be widespread in Africa. The Azande, for instance, maintain "that in sleep the soul is released from the body and can roam about at will and meet other spirits and have other adventures, though they admit something mysterious about its experiences. ... During sleep a man's soul wanders everywhere."[30]

The idea that some part of the soul leaves the body in sleep is not completely absent from the history of Western thought, even though, as Parrinder says, "the notion of a wandering soul is [are] foreign to the modern European mind."[31] The idea occurs, for instance, in Plato. In the *Republic* Plato refers to "the wild beast in us" that in pursuit of desires and pleasures bestirs itself "in *dreams* when the *gentler part of the soul* slumbers and the control of reason is withdrawn; then the wild beast in us, full-fed with meat and drink, becomes rampant and shakes off sleep to go in quest of what will gratify its own instincts."[32] The context is a discussion of tyranny. But Plato prefaces his discussion with remarks on the *psychological* foundation of the tyrannical man, and says that desire (Greek: *epithumia*) is the basis of his behavior.

It is not surprising that both scholars of Plato and modern psychologists have noted the relevance of the above passage to the analysis of the nature of the human psyche. On this passage the classical scholar James Adam wrote: "The theory is that in dreams the part of the soul concerned is not asleep, but awake and goes out to seek the object of its desire."[33] The classicist Paul Shorey observed that "The Freudians have at least discovered Plato's anticipation of their main thesis."[34] The relevance of the Platonic passage to Freud has been noted also by other scholars of Plato such as Renford Bambrough[35] and Thomas Gould,[36] and by psychologists. Valentine, a psychologist, observed: "The germ of several aspects of the Freudian view of dreams, including the characteristic doctrine of the censor, was to be found in Plato."[37]

It is clear that the passage in Plato indicates a link between dreams and (the gratification of) desires.[38] In Akan psychology the *sunsum* appears not only as unconscious but also as that which pursues and experiences desires. (In Akan dreams are also considered predictive.) But the really interesting part of Plato's thesis for our purposes relates to *the idea of some part of the human soul leaving the body in dreams*. "The wild beast in us" in Plato's passage is not necessarily equivalent to the Akan *sunsum*, but one may say that just as Plato's "wild beast" (which, like the *sunsum*, experiences dreams) is a *part* of the soul and thus not a physical object, so is *sunsum*.

It might be supposed that if the *sunsum* can engage in activity, such as traveling through space or occupying a physical location –

like standing on the top of a mountain – then it can hardly be said not to be a physical object. The problem here is obviously complex. Let us assume, for the moment, that the *sunsum* is a physical object. One question that would immediately arise is: How can a purely physical object leave the person when he or she is asleep? Dreaming is of course different from imagining or thinking. The latter occurs during waking life, whereas the former occurs only during sleep: *wõnda a wõnso dae*, that is, "Unless you are asleep you do not dream" is a well-known Akan saying. The fact that dreaming occurs only in sleep makes it a unique sort of mental activity and its subject, namely *sunsum*, a different sort of subject. A purely physical object cannot be in two places at the same time: A body lying in bed cannot at the same time be on the top of a mountain. Whatever is on the top of the mountain, then, must be something nonphysical, nonbodily, and yet somehow connected to a physical thing – in this case, the body. This argument constitutes a *reductio ad absurdum* of the view that *sunsum* can be a physical object.

But, then, how can the *sunsum*, qua nonphysical, extrasensory object, travel in physical space and have a physical location? This question must be answered within the broad context of the African belief in the activities of the supernatural (spiritual) beings in the physical world. The spiritual beings are said to be insensible and intangible, but they are also said to make themselves felt in the physical world. They can thus interact with the physical world. But from this it cannot be inferred that they are physical or quasi-physical or have permanent physical properties. It means that a spiritual being can, when it so desires, take on physical properties. That is, even though a spiritual being is nonspatial in essence, it can, by the sheer operation of its power, assume spatial properties. Debrunner speaks of "temporary 'materializations,' i.e., as spirits having taken on the body of a person which afterwards suddenly vanish."[39] Mbiti observed that "Spirits are invisible, but may make themselves visible to human beings."[40] We should view the "physical" activities of the *sunsum* in dreaming from the standpoint of the activities of the spiritual beings in the physical world. As a microcosm of the world spirit, the *sunsum* can also interact with the external world. So much then for the defense of the psychical, nonphysical nature of *sunsum*, the subject of experiences in dreaming.

As the basis of personality, as the coperformer of some of the functions of the õkra (soul) – undoubtedly held as a spiritual entity –

and as the subject of the psychical activity of dreaming, the *sunsum* must be something spiritual (immaterial). This is the reason for my earlier assertion that "spirit" might not be an inappropriate translation for *sunsum*. On my analysis, then, we have the following picture:

Ōkra (soul)   ⎫
Sunsum ("spirit")   ⎬ immaterial (spiritual)
Honam (body)   material (physical)

In their conception of the nature of the person the Akans distinguish the *ntoro* and the *mogya* (blood). In contrast to the *sunsum* and *ōkra*, which definitely are of divine origin, the *ntoro* and the *mogya* are endowed by human beings. The *ntoro* is held as coming from the father of the child. It has been confused with *sunsum*. Thus, Busia says that the two terms are synonymous, and hence renders *ntoro* as "spirit." He writes: "*Ntoro* is the generic term of which *sunsum* is a specific instance."[41] Rattray also translated *ntoro* by "spirit," though he thought it corresponded with the semen.[42] He said elsewhere that the *ntoro* is "passed into the woman by a male during the act of coition."[43] One of my discussants stated that *ntoro* is derived from the father's semen, but the *sunsum*, he said, comes from the Supreme Being.[44] The *ntoro* appears to be the basis of inherited characteristics and may therefore be simply translated as "sperm-transmitted characteristic," even though spiritual as well as physiological qualities are attributed to it. Both *ntoro* and *mogya* (blood, which is believed to be transmitted by the mother) are genetic factors responsible for inherited characteristics, on the basis of which the Akan thinkers have created proverbs such as:

> The crab does not give birth to a bird.
> The offspring of an antelope cannot possibly
>   resemble a deer's offspring.
> The antelope does not leap for its offspring to
>   crawl.[45]

The introduction of inherited characteristics into the constitution of a person introduces an element of complexity into the Akan concept of the person.

6.3. Relation of ōkra and sunsum

Having shown that the *sunsum* is in fact something spiritual (and for this reason I shall henceforth translate *sunsum* as "spirit"), we must examine whether the expressions *sunsum* and *ōkra* are identical in terms of their referent. In the course of my field research some discussants stated that the *sunsum*, *ōkra*, and *honhom* (breath) are identical; they denote the same object; it is one and the same object that goes under three names. I have already shown that although there is a close link between *ōkra* and *honhom*, the two cannot be identified; likewise the identification of *honhom* and *sunsum* is incorrect. What about the *sunsum* and *ōkra*? Are they identical?

The relation between the *sunsum* and *ōkra* is a difficult knot to untie. The anthropologist Rattray, perhaps the most perceptive and analytical researcher into the Ashanti culture, wrote: "It is very difficult sometimes to distinguish between the *'kra* and the next kind of soul, the *sunsum*, and sometimes the words seem synonymous, but I cannot help thinking this is a loose use of the terms."[46] Rattray was, I think, more inclined to believe that the two terms are not identical. Such a supposition, in my view, would be correct, for to say that the two are identical would logically mean that whatever can be asserted of one can or must be asserted of the other. Yet there are some things the Akans say of the *sunsum* which are not said of the *ōkra*, and vice versa; the attributes or predicates of the two are different. The Akans say:

A(1)   "His *'kra* is sad" (*ne 'kra di awerēhow*); never, "His *sunsum* is sad."

(2)   "His *'kra* is worried or disturbed" (*ne 'kra teetee*).

(3)   "His *'kra* has run away" (*ne 'kra adwane*), to denote someone who is scared to death.

(4)   "His *'kra* is good" (*ne 'kra ye*), referring to a person who is lucky or fortunate. [The negative of this statement is "His *'kra* is not good." If you used *sunsum* in lieu of *'kra*, and made the statement "His *sunsum* is not good" (*ne sunsum nnyē*), the meaning would be quite different; it would mean that his *sunsum* is evil, that is to say, he is an evil spirit, a witch.]

(5)   "His *'kra* has withdrawn from his body" (*ne 'kra afi ne ho*).

(6)   "But for his *'kra* that followed him, he would have died" (*ne 'kra dii n'akyi, anka owui*).

(7)   "His *'kra* is happy" (*ne 'kra aniagye*).

In all such statements the attributions are made to the *ōkra* (soul), never to the *sunsum*. On the other hand, the Akans say:

B(1)   "He has *sunsum*" (*ōwō sunsum*), an expression they use when they want to refer to someone as dignified and as having a commanding presence. Here they never say, "He has *ōkra*," soul, for it is believed that it is the nature of the *sunsum* (not the *ōkra*) that differs from person to person; hence they speak of "gentle *sunsum*," "forceful *sunsum*," "weak or strong *sunsum*," etc.

(2) "His *sunsum* is heavy or weighty" (*ne sunsum yē duru*), that is, he has a strong personality.

(3) "His *sunsum* overshadows mine" (*ne sunsum hyē me so*).

(4) "Someone's *sunsum* is bigger or greater than another's" (*obi sunsum so kyēn obi deē*). To say "someone's *'kra* is greater than another's" would be meaningless.

(5) "He has a good *sunsum*" (*ōwō sunsum pa*), that is, he is a generous person.

In all such statements the attributions are made to the *sunsum* (spirit), never to the *ōkra* (soul). Rattray also pointed out correctly that "an Ashanti would never talk of washing his *sunsum*."[47] It is the *ōkra* that is washed (*okraguare*). In the terminology of the modern linguist, sentences containing *ōkra* and *sunsum* differ, according to my analysis, not only in their surface structures but also in their deep structures.

It is pretty clear from this semantic analysis that *ōkra* and *sunsum* are not intersubstitutable in predications. Intersubstitution of the terms, as we saw above, leads either to nonsense as in B(4) or to change of meaning as in A(4) and B(1). Semantic analysis suggests a nonidentity relation between *sunsum* and *ōkra*. One might reject this conclusion by treating these distinctions as merely idiomatic and not, therefore, as evidence for considering *ōkra* and *sunsum* as distinct. Let us call this the "idiomatic thesis." In the English language, for instance, it is idiomatic to say "He's a sad soul" rather than "He's a sad spirit," without implying that soul and spirit are distinct. But in English the substitution of one for the other of the two terms – even if unidiomatic – will not lead to nonsense and would not change the *meaning*; in Akan it would.

The "idiomatic thesis" has been advanced by a former student of mine in an undergraduate "Long Essay" written under my supervision. He denied that any ontological distinctions can be made from the fact that attributions in some statements in Akan are made to the *ōkra*, whereas in others they are made to the *sunsum*. He wrote:

> If the Akans use *ōkra* instead of *sunsum*, or the latter instead of the former in expressions such as those given above, they do

so not because of their belief in the distinction between the *ōkra* and the *sunsum*, but merely as a matter of *locution*. The Akans do not say, *ne sunsum ye* simply because such expression is not *idiomatic*. In many instances the two terms are used interchangeably.[48]

He went on to say that "the words *sunsum* and *ōkra* refer to one and the same thing, the soul, the spiritual substance of a human being. Therefore any attribute predicated of the *ōkra* can be predicated of the *sunsum*."[49] My student's point is that the use of the terms *ōkra* and *sunsum* in different statements is a matter of usage and that no ontological distinction between *ōkra* and *sunsum* can be made on the basis of sentences in the Akan language. Sentences containing *ōkra* and *sunsum* differ in their surface structures but not, according to my student, in their deep structures (that is, meanings). Language, he would say, at any rate in the present context, is therefore a misleading guide to metaphysics. This view is plausible and ought not to be rejected cavalierly; it is the view of some of my discussants and others. This is not to say, however, that that view is not irrefutable. My refutation of it is grounded on, and strengthened by, what the Akans say regarding the nature and functions of *ōkra* and *sunsum*. That is, the distinction between *ōkra* and *sunsum* is not based solely on semantic grounds. It may be the easiest way out of an interpretative labyrinth to identify *ōkra* and *sunsum*,[50] but I do not think it is the most satisfactory way out. There are, I believe, other considerations for rejecting the "identity theory."

First, most Akans agree that in dreaming it is the *sunsum*, not the *ōkra*, that leaves the body. The departure of the *ōkra* (soul) from the body means the death of the person, whereas the *sunsum* can leave the body, as in dreaming, without causing the death of the person. Second, moral predicates are generally applied to the *sunsum*. Rattray wrote: "Perhaps the *sunsum* is the more volatile part of the whole 'kra," and ". . . but the 'kra is not volatile in life, as the *sunsum* undoubtedly is."[51] Moreover, the *ōkra* and *sunsum* appear to be different in terms of their functions or activities. The *ōkra*, as mentioned before, is the principle of life of a person and the embodiment and transmitter of his or her destiny (*nkrabea*). Personality and character dispositions of a person are the function of the *sunsum*. The *sunsum* appears to be the source of dynamism[52] of a person, the *active* part or force of the human psychological system; its energy is the ground for its interaction with the external world.

II. The Akan conceptual scheme

It is said to have extrasensory powers; it is that which thinks, desires, feels, etc. It is in no way identical with the brain, which is a physical organ. Rather it acts upon the brain (*amene, hon*). In short, people believe that it is upon the *sunsum* that one's health, worldly power, position, influence, success, etc. would depend. The attributes and activities of the *sunsum* are therefore not ascribable to the *ōkra*. Lystad was wrong when he stated: "In many respects the *sunsum* or spirit is so identical with the *ōkra* or soul in its functions that it is difficult to distinguish between them."[53]

Now, given *x* and *y*, if whatever is asserted of *x* can be asserted of *y*, then *x* can be said to be identical with *y*. If there is at least one characteristic that *x* has but *y* does not, then *x* and *y* are not identical. On this showing, insofar as things asserted of the *ōkra* are not assertable of the *sunsum*, the two cannot logically be identified. However, although they are logically distinct, they are not *ontologically* distinct. That is to say, they are not independent existents held together in an accidental way by an external bond. They are a unity in duality, a duality in unity. The distinction is not a relation between two separate entities. The *sunsum* may, more accurately, be characterized as a *part* – the active part – of the *ōkra* (soul).

I once thought that the *sunsum* might be characterized as a state,[54] an epiphenomenon, of the *ōkra*. I now think that characterization is wrong, for it would subvert the entitative nature of *sunsum*. The fact that we can speak of the inherence of the *sunsum* in natural objects as their activating principle means that in some contexts reference can be made to the *sunsum* independently of the *ōkra*. This, however, is not so in the context of the human psyche: In man *sunsum* is part of the *ōkra* (soul). Plato held a tripartite conception of the human soul, deriving that conception from his view of the functions said to be performed by the various parts of the soul. So did Freud. There is nothing inappropriate or illogical or irrational for some Akan thinkers to hold and argue for a bipartite conception of the human soul. Neither a tripartite nor a bipartite conception of the soul subverts its *ontic unity*. As already stated, the *ōkra* and *sunsum* are constitutive of a spiritual unity, which survives after death. Therefore the soul (that is, *ōkra* plus *sunsum*) does not lose its individuality after death. It survives individually. Beliefs in reincarnation (which I do not intend to explore now) and in the existence of the ancestors in the world of spirits (*asamando*) undoubtedly presuppose – and would be logically impossible without – the survival of each individual soul.

6.4. Relation of *ōkra*
(soul) and *honam* (body)

Understanding the *sunsum* and *ōkra* to constitute a spiritual unity, one may say that Akan philosophy maintains a dualistic, not a tripartite, conception of the person: A person is made up of two principal entities or substances, one spiritual (immaterial: *ōkra*) and the other material (*honam*: body).

But Akans sometimes speak as if the relation between the soul (that is, *ōkra* plus *sunsum*) and the body is so close that they comprise an indissoluble or indivisible unity, and that, consequently, a person is a homogeneous entity. The basis for this observation is the assertion by some discussants that "*ōkra* is blood" (*mogya*),[55] or "*ōkra* is in the blood." They mean by this, I think, that there is some connection between the soul and the blood, and that ordinarily the former is integrated or fused with the latter. I think the supposition here is that the blood is the physical or rather physiological "medium" for the soul. However difficult it is to understand this doctrine, it serves as a basis for a theory of the unity of soul and body. But Akan thinkers cannot strictly or unreservedly maintain such a theory, for it logically involves the impossibility of the doctrine of disembodied survival or life after death, which they tenaciously and firmly hold. The doctrine of the indivisible unity of soul and body is a doctrine that eliminates the notion of life after death, inasmuch as both soul and body are held to disintegrate together. The doctrine that the souls of the dead have some form of existence or life therefore cannot be maintained together with a doctrine of the indivisible unity of soul and body. The former doctrine implies an independent existence for the soul. I think their postulation of some kind of connection between the soul and blood is a response to the legitimate, and indeed fundamental, question as to how an entity (that is, the soul), supposed to be immaterial and separate, can "enter" the body. Though their response certainly bristles with difficulties and may be regarded as inadequate, like most theses on the soul, Akan thinkers had sufficient awareness to focus philosophical attention also on the intractable question regarding the beginnings of the connection of the soul to the body, of the immaterial to the material. Other philosophies attempt to demonstrate that man consists of soul and body, but they do not, to my knowledge, speculate on the manner of the soul's "entry" into the body.

II. The Akan conceptual scheme

In the Akan conception, the soul is held to be a spiritual entity (substance). It is not a bundle of qualities or perceptions, as it is held to be in some Western systems. The basis of this assertion is the Akan belief in disembodied survival. A bundle theory of substance implies the elimination of the notion of substance, for if a substance is held to be a bundle or collection of qualities or perceptions, when the qualities or perceptions are removed, nothing would be left. That is, there would then be no substance, that is, a substratum or an "owner" of those qualities.[56] Thus, if the soul is held to be a bundle of perceptions, as it is in the writings of David Hume, it would be impossible to talk of disembodied survival in the form of a soul or self since the bundle itself is an abstraction. One Akan maxim, expressed epigrammatically, is that "when a man dies he is not (really) dead" (*onipa wu a na onwui*). What is implied by this is that there is something in a human being that is eternal, indestructible, and that continues to exist in the world of spirits (*asamando*). An Akan motif expresses the following thought: "Could God die, I will die" (*Onyame bewu na m'awu*). In Akan metaphysics, as was explained in Chapter 5, God is held to be eternal, immortal (*Odomankoma*). The above saying therefore means that since God will not die, a person, that is, his or her '*kra* (soul), conceived as an indwelling spark of God, will not die either. That is, the soul of man is immortal. The attributes of immortality make sense if, and only if, the soul is held to be a substance, an entity, and not a bundle of qualities or perceptions (experiences).

But where in a human being is this spiritual substance located? Descartes thought that the soul was in the pineal gland. The Akans also seem to hold that the soul is lodged in the head, although they do not specify exactly where. But "although it is in the head you cannot see it with your natural eyes," as they would put it, since it is immaterial. That the soul is "in the head (*ti*)" may be inferred from the following expressions: When they want to say that a person is lucky or fortunate they say: "His head is well (good)" (*ne ti ye*), or "His soul is well (good)" (*ne 'kra ye*). From such expressions one may infer some connection between the head and the soul. And although they cannot point to a specific part of the head as the "residence" of the soul, it may be conjectured that it is in the region of the brain which, as observed earlier, receives its energy from the *sunsum* (spirit), a part of the soul. That is, the soul acts on the brain in a specific locality, but it is itself not actually localized.

The Akan conception of a person, in my analysis, is dualistic, not

6. The concept of a person

tripartite, although the spiritual component of a person is highly complex. Such dualistic conception does not necessarily imply a belief in a causal relation or interaction between the two parts, the soul and body. For instance, some dualistic philosophers in the West maintain a doctrine of psychophysical parallelism, which completely denies interaction between soul and body. Other dualists advance a doctrine of epiphenomenalism, which, while not completely rejecting causal interaction, holds that the causality goes in one direction only, namely, from the body to the soul; such a doctrine, too, is thus not interactionist. Akan thinkers, however, are thoroughly interactionist on the relation between soul and body. They hold that not only does the body have a causal influence on the soul but also that the soul has a causal influence on the body (*honam*). What happens to the soul takes effect or reflects on the condition of the body. Thus, writing on Akan culture, Busia stated:

> They (that is, Akans) believed also that spiritual uncleanness was an element of ill-health and that the cleansing of the soul was necessary for health. When, for example, a patient was made to stand on a broom while being treated, it was to symbolize this cleansing. The broom sweeps filth away from the home and keeps it healthy; so the soul must be swept of filth to keep the body healthy.[57]

Similarly, what happens to the body reflects on the conditions of the soul. It is the actual bodily or physical behavior of a person that gives an idea of the condition of the soul. Thus, if the physical behavior of a man suggests that he is happy they would say, "His soul is happy" (*ne 'kra aniagye*); if unhappy or morose they would say, "His soul is sorrowful" (*ne 'kra di awerehow*). When the soul is enfeebled or injured by evil spirits, ill health results; the poor conditions of the body affect the condition of the soul. The condition of the soul depends upon the condition of the body. The belief in psychophysical causal interaction is the whole basis of spiritual or psychical healing in Akan communities. There are certain diseases that are believed to be "spiritual diseases" (*sunsum yare*) and cannot be healed by the application of physical therapy. In such diseases attention must be paid to both physiological and spiritual aspects of the person. Unless the soul is healed, the body will not respond to physical treatment. The removal of a disease of the soul is the activity of the diviners or the traditional healers (*adunsifo*).

101

6.5. Akan psychology and Freud

There are some similarities between the functions and activities of the *sunsum* of Akan psychology and the ego of Freud. An essential task of the ego is to engage in intercourse with the external world. Like the *sunsum*, it directs the business of everyday living; it is the executive of the personality and the representative of the id in the external world. An aspect of the *sunsum* is or may be similar to the ego. The *sunsum* is not always conscious, and a person does not always know what the *sunsum* wants. It is the *sunsum* with which the Akan diviner (*ɔkɔmfo*), believed to possess extrasensory abilities, communicates. It tells the diviner what it really wants without the person knowing or being aware of what he or she wants: Thus, the *sunsum* may be unconscious. Freud said: "And it is indeed the case that large portions of the ego and super-ego can remain unconscious and are normally unconscious. That is to say, the individual knows nothing of their contents and it requires an expenditure of effort to make them conscious."[58] It is, I suppose, for these reasons that some scholars have not hesitated to identify the *sunsum* with the ego of Freud, and having done so to go on to identify the *ɔkra* with the id.[59]

There are, however, dissimilarities as well. First, in Freud the id is the original system of the psyche, the matrix within which the ego and the superego become differentiated. In the Akan conceptions both the *ɔkra* and *sunsum* at once constitute the original system of the psyche. Unlike the id, the *ɔkra* is not the only entity present at birth. Second, in Freud the ego and the superego are formed or developed later. In Akan the *sunsum* is not formed later; it is a constitutive part of the original psychical structure, the *ɔkra*, soul. At birth the child possesses a *sunsum* as well as an *ɔkra*. Freud thought in fact that the mental structure of the person was pretty well formed by the end of the fifth year of life. Third, the superego is the moral dimension of personality; it represents the claims of morality.[60] In the Akan system moral attributes are generally ascribed to the *sunsum*. Thus, the *sunsum* of the Akan seems to perform aspects of the functions of both the ego and the superego.

6.6. Conclusion

The Akan conception of the person, on my analysis, is both dualistic and interactionist. It seems to me that an interactionist psychophysical dualism is a realistic doctrine. Even apart from the prospects for disembodied survival that this doctrine holds out – prospects that profoundly affect the moral orientation of some people – it has had significant pragmatic consequences in Akan communities, as evidenced in the application of psychophysical therapies. There are countless testimonies of people who have been subjected to physical treatment for months or years in modern hospitals without being cured, but who have been healed by traditional healers applying both physical and psychical (spiritual) methods. In such cases the diseases are believed not to be purely physical, affecting only the body (*honam*). They are believed rather to have been inflicted on the *sunsum* through mystical or spiritual powers, and in time the body also gets affected. When Western-trained doctors pay attention only to the physical aspects of such diseases, they almost invariably fail to heal them. The fact that traditional healers, operating at both the physical and psychical levels, cope successfully with such diseases does seem to suggest a close relationship between the body and the soul.

From the point of view of the Akan metaphysics of the person and of the world in general, all this seems to imply that a human being is not just an assemblage of flesh and bone, that he or she is a complex being who cannot completely be explained by the same laws of physics used to explain inanimate things, and that our world cannot simply be reduced to physics.

7

Destiny, free will, and responsibility

Although much has been written about it, the Akan concept of destiny (*nkrabea*: also fate) has not been thoroughly analyzed. Many of the attempts to define it have been thin and pedestrian. There have been a number of different interpretations of the concept, resulting either from the ambiguity of the concept among the Akan thinkers themselves, or from the lack of profound and satisfactory analysis by scholars. My intention in this chapter is to clarify fully the nature of the concept and to explore its implications for human freedom and responsibility.

7.1. Basis of belief in destiny

Akan thinkers hold that every human being has a destiny that was fixed beforehand. As noted in Chapter 6, the soul (*ɔkra*) is thought to be the bearer of the destiny of man. It is held that before the soul sets out to enter this world, it takes leave of or bids farewell (*kra*) to the Supreme Being, Onyame. At this juncture it receives from Onyame the message (*nkra*) that will determine the course of the individual's life on earth. From the outset, that is, in Akan conceptions there is a close link between destiny and the soul. Here are some proverbs that underline this belief:

There is no bypass to God's destiny.
No living man can subvert the order of God.
Unless you die of God, let living man attempt to
   kill you and you will not perish.

7. Destiny, free will, and responsibility

The yam that will burn when fried, will also burn
  when boiled.
The tree that will shed its leaves, knows no rainy
  season.
If you are destined to die by the gun, you will not
  die by the arrow.
What is destined to prosper or succeed cannot be
  otherwise.
If a piece of wood remains in a river for thousands
  of years, it cannot become a crocodile.
If you are destined to gain fortunes, the vulture will
  not be abominable to your soul.[1]

What is the basis of Akan belief in destiny? In his critical examination Wiredu stated: "There is however a very much more intractable difficulty which emerges when we ask the question why it comes to be supposed in the first place that man has unalterable pre-appointed destiny. A question of this sort is of the last consequence in the assessment of a philosophy, for the real meaning of a philosophical thesis remains more or less hidden until the *reasoning* behind it is known."[2] Wiredu's point is of course fundamental and applies to a great number of beliefs and assumptions. However, before I take up the reasoning of the Akan thinkers concerning the basis of their belief in human destiny, I should like to make one general remark.

The belief in destiny is of course not peculiar to the Akan people; it is probably found in all cultures. The question of destiny is of great import for human beings, and hence has been raised and explored by thinkers and theologians in all philosophies and religions. It is enmeshed with such genuine philosophical themes as determinism, freedom of the will, punishment, moral responsibility, etc. Regarding the reasons for this universal belief in destiny two observations may be made.

The first relates to the link that a number of thinkers find between language and thought, or more precisely in the present context, between language and metaphysics. They claim that there is some kind of reality antecedent to language that language is developed to express or depict. Language or linguistic structure, they hold, reflects a deep-lying structure of reality (or being). On this showing, the Akan expression *nkrabea* was developed to depict a reality. Thus, a well-known discussant stated that "if there were

105

no accident (*asiane*), the word *asiane* would not exist in the Akan language."[3] He stated that "the situation or matter that is not real has no name" (*asєm a enni hɔ no enni din*). In other words, anything that is named must be presumed to be real.

Second, the universal belief in destiny derives from another belief, namely, that humans are the product of a Creator. It is possible to assume that if humans were fashioned, they were fashioned in a way which would determine their inclinations, dispositions, talents, etc. Thus, an Akan fragment says: "All men have one head but heads[4] differ" (*nnipa nyinaa wɔ ti baako nanso wɔn ti nsє*). That is, all people are basically alike as people – they are all created in the same way – but they differ in their fortunes, luck, capacities, etc. Just as the maker of a car can determine its speed, size, and shape, so the Creator can determine a number of things about human beings. The notion of a preappointed destiny, therefore, may also have arisen in this way. It might not have arisen if man were supposed to have evolved and not been created by a Creator. Thus, Western humanism that maintains "that man is an evolutionary product of the Nature of which he is part" goes on appropriately to deny "that there is any overarching fate, either in the form of a Divine Providence or a malignant Satanism, that is either helping or hindering man's progress and well-being."[5]

How did the Akan thinkers come by their concept of destiny? What is the basis or reasoning behind their concept of destiny? The basis of the Akan concept of destiny, like the bases of most of their concepts and thoughts, is essentially experiential. Human life (*abrabɔ*) itself, therefore, provides the setting for their thought on destiny. A well-known researcher on Akan language and culture said in a discussion: "It is in *life* itself that we see that there is destiny."[6] Another discussant stated: "Destiny reveals itself clearly in life"[7] (that is, in human experiences). Patterns of individual lives, habitual or persistent traits of persons, fortunes and misfortunes, successes and failures, the traumas and enigmas of life; the ways in which propensities, inclinations, capacities, and talents show themselves in individuals; the observed uniqueness of the individual – all these suggest to the Akan that there is and must be some basis or reason for this individuality. That basis is destiny.

For the Akan, the striking features of these phenomena do much to clinch the idea about destiny. These features include the repetition and persistence of particular actions of the individual, the apparent unalterability and inexplicability of elements in one's character, the inexplicability of events in the life of an individual, the apparent irremediability of particular failures in the life of an individual, the constancy of one's good fortunes, and so on. It is the existence of such features of their experiences that, in the view of Akan thinkers, suggests the reality of a concept of destiny. With regard to the unalterability of a trait in one's character, for instance, it is held that if a person commits an accidental act (*asiane*), which for them means not influenced by destiny, he or she will not commit it again; that action is thus easily corrigible. A discussant[8] explained that if one day the cocoa bags of a farmer who has become wealthy through buying and selling cocoa catch fire, the occurrence would be considered an accident. On the other hand, if every time he buys cocoa it catches fire, then this repeated event will be ascribed to his destiny: Selling and buying cocoa is just not his destined occupation; he ought to give it up and look elsewhere for his "real" occupation. In other words, it is the persistence of an action or a behavior pattern or the inexplicability of an event that induces a belief in destiny.

The Akan concept of destiny is thus not mysterious; it is reached through a profound analysis of the realities of human life. The reasoning behind the concept, like all reasoning based on experience, is inductive. This does not, however, detract from its plausibility or validity, and supports the view that the philosophical enterprise proceeds from experience.

The concept of destiny is thus reached by reflecting upon the experiences of individuals. This implies that destiny is that which determines the uniqueness and individuality of a person. It is your destiny (*nkrabea*) that makes you you, and my destiny that makes me me. The *nkrabea* of a person is unique and idiosyncratic, as we see in the following proverbs:

> Each destiny is different from the other.
> All men have one head but heads differ.
> Antelope's soul (destiny) is one, duiker's another.[9]
> Oh cock, do not compare your destiny with that of
> the hen.

In Akan conceptions each person is unique, for, as they often say, "each and his destiny," that is, each person has his own destiny (*obiara ne ne nkrabea*). A person's destiny is the crucial determinant or basis of individuality and uniqueness. The characteristics of individuals reflect the differences in their destiny.

7.2. Nature of the concept

7.2.1. On the two Akan words for destiny

The two Akan words used to denote destiny are *nkrabea* and *hyēbea*. *Nkrabea* is composed of two words *nkra*, message, and *bea*, manner. *Nkrabea* therefore literally means "the manner of the message," and it has come to mean the message given by the Supreme Being to the individual soul, which (message) was to determine the manner in which the individual was to live in the world. As Bishop Sarpong correctly pointed out, though in a different context: "Mothers are wont to shout at their children: 'What *kind* of destiny have you brought into the world?' "[10] The word *nkrabea* has thus come to be translated as destiny or fate.[11] The other word used synonymously with *nkrabea*, though this synonymy has been doubted or variously interpreted, is *hyēbea*, also composed of two words: *hyē*, to fix, arrange [*not* to command, as Meyerowitz[12] thought, or to make law, to order (in the sense of command), as Danquah[13] thought], and *bea*, manner. The word indicates the manner in which one's destiny was fixed or arranged.

A further discussion of the words *nkrabea* and *hyēbea* is necessary here, as different philological interpretations of these terms have led to incorrect or farfetched conclusions. First, the *bea* component. The dictionary gives two meanings of *bea*, namely (a) place, and (b) manner or state.[14] Some scholars[15] have preferred the "place" meaning, intending to imply that *nkrabea* indicates a person's place (that is, position, rank) in the world. In Akan, however, *bea* as "place" refers only to a specific spatial locality, whereas in English "place," in addition to denoting a spatial locality, also denotes rank, status, situation, circumstances, etc. For purposes of clarity, let us use $place_2$ for the comprehensive meaning and $place_1$ for the narrow meaning. $Place_1$, is the only meaning in Akan; therefore, *bea* as $place_2$ – that is, rank, status, condition, – does not work within the context of Akan. Moreover, if we took *bea* to be place rather than manner or state, *nkrabea* would literally mean "the place of taking leave," which makes *nkrabea* a physical concept, whereas it is in fact metaphysical.

There are Akan words with *bea* as a component in which the spatial meaning of "place" does not figure at all. As examples:

bōbea	:	nature
kabea	:	manner of speaking

| *yēbea* | : | manner of doing or making, performance, style, fashion |
| *dibea* | : | position (in the sense of rank), occupation |

There is another group of expressions which connote both place (in the spatial sense) and manner. As instances:

gyinabea	:	standing place; stand, state; attitude
dabea	:	sleeping place; position, situation
tobea	:	place or manner of lying
tebea	:	a place of existence, abode; manner, nature, condition, rank[16]

In the first group of words, the *bea* component does not mean place$_1$ (that is, in the spatial sense), but manner, nature, quality, rank. In the second group, the *bea* component carries both meanings, that is (spatial) place and manner. But if by "place" the interpreters of *bea* as place have the comprehensive meaning (that is, place$_2$) in mind, as I believe they do, only *bea* as "manner" is relevant, for *bea* (place) in Akan only means, a specific physical space, as in sleeping place, and standing place. The words in the first group all indicate in different ways the "manner" of one's faring in the world. Therefore the "place" interpretation of the *bea* component of *nkrabea* must be rejected. If the place or the spatial region a person is born in or resides in is decreed or involved in his *nkrabea*, it is merely one of the several elements of the concept, merely a logical consequence of the concept of destiny. *Bea*, then, must be taken to mean *manner*, indicating the way an individual soul was to express itself in the world.

I now turn to the distinction that has been made by some scholars between *nkrabea* and *hyēbea*.[17] Hagan has argued that the two expressions denote different concepts. In his view, *hyēbea*, which he takes to be *hyēbere* and renders as "appointed time," denotes the temporal dimension of a person's life, whereas *nkrabea* denotes the nontemporal attributes of a person – status, rank, occupation, success. Not one of my discussants thought that the two expressions denote different concepts. For all of them, the two expressions have identical referents. One discussant,[18] who had some knowledge of English, pointed out that the two words are like the expressions "you" and "thou" in English.

Both philological and philosophical objections may be raised against Hagan's thesis. First, the philological caveat: In some parts

II. The Akan conceptual scheme

of the Akan land the *bea* component is pronounced and written as *bere* (sometimes *brē*). Examples of such expressions follow:

bōbrē	:	that is, *bōbea*
dibere	:	that is, *dibea*
dabere	:	that is, *dabea*
gyinabere	:	that is, *gyinabea*
tebere	:	that is, *tebea*

One discussant[19] stated that in the Kwahu area, *nkrabea* is pronounced *nkraberē*. The *berē* component of such words does *not* indicate time as such, as Hagan thought, although the usual Akan expression for time is *berē*. The *berē* in the above words is another form of *bea*, meaning "manner." Therefore, it is wrong to associate a concept of time with *hyēbea* (or *hyēberē*).

Now, the philosophical objection: Hagan's thesis implies that the Akan concept of destiny or fate is two-pronged, one prong directed at the temporal aspects and the other at the nontemporal aspects, of one's life on earth. This is a philosophical aberration; for the concept of destiny, that is, the message (*nkra*) borne by the soul (*ōkra*), must necessarily embrace all aspects of the person's life, temporal and nontemporal, even if not in detail. The temporal dimension of one's life, indicating, according to Hagan, the temporal order of events in one's life, must therefore already be involved in one's *nkrabea*, destiny. The message would perhaps be incomplete without the inclusion of the element of time. The Akan proverb, "We offer advice in order to reform a person, but not to change his destiny;" (*yetufo, yentu hyēberē*), refers of course to the whole of a person's destiny, not only to its temporal element. Why should the offer of advice be contrasted with only the time dimension of one's destiny? The concept of destiny is not two-pronged but many-pronged, involving the individual's status, rank, and occupation, as well as the fixed time when the soul must depart this world. Although destiny is conceived by Akan thinkers to be of a general nature, so that not everything is "stated" in the message, nevertheless the general Akan view is that the time of a person's death is definitely stipulated in the scroll of destiny. Nevertheless, this fact does not justify singling out the time element and subsuming it under a different, autonomous concept, for time is no more significant than the other elements of destiny. Time is only one atom in the molecular life of the individual. There is no evidence in the sources I have examined that the soul, the bearer of destiny, bears two messages, a temporal one and a nontemporal one. Nor does philosophical analysis lead us to a two-message concept of destiny in Akan thought.

Eva Meyerowitz, Danquah, and Bishop Sarpong also attempt to separate *nkrabea* and *hyēbea*, but with different aims. In their interpretations, however, time is not separated from the other elements and subsumed under an autonomous concept. In *nkrabea*, Meyerowitz sees the conscious, personal will, and in *hyēbea*, the unconscious drives and impulses.[20] Elsewhere she identifies the conscious personal will with the *sunsum*, and the unconscious drives and impulses with the *ōkra*.[21] Thus, she sees some connection between *nkrabea* and *sunsum* on the one hand, and *hyēbea* and the *ōkra* on the other hand, although she does not explain the basis for making such connections. Her interpretations, however, are incorrect insofar as they imply a dichotomy between *nkrabea* and *hyēbea*. In my view, there is a definite connection between personality (*sunsum*) and destiny (*nkrabea* or *hyēbea*). An attempt will be made directly, in dealing with Danquah's discussion, to explain why a connection of some sort between *sunsum* and *nkrabea* (destiny) may in some sense be allowed, although the explanation cannot be taken to imply that a connection may also be correctly made between *ōkra* and *hyēbea*.

Danquah may have been the source, in whole or in part, of Meyerowitz's interpretations. He speaks of the *sunsum* as conscious and the *ōkra* as unconscious.[22] He also uses *nkrabea* and *hyēbea* to designate different concepts. He says that the destiny of man is of two parts,[23] and speaks of "the *nkrabea* of the *sunsum*" and "the *hyēbea* of God."[24] These two expressions of Danquah's are misleading. We cannot strictly speak of "the *nkrabea* of the *sunsum*" since, it is the *ōkra* (soul) that bears the *nkrabea* of a person.[25] Nevertheless, it is not absolutely incorrect to speak of "the *nkrabea* of the *sunsum*," for – and this applies as well to Meyerowitz's connection of *sunsum* and *nkrabea* – it is the *sunsum*, the active part of the psychical system, that makes possible the realization of the *nkrabea* on earth, because it is the *sunsum* that interacts with the external world. Thus interpreted, Danquah's expression "the *nkrabea* of the *sunsum*" makes sense. The expression "the *hyēbea* of God" makes sense only when it is taken to mean the destiny of God, where destiny is designated by both *nkrabea* and *hyēbea*. Nevertheless, my main objection to Danquah's use of these two expressions, as to Meyerowitz's, is the implication that *nkrabea* and *hyebea* denote different concepts.

All these confusions stem from holding that the words *nkrabea* and *hyēbea* refer to different concepts. According to my discussants, the two are identical in their referent; and it is also the view that is philosophically attractive. There is no evidence in the sources that leads one to believe that two different "messages," that is, scrolls of destiny, are borne by the individual into the world. The message, whether determined by the individual's own soul or given to it by the Supreme Being, is a single message, but its content is many-faceted. *Nkrabea* (or *hyēbea*) therefore expresses a concept of destiny that is totalistic, encompassing all aspects, temporal and nontemporal, though not in detail, of an individual's mundane existence.

7.2.2. Is it a concept of double destiny?

The question has arisen whether the individual's soul states the destiny message to God or receives it from God. In this connection, some scholars find a conception of double destiny in Akan thought. Bishop Sarpong makes a distinction between *nkrabea*, which he regards as the divinely imposed destiny, and *hyēbea* (or *hyēbrē*, as he reads it), as the self-determined destiny: "Neither the divinely imposed Fate (*Nkrabea*) nor the self-determined Destiny (*Hyēbrē*) is avoidable. . . ."[26] Although Bishop Sarpong is perceptive enough to see that this concept of "double destiny [is] fraught with many logical problems,"[27] yet he does nothing to disentangle those problems and continues to hold that view in a later publication.[28] Bishop Sarpong's position was taken also by some informants of Helaine Minkus, who stated that "*nkrabea* refers to the message the individual gives to God . . ." while "*hyēbea* is the message given by God. . . ."[29] (Some of her informants claimed, however, that the two expressions were synonymous.) Bishop Sarpong and Minkus's informants differ as to which is the divinely imposed destiny and which the self-determined destiny. But all is a muddle. Which aspects or elements of a person's destiny are determined or chosen by the soul, and which are given by God? How much of the message is decided on by the soul and how much by God? Double destiny is a conceptual blunder. The concept of destiny makes sense only when it is held to be either wholly self-determined or wholly divinely imposed, but not both.

The concept of double destiny bristles with difficulties, as Bishop Sarpong saw. Its proponents use the self-determined theory of destiny to argue for human freedom and responsibility. This misfires, however, because in the context of a philosophy of double destiny, how can an individual in this world know that a particular action one takes stems from the "part" of destiny that was chosen and not the "part" that was divinely imposed? Akan thought offers a more satisfactory basis for the concept of human freedom and responsibility than a double destiny theory.

In the course of my field research I often found conflicting views or statements. Some discussants claimed that the individual states his or her destiny to God, and others claimed that it is God who gives the destiny. The analyst must provide reasons for preferring one point of view to the other. I have three reasons for thinking that an individual's destiny is given by God. The first reason, a subtle one, derives from such proverbs as these:

> There is no bypass to God's destiny.
> (*Onyame nkrabea nni kwatibea*)
>
> God's destiny cannot be altered.
> (*Onyame hyēbea yennae no*)
>
> No living man can subvert the order (arrangement)
>   of God.
> (*ade a Onyame ahyehyē ōdasani ntumi nsēe no*)

These clearly refer to *God's* destiny (*Onyame nkrabea, Onyame hyēbea*), which suggests that God gives the destiny. The destiny is his, in the sense that he decrees or determines it. Thus, the language of some proverbs suggests or supports the divinely imposed theory of destiny.

Second, an Akan myth expresses the idea of God determining an individual's destiny. The myth is as follows:

> The rivers Tano, Bea, the Bosomtwe Lake and the sea were children of the Supreme Being. The latter decided to send these his children to the earth. The Supreme Being himself had planned where he would send each of the children. The goat got to know of the plans of the Supreme Being. He, the goat, and Bea were great friends, so he told Bea of the plans of the Supreme Being, urging him to arrive before his brothers if their father sent for them. One day the Supreme Being sent for his children and Bea ran quickly and got there first; so the Supreme Being assigned to him the cool and shady forest country which had been intended for Tano, the favorite son of the Supreme Being. Tano therefore was sent to the grassy plains, and each in turn was given a place different

from the original plan, due to the goat having revealed the plan to Bea.[30]

There is no direct evidence here that God's children – the river spirits – have a destiny in the sense that human beings do. But it is clear from the myth that God determined the place of each river spirit (that is, place$_1$, where place$_1$ is logically a part of the comprehensive concept of destiny). God's action in determining the place of the river spirits can be seen as an analogue of his determination of human destiny, which of course comprehends more than just place$_1$. This myth suggests that there is no choice of destiny for individuals, for the Supreme Being had already decided where each of the children would be settled. Although, as Rattray pointed out, "Owing to the machinations of the goat the final resting-place of all the waters was not as really intended by Nyame,"[31] nevertheless upsetting the intentions of God (Nyame) did not imply that his children had the opportunity to decide on their resting places. God had already decided that whoever got to him first would be given the most congenial place, and the subversion of his intentions was the result not only of the goat having revealed God's plans but also of his own firmness and fairness. To the extent that the myth can be applied to human beings, it suggests that destiny is given by God.

The third and perhaps most telling reason is this: The soul setting foot into the world must be presumed to be completely without knowledge of the conditions of this world. This being so, how can the soul possibly choose or indicate its own destiny? It is the omniscient God who, of course, knows of such conditions. The ignorance of the soul regarding the world suggests both the implausibility of the self-determined theory of destiny and the plausibility of the divinely imposed theory of destiny.

7.2.3. The general nature of destiny

The conception of destiny held by most of the traditional wise persons with whom I had discussions makes the destiny of man a *general* destiny. That is, the message (*nkra*) borne by the soul is said to be comprehensive; it determines only the broad outlines of an individual's mundane life, not the specific details. It follows that not every action a person performs or every event that occurs in one's life comes within the ambit of his destiny. Two problems, perhaps the most difficult problems in the Akan conception of destiny, immediately come up. The first is: How can we determine the exact level of generality of one's destiny? The second is: What are the elements of destiny, that is, what attributes are contained in the message of destiny? The second question appears to be more fundamental, for if we can determine the nature of the content of the message, we have some idea of the level of generality of destiny. I shall therefore attempt the second question first.

My discussants were generally unsure about the elements that are included in one's destiny. They were, however, unanimous in claiming that the time of a person's death and possibly also the manner and place of death are stipulated in his destiny. Rank and occupation are included, according to two discussants.[32] Thus the level of the generality of destiny remains vague. All the discussants, however, agreed that the inexplicable events in one's life, the unalterable and persistently habitual traits of character, the persistent actions and behavior patterns of an individual are all traceable to destiny. It is important to note that only when all human or physical explanations for events or actions are exhausted that recourse is had to a person's destiny. This being so, one might say that only certain "key" events and actions are embodied in destiny. Perhaps better, the destiny of an individual comprises certain basic attributes. The proverbs on destiny quoted in section 7.1 refer to such key events or basic attributes. What these basic attributes are is of course difficult to say with certainty. Nevertheless, it is clear that the Akan notion of destiny is a general one, which implies that not everything that a person does or that happens to him or her represents a page from the "book of destiny."

Construing the message (*nkra*) of destiny in terms of basic attributes provides a solution for another knotty problem in the Akan conception of destiny. The problem is that of the alterability or unalterability of one's destiny. This problem is of great consequence, for it has been supposed that its solution determines the place of human effort in human activities and the development of society. It will be shown, however, that the place of human effort depends on something other than the alterable or unalterable nature of one's destiny. On the question of whether or not one can alter one's destiny, my discussants were about equally divided. Bishop Sarpong[33] claims that destiny can be changed by magic or religious means. Opoku,[34] however, denies that it can be changed. The Akan proverbs on destiny I have examined seem to imply the unalterability and unavoidability of destiny. Perhaps there are some proverbs that imply otherwise. But if the message of destiny is conceived in terms of basic attributes, as I am construing it, it is clear why destiny cannot be changed: Basic attributes do not change. Moreover, if as I have argued destiny is determined by the *omnipotent* Supreme Being, it obviously cannot be changed. Hence, the insistence of the proverbs I have seen that God's destiny cannot be avoided or changed is logical.

Changing one's destiny is not only an impossible idea, but it is also one that should, strictly speaking, not arise in a system in which destiny is divinely determined. The reason is, since the Supreme Being is regarded in Akan thought as good – a view that is expressed in these proverbs:

> Goodness is the prime characteristic of God.
> The hawk says: "Whatever God does is good."

– the destiny fixed by God must be good. My discussants were unanimous in asserting that "everyone's leave-taking was good" (*obiara kraa yie*); "nobody's leave-taking was evil" (*obiara ankra bōne*); "God created everyone well" (*Nyame bōō obiara yie*). Thus, bad things are not included in the message of destiny. Wherein, then, lies the necessity for changing one's destiny, for changing what is good? There is really no such necessity, for the talk of changing destiny really refers to the attempt to better one's condition. For instance, a person's path may be strewn with failures, either because of his or her own actions, desires, decisions, and intentions, or because of the activities of some supposed evil forces. A person in such a situation may try to do something about the situation by, say, consulting priests and diviners. But in so doing he or she would certainly not be changing destiny as such; rather, he or she would in fact be trying to better the conditions of life (*abrabō*) by some means. Therefore one should speak of improving one's circumstances in life rather than of "changing" one's destiny.

Destiny in Akan thought, interpreted as the basic attributes of an individual, may be contrasted with the German philosopher Leibniz's (1646–1716) concept of the individual. Leibniz wrote:

> We have said that the concept of an individual substance includes once for all everything which can ever happen to it, and that in considering this concept one will be able to see everything which can truly be said concerning the individual, just as we are able to see in the nature of a circle all the properties which can be derived from it.[35]

The view that the concept of the individual "includes once for all everything which can ever happen to it" is in fact antithetical to the message of destiny, the basis of individuality in Akan thought. For the Akan notion does not include everything that can ever happen to the individual.

Akan thinkers maintain that the message of destiny of an individual is not known by any living man, a view that is expressed, for instance, in the proverb:

When someone was taking leave of the Supreme
Being, no one else was standing by.

(*obi kra ne Nyame no na obi nnyina hɔ bi*)

Since no one else observed the act of leave-taking of another person, no one knows the destiny of any other person. The individual does not know his or her own destiny either; the message of destiny cannot be remembered since a large portion of the soul (*ɔkra*) is said to remain unconscious. Only the Supreme Being (Onyame) knows an individual's destiny. But divine knowledge of an individual's destiny does not appear to be fatal to the latter's exercise of free will, since the individual does not presume to have access to this knowledge of God. More on free will in Akan thought anon.

Finally, we turn to the resignation that is alleged to be involved in, or induced by, the Akan concept of human destiny. Wiredu wrote:

... adversity may lead a man to resignation. This happens every where and in all cultures. *But in our culture the notions about destiny just mentioned are apt to facilitate the resignation of a despairing soul.*[36]

Again:

But our traditional philosophy is probably highly remarkable in the personal directness and individual immediacy of the doctrine of fate and, further, in the sincerity and practical seriousness with which it is entertained in the day to day life of our people.[37]

Kwesi Dickson has argued successfully against the view that the Akan concept of *nkrabea* induces resignation. Referring specifically to the Akan notion of destiny, *nkrabea*, he wrote: "Resignation, with its consequent passivity, does not appear to be encouraged in African thought."[38] Some of the arguments I advance against the view that the Akan concept of destiny induces an immediate feeling of doom have been made by Dickson.

117

II. The Akan conceptual scheme

First, only after *repeated* attempts in the pursuit of some aim have failed do the Akans normally blame a person's failure on destiny, *nkrabea*. This means that striving is highly esteemed by the Akans and that it is never considered normal to give up easily or immediately unless one is brought to a situation from which there is no escape. Resignation should not be the immediate response to failure; it is appropriate only after all possible recourse has been exhausted. Resignation is thus a response or attitude to a humanly impossible situation. In such a situation the Akans would say:

Man came to play only a part of the drama of life,
not the whole.
(onipa bēyēē bi, na wōammēyē ne nyinaa)

On this saying Antubam comments: "*When after a sincere strenuous effort* the Ghanaian fails to reach the highest height in a competition, he cheers himself up in resignation by saying to himself" the above proverb.[39] It is implicit in the proverb that something must have been achieved, some effort expended. The feeling of resignation wells up only when one recognizes that one's efforts have been misplaced, or are otherwise unavailing. Such resignation, however, does not imply a feeling of doom or a belief that future success is impossible, nor does it induce in that individual the feeling that trying other pursuits would be useless. After repeated failure, resignation is a rational, realistic, and necessary attitude for an individual who believes that luck, success, and fortune are to be looked for elsewhere.

Second, everyone wishes to avoid evil and escape disaster; hence the strong belief in the beneficial activities of the traditional diviners and priests. In all libation prayers, the spiritual beings, from Onyame down to the ancestors, are implored to avert disaster (*musuo*) and to bring peace, happiness, prosperity, good harvest, etc.

Third, as observed earlier, Akans believe in the existence of accidents (*asiane, akwanhyia*) – events or actions that are not "in one's destiny." As one discussant put it, "Accident is not in the *nkrabea*" (*asiane, enni nkrabea no mu*).[40] The word *asiane* is generally used to refer to an unintended effect, although this does not mean that it is uncaused, or occurring by chance. An Akan proverb has it that,

The death of *funtum* affects *mmatatwene*.
(funtum wuo saa mmatatwene)

Funtum is a tree. *Mmatatwene* is a creeping plant that grows along and around the main stem of the *funtum* tree. Now, if one fells the *funtum* tree, at the same time, though unintentionally as far as one is concerned, one destroys the *mmatatwene* plant around it. Thus, the destruction or death of the *mmatatwene* plant is an accident, that is, an effect not intended by the person who felled the *funtum* tree. The proverb makes it clear that there are, according to the Akan thinkers, accidents or contingencies in human life, a fact also recognized or implicit in the general character of *nkrabea*.

Finally, by stressing the uniqueness and individuality of people, the Akan concept of destiny implies that each individual is naturally fitted for a particular sphere of action, and that he or she has capacities and aptitudes for the activities of that sphere. This means that while one does not have a capacity or talent for every conceivable or desirable pursuit, one certainly has capacities for particular pursuits or endeavors. This position emerges in such proverbs as:

> If God did not give the swallow anything, He gave
>   it agility.[41]
> If the cat does not have anything, it has swiftness.

Since each individual has some talents, a series of failures would suggest that he or she might be in the wrong sphere of action and that those talents are therefore misplaced and are consequently being denied the opportunity for their full exercise. Thus, if the Akan concept of destiny is fully and properly understood, it would have far-reaching beneficial consequences for individuals in society.

7.3. Causality, fate, free will, and responsibility

I now turn to the external and internal influences on human life and the implications of these for free will and moral responsibility. Chapter 5 made clear that Akan thinkers hold a strongly deterministic conception of the world: For them every event has a cause; nothing is attributable to chance. We learned in our analysis of the Akan concept of a person (Chapter 6) that some characteristics, due to the *ntoro* and *mogya* elements, are inherited from parents or relatives and that moral attributes are generally ascribed to the *sunsum* (spirit). In section 7.2.3 we saw that fate or destiny is unalterable. Even an individual's day of birth, called *krada*, is thought to influence one's personal characteristics. Thus, people born on Monday are said to be calm (*odwo*), those born on Thursday are said to be courageous (*prĕko*: warlike), and so on. One's *krada*, and hence time, is believed to be a factor in determining one's individuality and uniqueness. In the light of such a deterministic conception of the world and of life, can humans be said to be free in their actions and behavior? Can they be moral agents? Akan thinkers answer these questions in the affirmative.

The argument in Western philosophy pertaining to human free will and responsibility is this: If every event is caused, as determinism holds, then human action and behavior too are caused, and hence we cannot be held to be free and therefore cannot be held morally responsible for those actions. There is a suppressed premise in the argument, which is that human actions are (a species of) events. This premise is, in my view, not wholly correct. There is a sense in which human actions cannot be considered as events. Events are mere happenings or occurrences, which do not have their origin in human design and motivation. Thus, we speak of the flooding of a river, the erosion of the sea, a tremor of the earth, the capsizing of a boat during a storm, the disruption of electrical supply following lightning, and the crash of an aircraft during a thunderstorm, as events. Human "events," insofar as they originate in human thought, deliberation, desire, etc., cannot strictly be regarded as events. Although the word "event" may be used to refer to humanly motivated action, as in "The French Revolution was a momentous *event* in the history of France," "The Bond of 1844 was a significant *event* in the history of Ghana," "Intertribal wars in Africa were tragic *events*," "Egyptian President Sadat's visit to Jerusalem in December 1977 was a historic *event*," the sense of "event" in these statements is plainly different from the sense it has in the occurrences mentioned earlier. The flooding of a river and the warring among ethnic groups in Africa are different kinds of "events." The former is an event simply: It just occurred, without any human intervention. The latter is, strictly speaking, not an event, for it did not simply occur; it was an *action* brought about as a result of human deliberation, intention, decision, and desire; it was planned and executed by people. The French Revolution did not erupt by itself, like a volcano; it was planned and executed by humans. Sadat's historic visit to Jerusalem resulted from his desire for peace in that area of the world. Such human actions may later be described as "events," but they are not events, properly speaking.

7. Destiny, free will, and responsibility

As noted in Chapter 5, Akan thinking about causation is confined to events, natural and nonhuman, that are beyond the control or power of people, to the exclusion of human actions (*nneyēe*). I think it is correct to maintain that in Akan thought the doctrine of causality or determinism is irrelevant as far as human actions are concerned. This means that the doctrine of determinism is not fatal to the freedom a person has in actions and behavior. For the fact that every event is caused does not, in the Akan system, eliminate or subvert the role of the individual in human actions. Now Akan thinkers conceive of cause in terms of spirit or power (*sunsum*), and humans also have a spirit, even if of a lower potency, that is the basis of thought, deliberation, will and so on. It follows that man also is a causal agent. Determinism therefore does not negate the effectiveness of human beings as causal and therefore moral agents. The *sunsum* of a person is held to be developable; a weak power or capacity can be improved or strengthened. Moral failures, then, which are in fact spiritual defects, can be rectified. Therefore, neither the Akan deterministic conception of the world nor Akan moral psychology is fatal to human free will and responsibility.

The concept of destiny (*nkrabea*) might be held to be subversive of the reality of humans as causal free agents. For if actions are predetermined, then thoughts, deliberations, decisions are of no consequence; there is nothing that a person might think of or do that will affect the result. Therefore, the effects of the concept of destiny on volitional causality are relevant to the questions of free will and moral responsibility. Is the Akan concept of destiny destructive of human free will?

Because *nkrabea* (destiny) expresses only the basic attributes of the individual, and because *nkrabea* is *general* and not specific, human actions are not fated or necessitated; this fact gives viability and meaningfulness to the concept of choice. Even if one considered free will not to be absolute in the light of human creatureliness, it must nevertheless be granted that the individual can make his or her own existence meaningful through the exercise of free will within the scope of destiny.

That actions and behavior originate from thought, desire, choice, etc., is implicit in the concept of *asiane*, accident, which is invariably tied to the concept of *nkrabea*. In Akan thought, "accident" refers to an action or event that is unintended but that has a cause. As far as human actions are concerned, the cause is, of course, the person him- or herself. Consequently, if a hunter, for instance, accidentally mistakes a man for an animal and shoots him, he is held responsible, even though as far as he is concerned it was an unintended action. It was his action in that he was the cause of it; he should or could have been more careful. Also relevant here is that of "doing something premeditatedly or purposely" (*se wo hyēda*). However, for it to be applicable here, it appears in the negative: *wōanhyēda*, that is, "He did not do it premeditatedly (or deliberately)." But it is implicit that this does not mean that action is automatic or predetermined. Our hypothetical hunter cannot absolve himself of the responsibility by claiming that his action was unpremeditated; he accepts the responsibility for the action because he willed and executed it, even though the consequences of his action turned out to be different from what he intended. Thus, the general nature of *nkrabea* allows room for the exercise by the person of free will and, consequently, "accidental" and "unpremeditated" actions are considered as deriving from the exercise of free will and hence are the person's responsibility.

Humanity is endowed with capacity (or power) for thought and action. This capacity is implied in the concept of *sunsum*. Humans then should employ this capacity to improve themselves. The Akans highly esteem effort, for as the proverb has it,

> Trying hard breaks the back of misfortune.
> (*mmōdenbō bu musuo abasa so*)

Thus, if a person fails to do the right thing either in a moral situation or otherwise he or she should be held responsible, for it was within human capacity to do it correctly.

Akan thinkers maintain that character, which is given an important place in the ethical life of a person, is reformable; it can be trained and developed. Moral habits are acquired through habituation and obedience to good advice. Thus, they say:

> We offer advice (in order to reform one's character),
>   but we do not change destiny.
> (*yetufo, yentu hyēbrē*)
> One is not born with "bad head" but one takes it
>   on the earth.
> (*ti bōne wofa no fam, wōmfa nnwo*)

The latter proverb means that bad habits are acquired by people; misfortunes and failures are their own making. Accordingly, an unhappy or miserable life is attributed to a person's behavior or conduct:

7. Destiny, free will, and responsibility

If a man is unhappy, his conduct is the cause.
(*onipa ho antō no a, na efi n'asēm*)

Because character can be reformed, such an attribution, it seems to me, is appropriate. A person is responsible for the state of his or her character, for he or she is endowed with the capacity to reform and to improve. In sum, then, Akan philosophy maintains that human beings are free and must therefore be held morally responsible for their actions and behavior.

7.4. The problem of evil

Because Akan thinkers hold that moral evil stems from the exercise of man's free will, it is appropriately treated here. The problem of evil appears to be more complex in Akan thought than Western thought. The reason is that whereas in Western thought the problem centers round God, in Akan thought the problem centers round both the Supreme Being (God: Onyame) and the deities (that is, lesser spirits). In Western thought the problem arises out of seeming conflicts between the attributes of God and the existence of evil. In Akan thought the problem is conceived in terms not only of the attributes of God but also of those of the deities. When the problem of evil in Akan thought is pushed to its logical limits, however, its philosophical nature is quite similar to that in Western philosophy and theology.

The problem of evil in Western philosophy arises out of the contradiction between God's attributes of omnipotence and goodness (benevolence) on the one hand and the existence of evil on the other hand. Thus, given the three propositions:

A. God is omnipotent,
B. God is wholly good,
C. evil exists,

C is considered to be incompatible with *A* and *B*, individually or jointly. If God is omnipotent, then He can completely eliminate evil, since there are no limits to what an omnipotent being can do, and if God is wholly good or benevolent then He would be willing to eliminate evil. Yet evil exists. The existence of evil, it is argued in Western philosophy, implies that either God does not exist or if He does exist He is not omnipotent or not wholly good or both. Of course various attempts have been made by philosophers and theologians to explain the sources of evil in this world.

II. The Akan conceptual scheme

In Akan philosophy and theology God is conceived as omnipotent and wholly good. Yet the Akan thinkers do not appear to find these attributes of God incompatible with the fact of the existence of moral evil. One might suppose that the Akan thinkers are dodging the philosophical issue here, but this is not so. Rather, they locate the source of the problem of evil elsewhere than in the logic of the relationships between the attributes of God and the fact of existence of evil.

For the Akan, evil is not a creation of God; that would be inconsistent with the goodness of God. Akan thinkers generally believe that it was not God who created evil (*Nyame ambõ bõne*). Then how is the existence of evil explained? According to them, there are two main sources of evil: the deities (*abosom*, including all supernatural forces such as magical forces, witches, etc.) and mankind's own will. About half a dozen assembled discussants were unanimous in asserting that "evil derives from evil spirits" (*bõne firi obonsam*).[42] The deities are held either to be good and evil or to have powers of good and evil. Thus, unlike Onyame (God), they are not wholly good, and hence they are the authors of evil things. Although the deities were created by God, they are considered in Akan theology and cosmology to have independent existence of some sort; they operate independently of God and in accordance with their own desires and intentions.

Since the deities that constitute one source of evil in this world are held not to be wholly good, one might suppose that the problem of evil is thereby solved. Busia, for instance, thought that

> . . .the problem of evil so often discussed in Western philosophy and Christian theology does *not* arise in the African concept of deity. It is when a God who is not only all powerful and omniscient but also perfect and loving is postulated that the problem of the existence of evil becomes an intellectual and philosophical hurdle. The Supreme Being of the African is the Creator, the source of life, *but between Him and man lie many powers and principalities good and bad, gods, spirits, magical forces, witches to account for the strange happenings in the world.*[43]

It is not clear what Busia means by "deity" here; perhaps he means the Supreme Being, God. If so, his view of the attributes of the Supreme Being – a view that implies some limitation on the Supreme Being as conceived in African thought – is disputable. Be that as it may, the view that the African concept of the Supreme Being does not give rise to the problem of evil is of course predicated on the assumption that the lesser spirits created by Him are conceived of as good *and* bad, so that the quandaries arising out of the conflict of omnipotence and perfect goodness on the one hand and evil on the other hand cease to exist. But this conclusion is premature and unsatisfactory philosophically.

The immediate question that arises is this: Why should a wholly good God create a being that embodies in itself both good *and* evil powers or dispositions? One possible answer may be that it was not God who created the evil powers or actions of a lesser spirit, but that these result from the operations of the independent will of the spirit itself. But this answer is not wholly satisfactory either. First, God, being a higher entity, can destroy the lesser spirits as well as the other powers and forces. Consequently, God has the power to eliminate or control the evil wills and actions of the lower beings such as the lesser spirits and so to eliminate evil from the world. Second, since God is wholly good and eschews evil (*Nyame mpē bōne*), as an Akan proverb has it, he would not refrain from eliminating evil or controlling evil wills. Even if it were granted that God endowed the lesser spirits with independent wills, it might be expected that the wholly good God would be willing to intervene when he sees them using their wills to choose to act wrongly and so to cause evil. Would it have been wrong for God to intervene in the evil operations of the independent free wills of the lesser spirits in order to eliminate evil? But if he had done so, would he not have disrupted the free wills with which he endowed them? (These questions come up again in discussing mankind as a source of evil.) Thus, contrary to Busia's assertion, it is clear that the Akan concept of deity does generate the philosophical problem of evil. Busia's assertion would be true only if a lesser spirit, held to be both good *and* bad, were considered as the supreme or ultimate spiritual being. But this, as we saw in Chapter 5, is not the case. It is Onyame who is the Supreme and Absolute Being.

The other source of evil, according to Akan thought, is human will. On this some of my discussants advanced the following views:

> Evil comes from man's character.
> (*bōne fi onipa suban*)[44]

In the view of this discussant, character determines the nature of our actions; bad character gives rise to evil actions, and good character gives rise to good actions. The person with bad character, he asserted, thinks evil, and it is such evil thoughts that translate or issue in morally evil actions. According to him, it is impossible for evil to come from Onyame (God) because (1) Onyame is good (*Onyame ye*), and (2) our character, from which evil proceeds, is of our own making; what our character is, or will be, is the person's responsibility, not God's. In a discussion with a different group of three elders,[45] two of them also blamed evil on human character, but the third one, criticizing the other two, asked: "Is it not *Onyame* who created the world and us and all that we are?" He answered his own question by saying: "If Onyame made us what we are, then he created, along with everything else, evil too." To this one of the others retorted: "It is surely *not* Onyame who tells or forces a person to go and rape, steal, and kill. It is the person's own desires and mind" (*n'apēde ne n'adwen*). But the conception of the human source of moral evil was shared by two other discussants, both from different communities. One of them maintained that "Onyame did not create evil; evil comes from man's own actions" (*Onyame ambō bōne; bōne firi onipa nneyēe*),[46] and the other that "Onyame is not the cause of evil, but our own thinking and deliberation" (*bōne mfi Onyame; efi yēn ankasa adwendwen mu*).[47]

Arguing that God is not the author of evil, another discussant maintained that "evil comes from man's conscience" (*tiboa*).[48] His position is that a human being has what is called *tiboa*, conscience (moral sense, that is, a sense of right and wrong), which enables one to see the difference (*nsoe*) between good and evil. Putting it bluntly, he said, "Man is not a beast (*aboa*) to fail to distinguish between the good and evil." The comparison between man and beast is intended as a distinction between moral sense and amoral sense on the one hand, and between rationality (intelligence) and irrationality (non-intelligence) on the other hand. The implication is that it is only conscienceless, irrational beasts that cannot distinguish between good and evil. Since, according to this traditional thinker, our possession of *tiboa* enables (or, should enable) us to do correct moral thinking, evil stems from our inability to exercise the moral sense. But this argument is not persuasive. Having the ability to do correct moral thinking, or to distinguish between good and evil, does not necessarily imply possession of the moral will to carry out the implications of the distinction. This traditional wise man assumes that it does, but this assumption, I think, is mistaken. So that the statement "Evil comes from man's conscience" must

7. *Destiny, free will, and responsibility*

perhaps be taken to mean that evil stems from the inability to exercise either our moral sense or our moral will.

In sum, the basic premise of the arguments of the Akan thinkers on the problem of evil is generally that God does not like evil (*Nyame mpɛ bɔne*) and hence did not create it (*Nyame ambɔ bɔne*). Evil, according to most of them, proceeds from man's character, conscience, desires, and thoughts – all of which suggest, within the Akan conceptual system, that evil stems from the exercise by the person of his or her own free will (*onipa ne pɛ*), as was in fact explicitly stated by a discussant.[49]

It was made clear in section 7.2.3 that the general nature of destiny (*nkrabea*) allows for the concept of human freedom, and therefore of choice, and that within the context of human actions – which are *not* to be considered as events – the concept of determinism is inapplicable. Thus, the view of the human source of moral evil appears to stem from a set of related concepts in the Akan metaphysical system.

This argument seems to me a potent one. Nevertheless, some difficult questions might be raised against it. For instance: Why did not God, if he is omnipotent and wholly good, make human beings such that they always choose the good and avoid the evil? Or, having endowed them with freedom of the will, why does God not intervene when he sees them using this freedom to choose the wrong thing and so to cause evil? Is God unable to control human will? Is he unable to control what he has created? And if he is able, why does he not do so? Can the argument that evil results from the exercise of human free will really be sustained?

If God is omnipotent, then he certainly could have made human beings such that they always choose the good and avoid the evil, that he could also intervene in the event of human freedom of the will leading to evil, and that he could thus control human will. But if God had done all this, humans would act in a wholly determined way, without any choice whatever – a situation that would run counter to the *general* nature of the concept of destiny and the notion of human action as held by Akan thinkers. That would also have led to the subversion of rationality, which not only distinguishes human beings from beasts, but also enables human beings generally to judge before acting. The argument that God should have made humans such that they always choose the good implies that God should have made them nonrational and thus less human, wholly without the ability to choose. Thus, the subversion of

127

rationality together with its concomitants of choice, deliberation, judgment, etc., constitutes a *reductio ad absurdum* of the view that the wholly good God should have created humans such that they always choose the good. The Akan thinkers, like thinkers in most other cultures, would rather have humankind endowed with rationality and conscience than to have them fashioned to behave like a beast. Hence, God's provision of rationality and freedom of the will and of choice is justified. If humans debase this provision, knowing that this would bring evil in its wake, then they, not their Creator, should be held responsible.

What if God made humans such that they use their rationality always to choose the good? Would they have been free under such circumstances? The answer must be no, inasmuch as the choice of the good would have been predetermined, which means that no choice ever existed.

This discussion shows that the problem of evil does indeed arise in Akan philosophy and theology. The Akan thinkers, although recognizing the existence of moral evil in the world, generally do not believe that this fact is inconsistent with the assertion that God is omnipotent and wholly good. Evil, according to them, is ultimately the result of the exercise by humans of their freedom of the will with which they were endowed by the Creator, Ōbōadeē.

8

Foundations of ethics

This chapter is in two main sections. The first takes up the question of the relation between religion (or God, deities) and morality as conceived in Akan moral thought and practice. The second, rather brief, deals with the social and humanistic foundations of Akan morality.

8.1. Religion and morality in Akan thought

Several writers have remarked that Africans are a very religious people, and that religion permeates all aspects of their lives (see section 12.3.3). This attribution of religiosity to African peoples, though a general one, may be said to be true of the Akan people. Thus, Opoku observed:

> The phenomenon of religion is so pervasive in the life of the Akan, and so inextricably bound up with their culture, that it is not easy to isolate what is purely religious from other aspects of life. It may be said without fear of exaggeration that life in the Akan world is religion and religion is life.[1]

In the light of the alleged religiosity of the Akan people, writers have not hesitated to establish some kind of necessary connection between the religion and the morality of the Akans. These writers maintain that the Akan moral system derives from, or is based on, religion. Thus, writing on Akan morality, Opoku stated: "Generally, morality *originates* from religious considerations, and so pervasive is religion in African culture that ethics and religion cannot be separated from each other. . . . Thus, *morality flows out of religion.*"[2] Bishop Sarpong also stated: "Ethics here merges with religion and religious practices, and assumes communal proportions. Among the Akan, every ethical conduct may be said to be religiously orientated."[3] Busia, a notable scholar of Akan culture, thought that "religion *defined* moral duties for the members of the group or tribe."[4] And Danquah said that "Everything else has value only in its relation to the *ideal* of the great ancestor."[5] This "great ancestor" he identified with God.[6]

All such statements are, in my view, mistaken, for reasons I shall state directly. I think that a more penetrating investigation must be made into the relation between religion and morality in Akan ethics, with a view to clarifying the Akan conception of the basis of morality and the roles, if any, played, or supposedly played, by the spiritual beings (God, deities, and ancestors) in the Akan moral universe.

However, before I examine the alleged religious basis or religious dependence of Akan morality, I wish to turn briefly to the meaning of any statement about the religious basis or dependence of morality. It must mean or imply: (1) that moral concepts such as "good," "bad," "right," "wrong," and "ought" are (to be) defined in terms of religious prescriptions or the commands of some supernatural being; (2) that moral beliefs, principles, and ideals derive logically from those of religion, and hence, (3) that religious prescriptions provide the necessary justification for moral beliefs, principles, and judgments. Finally, (4) the moral conduct of individuals is determined or greatly influenced by their religious beliefs.

These implications are of course intimately bound up with the concept of morality itself. Morality refers either to a set of social rules and norms for guiding and regulating the conduct of people in a society, or to behavior patterns, that is, responses or attitudes to such rules and norms. Thus, we speak not only of moral rules, beliefs, and prescriptions, but also of moral behavior, meaning behavior in conformity with accepted moral beliefs and rules: The moral person is one whose attitude or response to moral rules is satisfactory and commendable. So that the idea of the religious dependence of morality involves not only the sources of moral rules and principles, but also the influences that affect patterns of behavior.

These two meanings or implications of the notion of the religious dependence of morality must be kept distinct. Failure to recognize such a distinction has led some scholars to make mistakes. For instance, in an article that seeks to establish that several factors, including religion, inform the morality of a people, Kudadjie wrote:

> Where we are thinking of the origin of influences that mold behavior, or the factors that enable one to lead the morally worthy life, or indeed, the determinants of what is right or wrong, good or bad, or obligation, there are factors other than religion which come into play.[7]

This statement conflates two issues, namely, the sources or constituents of moral rules – what the author calls "the determinants of what is right or wrong, good or bad, or obligation" *and* what makes one observe moral rules – what the author refers to as the "influences that mold behavior or the factors that enable one to lead the morally worthy life." Parrinder also wrote (of Africans as a whole): "Morality is bound up with religion and receives its sanction from the Creator who gives the order of the world."[8] It is not clear whether Parrinder means that morality is genetically bound up with religion or that religious beliefs influence people's moral conduct, or both. There is, thus, a need to distinguish between the role of religion in the genesis of moral beliefs and principles and the role of religion in the moral conduct of people.

I wish now to explain why I reject the view that religion constitutes the basis of Akan morality. (For purposes of clarity and to save space, I shall in this chapter write "morality₁," to refer to moral beliefs, norms, rules, principles, ideals, and "morality₂," to refer to patterns of behavior, that is, attitudes or responses to moral norms, rules, etc.; moral practice or commitment. Where I mean both aspects, I shall write "morality" without subscripts.)

8.1.1. The concepts of good and evil

I shall begin with the Akan moral concepts of good (or goodness: *papa*) and evil (*bône*), which are fundamental in the moral thought and practice of any culture. In Akan thought goodness is not defined by reference to religious beliefs or supernatural beings. What is morally good is not that which is commanded by God or any spiritual being; what is right is not that which is pleasing to a spiritual being or in accordance with the will of such being. In the course of my field research none of my discussants referred to Onyame (God) or other spiritual entities in response to the questions What is good? What is evil? None of them held that an action was good or evil because Onyame had said so. On the contrary, the views that emerge in discussions of these questions reveal an undoubted conviction of a nonsupernaturalistic – a humanistic – origin of morality. Such views provide insight into the Akan conception of the criterion of moral value.

In Akan moral thought the sole criterion of goodness is the welfare or well-being of the community. Thus, in the course of my field research, the response I had to the question, "What do the Akan people mean by 'good' (or, goodness)?" invariably included a list of goods, that is, a list of deeds, habits, and patterns of behavior considered by the society as worthwhile because of their consequences for human well-being. The list of such goods invariably included: kindness (generosity: *ayamyie*), faithfulness (honesty, truthfulness: *nokwaredi*), compassion (*mmɔ̄-brōhunu*), hospitality (*ahōhoyē, adōe*), that which brings peace, happiness, dignity, and respect (*nea ede asomdwee, ahomeka, anuonyam ne obuo ba*), and so on. The good comprehends all the above, which is to say that the good (*papa*) is explained in terms of the qualities of things (actions, behavioral patterns). Generosity, hospitality, justice are considered (kinds of) good. Generosity is a good thing, but it is not identical with goodness. Goodness (or the good), then, is considered in Akan moral thinking as a concept comprehending a number of acts, states, and patterns of behavior that exemplify certain characteristics.

On what grounds are some acts (etc.) considered good? The answer is simply that each of them is supposed (expected or known) to bring about or lead to social well-being. Within the framework of Akan social and humanistic ethics, what is morally good is generally that which promotes social welfare, solidarity, and harmony in human relationships. Moral value in the Akan system is determined in terms of its consequences for mankind and society. "Good" is thus used of actions that promote human interest. The good is identical with the welfare of the society, which is expected to include the welfare of the individual. This appears to be the meaning or definition of "good" in Akan ethics. It is clear that this definition does not at all refer to the will or commands of God. That which is good is decreed not by a supernatural being as such, but by human beings within the framework of their experiences in living in society. So that even though an Akan maxim says

8. Foundations of ethics

I am doing the *good* (thing) so that my way to the
world of spirits might not be blocked,
(*mereye papa na ankosi me nsaman kwan*)[9]

what constitutes the good is determined not by spiritual beings but
by human beings.

Just as the good is that action or pattern of behavior which
conduces to well-being and social harmony, so the evil (*bōne*; that is,
moral evil) is that which is considered detrimental to the well-being
of humanity and society. The Akan concept of evil, like that of
good, is definable entirely in terms of the needs of society. Thus,
even though one often hears people say "God does not like evil"
(*Onyame mpē bonē*), yet what constitutes evil is determined by the
members of the community, not by Onyame.

Akan ethics recognizes two categories of evil, *bōne* and *musuo*,
although *bōne* is the usual word for evil. The first category, *bōne*,
which I shall call "ordinary," includes such evils as theft, adultery,
lying, backbiting (*kōkōnsa*), and so on. The other category of evil,
musuo, I shall call "extraordinary." As described by a group of
discussants, "*musuo* is an evil which is great and which brings
suffering (*ōhaw, ahokyerē*: disaster, misfortune) to the whole community, not just to the doer alone."[10] Another discussant also stated
that "the consequences of committing *musuo* affect the whole
community."[11] *Musuo* was also defined as an "uncommon evil" (*bōne
a wōntaa nhu*),[12] and as an "indelible evil" (*ade a woye a wompepa da*),
"remembered and referred to by people even many years after the
death of the doer."[13] Thus, *musuo* is generally considered to be a
great, extraordinary moral evil; it is viewed by the community with
particular abhorrence and revulsion because its commission is
believed not only to bring shame to the whole community, but
also, in the minds of many ordinary people, to invite the wrath of
the supernatural powers.

The category of *musuo* includes such acts as suicide, incest, having
sexual intercourse in the bush, rape, murder, stealing things dedicated to the deities or ancestral spirits, etc. Moral evils that are
musuo are also considered as taboos (*akyiwade*: abominations, prohi-
bitions), a taboo being, to most people, an act that is forbidden or
proscribed just because it is supposedly hateful to some supernatural being. That *musuo* are classifiable as taboos was in fact the view
of some discussants: "*musuo* is something we abominate" (*musuo ye
ade a yekyi*);[14] "*musuo* is a taboo" (*akyiwade*).[15] Now, it is remarkable

that the same evils considered as taboos by Bishop Sarpong, such as murder, sexual intercourse with a woman impregnated by another man, suicide, incest, words of abuse against the chief, and stealing from among the properties of a deity are all *musuo*. This gives the impression that the category of extraordinary moral evils (*musuo*) is coextensive with the category of taboos (*akyiwade*).[16] But in reality this is not so. The *musuo* are indeed taboos, but from this we can only infer that some taboos are *musuo*; since *musuo* are moral evils, such taboos (as are *musuo*) are also moral evils.[17] It seems to me that extraordinary moral evils (which include both *musuo* and moral taboos) are the kinds of moral evil that are *never* to be committed under any circumstances. This view is based on the force of the word *kyi*, to abhor, hate, from which *akyiwade* (hateful things, taboos) derives. Henceforth, I shall simply use the expression "moral taboos" to cover both *musuo* and *akyiwade*.

In view of the fact that breaking a moral taboo by any member of the community is followed by the performance by the elders of purificatory rites in order to avert possible (or imagined) disasters, it would seem to follow that the moral evils referred to as moral taboos are believed by most of the community to be especially hateful to the supernatural beings. But understanding moral taboos in terms of supernaturalism does not accord with the fundamentally humanistic thrust of Akan culture and thought (see section 8.1.2); it is the humanistic, nonsupernaturalistic outlook of Akan morality that in fact underpins the reasons offered by Akan thinkers for considering some things as morally taboo.

How would the traditional Akan thinker explain the origin and role of taboos in Akan morality? In connection with taboo, Bishop Sarpong observed: "If one were to ask the Ashanti why he keeps these taboos, he will probably not be able to give the reasons I have propounded. All he is likely to assert is that they existed from time immemorial, that the ancestors want him to observe them."[18] Bishop Sarpong is right as far as the ordinary Akan is concerned; but the wise persons (*anyansafo*) among them would be able to furnish the underlying reasons for considering such acts as moral evils of a high order. Their statements quoted above indicate clearly that they believe that committing a taboo act affects the welfare of the whole community. Moral taboos are thus explained by reference to their social function and purpose. Communal well-being, then, appears to be the principal reason for the proscription of the category of moral evils referred to as moral taboos (*musuo* and *akyiwade*). The following explanation given by Bishop Sarpong for tabooing sexual intercourse in the bush is in line with the thinking of the Akan thinkers:

> Those who indulge in it expose themselves to the risk of being bitten by venomous creatures like the snake, the scorpion, and the spider. (It should be borne in mind that Ashanti is a forested region with dangerous creatures whose bites may easily be fatal.) Let a mishap of this nature take place and there is every likelihood that misapprehensions are conceived about the conjugal act itself. That this would be detrimental to the human species is too obvious to emphasize.[19]

In the view of Akan thinkers, the real, underlying reason for regarding sexual intercourse in the bush as a great moral evil and thus for tabooing it is not that it is hated by the earth goddess (*Asase Yaa*), but that it has undesirable social consequences. Their position is plainly that the acts classified as moral taboos were so regarded simply because of the *gravity* of their consequences for human society, not because those acts were hateful to any supernatural beings.

8.1.2. Morality in the context of a nonrevealed religion

The conclusion regarding the nonsupernaturalistic foundation of Akan morality₁ is buttressed by the nature of Akan religion itself. Akan religion, like any other indigenous African religion, is not a revealed religion such as Islam or Christianity. In this connection, Danquah observed that

> ... the original Akan society did not act according to any Christian conception. We have never had a Christ or a Buddha or a Mohammed. Never in the history of the Akan people, so far as we know, have we had what is known as a revealed religion, a revelation to, or by, a prophet, of a Supreme Master or Lord, residing in your heart or residing in Heaven, who sits there waiting for you at the end of your life to judge you as either a goat or a sheep, and to send you to Paradise or to Hell, according as you are a sheep or a goat.[20]

In a revealed religion divine truth is revealed to a single founder; others must know it through him. In such cases, what is revealed is generally elaborate, and there is inevitably a moral dimension to the detailed will of God so revealed. A system of morality grounded in religion is a necessary offshoot and concomitant of a revealed religion. The morality₁ of the Decalogue, the Sermon on the Mount, and the Koran are obvious cases in point. The elaborate moral prescriptions contained in Scriptures are held to derive from the commands of God.

Given that Akan religion is not a revealed religion, how could the Akans have had access to the will of God on which to erect a moral system? It is true that a deity in some Akan locality may, from time to time, reveal through its priest that, for instance, a particular man died because he committed a wrong act in secretly selling a portion of an ancestral land, or that he had appropriated a great part of the income from the sale of family property before distributing the rest to the other members of the family – revelations that would embody or imply moral rules or prescriptions that ought to be observed. Yet such revelations in Akan communities are so few and far between that they cannot constitute a basis for a coherent moral system. Moreover, such revelations would be made to a community already in possession of moral beliefs and ideals, moral beliefs and values whose grounds were independent of any revelation. In consequence, then, any moral relevance that may have been attached by the Akans to revelations would have had to be derived from their own insight and understanding of the moral issues involved. If the quality of moralities₁ derived from, or connected with, a revealed religion such as Christianity has to be independently judged by people on the basis of their own moral knowledge and intuitions, as is usually maintained by Western philosophers,[21] this would be even more so in the case of a morality₁, like the Akan morality₁, that is not related to a revelation. It should be clear from my analysis that the Akans hold morality₁ to be logically independent of nonhuman (supernatural) powers.

It follows from the foregoing that it is through their own moral perception or understanding or knowledge that the Akans have come to ascribe moral attributes to Onyame, the Supreme Being (God). For instance, God is considered to be good. Thus, the proverb,

> Goodness is the prime characteristic of God.
> (*papa yē Nyamesu a edi kan*)

God is identified with goodness (*Nyame ne papa*).[22] God is also held as compassionate, as the following proverbs illustrate:

God pounds the one-armed person's *fufu* for him.[23]
God drives away the insects from the tailless
  animal.

God is referred to as *Abommubuwafrē*, that is, "He upon whom you
call in your experience of distress." As *Nyaamanekōse*, he is one "in
whom you confide troubles which come upon you";[24] thus, he is
one ready to offer help. Thus, God is regarded by the Akans as
good, compassionate, merciful, just, benevolent, comforting, etc.
But the meanings of these moral terms must have been appreciated
by them independently before their application to God: That is,
what would count as "good," "compassionate," etc., would logically have been known prior to their ascription to God. The
criterion by which the Akans evaluate the actions not only of God
but also of the other spiritual powers and which often influences
their attitudes springs from the attribution of a moral character to
these spiritual powers. Clearly that criterion is established through
their own understanding and appreciation of moral concepts.

Another argument against the religious basis of Akan morality₁
can be derived from the relationships between the deities and their
devotees, or more specifically from the attitudes of devotees to the
deities in certain situations. Much evidence indicates that in the
event of a deity failing to fulfill a promise, for instance, that deity
would be censured and abandoned by the people. The obvious
implication here is that the deity's action is considered *unethical*; the
deity would have therefore forfeited its moral right to command
and to be obeyed. This independent moral attitude with regard to
the conduct of the spiritual powers is unrelenting. Busia observed:
"The gods are treated with respect if they *deliver the goods*, and with
contempt if they fail. . . . Attitudes to [the gods] depend upon their
success, and vary from healthy respect to sneering contempt."[25]
Abraham wrote: "Minor gods are artificial means to the *bounty* of
Onyame . . . The institution of minor deities thus appears as an
attempt to make sure of God's *succour*. . . ."[26] The expectation of
goods and bounty from the deities is of course based on the Akan
assumption about the deities' moral esteem, an esteem that suffers
in the eyes of the Akans in the event of the inability (or unwilling-
ness) of the deities to deliver. (I have reason to believe that some of
the deities in the Akan pantheon have become extinct due to the
moral disapprobation of the people.) The fact that the behavior of a
supernatural being is thus subject to human censure implies that it

is possible for a deity to issue commands that can be considered unethical. This being the case, the criterion of moral right and wrong for the Akan must be located elsewhere than in the notion of "commanded by God," or any other spiritual power for that matter. Finally, it should be clear from the above that rather than saying that Akan morality₁ is grounded in religion, one should say that Akan religion is moral; that is, it is founded upon morality₁.

It follows from what has been said that to the question asked by Socrates (in Plato's *Euthyphro*) whether something is good because God approves of it or whether God approves of it because it is good, the response of the Akan moral thinker would be that God approves of the good because it is good. The reason is, if something is good because God approves of it, how would that good thing be known to them (that is, Akans)? How would they know what God approves in a nonrevealed religion? On the contrary, their ascription of moral attributes to God and the sanctions that he is believed to apply (see section 8.1.3) in the event of a breach of the moral law clearly suggest the Akan conviction that God approves of the good because it is good and eschews the evil because it is evil.

8.1.3. Religion, sanctions, and moral practice

To one who believes that a religious people, such as the Akans are supposed to be, can hardly do away with supernatural beings in matters of morality₁, the conclusion that Akan morality₁ is not grounded in religion and is thus independent of nonhuman sources may appear bizarre, even paradoxical. Yet that conclusion is logical. There is, however, another aspect of the question of the relation between morality and religion that needs to be examined more closely. It relates to morality conceived not as a set of rules of good conduct as such, but as patterns of behavior, as responses to the rules and norms – morality as commitment (that is, morality₂). The question is whether in the Akans' moral practice, in their response to the moral rules of society, supernatural influences and sanctions come into play.

It was indicated in the previous section that the moral intuitions of the Akans led them to attribute a moral character to God. This moral attitude in turn led them to consider God as the upholder of the moral law, even if he is not the immediate giver of that law, and, consequently, to consider the virtuous God as concerned with the moral life of humanity, even if he has not specifically told them what to do or what not to do. Consequently, an individual wronged in some way by another individual would invoke curses such as, "God will give you due recompense" (*Nyame betua wo ka*). Busia stated that "the ancestors and gods punish those who violate the traditionally sanctioned code, and reward those who keep it. . . . It will be seen from their prayers that the gods are expected . . . to see that proper behavior is rewarded and offenses are punished."[27] Bishop Sarpong also observed that religion served "as a deterrent against aberrant behavior and an incentive to good conduct."[28]

The role of sanctions in the moral conduct of the Akan must be examined more closely. Note first that the sources of sanctions do not have to be supernatural or nonhuman. Along with the nonhuman sources of sanctions in Akan moral practice, there are human sources as well: In a communal society like the Akan, containing a network of complex relationships, the opinions of kinsmen, parents, and heads of lineage and clan powerfully influence the moral behavior of the individual.

The possibility of undergoing shame, disgrace, or dishonor in consequence of unethical behavior is a real sanction in Akan moral practice. The moral maxim, "It is unbecoming of the Akan to be in disgrace" (or "Disgrace does not befit the Akan": *animguase mfata okanniba*), is so ever-present in the consciousness of every adult Akan that it undoubtedly constitutes a potent influence on moral conduct. A similar moral maxim is "Given a choice between disgrace and death, one had better choose death" (*aniwu ne owu, na efanim owu*). That one ought to behave so as not to bring dishonor or disgrace to oneself and one's group is ingrained in the moral consciousness and motivation of the Akan. It can be said that any wrong act is disgraceful, but the pertinent question is whether it should be avoided in order to avoid disgrace or because it is wrong in itself. Akan moral thought leans heavily, I think, to the former alternative. The consequentialistic stamp of Akan morality$_2$ thus appears glaring.

Is a person, Akan or anyone else for that matter, moral who does the right thing or avoids the wrong thing because of, or after thinking about, sanctions? Sanctions, whether human or nonhuman (supernatural), may be said to be extrinsic to morality$_2$, and so they are generally impugned by those moral philosophers who are given to defending the autonomy of ethics. For such philosophers it is not only moral rules and principles that are logically independent of religion or metaphysics, but our moral conduct as well. According to them, a person does or ought to do that which is right and avoid that which is wrong for no other reason than that the action is right in one case and wrong in the other. If a person does the right thing in order merely to avoid possible sanctions or undesirable consequences, then such conduct is not to be considered moral; to observe a moral rule just because of the consequences is not to act morally. Thus, Bernard Williams maintains that "genuinely moral action must be motivated by the consideration that it is morally right, and by no other consideration at all. So, taking this all together, we reach the conclusion that any appeal to God in this connection either adds nothing at all, or it adds the wrong sort of thing."[29] This, many people will agree, is the ideal moral life.

It seems to me that the case regarding the alleged immoral character of an action done because of, or after thinking about, or under the influence of sanctions, is unduly overstated and made without adequate consideration of the question of moral motivation. The factors that motivate a person to do the right thing are complex, so complex that they cannot so easily be unraveled and identified. In certain situations, therefore, much more may be involved in a person's motivation than the consideration whether an action is morally right. The complexity of the question of moral motivation is related to the rise and function of morality$_1$.

The British philosopher G. J. Warnock[30] has argued persuasively that the rise of morality$_1$ is in response to what he calls the "human predicament" of having to make moral choices based on "limited resources, limited intelligence, limited rationality, limited sympathies."[31] Regarding the limitations of human sympathies, Warnock writes: "One may say for a start, mildly, that most human beings have some natural tendency to be more concerned about the satisfaction of their own wants, etc., than those of others."[32] The general object of morality, then, he concludes, ". . . is to countervail limited sympathies and their potentially most damaging effects."[33] Following Warnock, J. L. Mackie writes: "The function of morality is primarily to counteract this limitation of men's sympathies."[34] All this is probably true.

Yet it is certainly disputable that morality – in the sense of moral rules – ipso facto alleviates the "human predicament" and thus enhances or expands human sympathies; otherwise we would not have such moral problems as selfishness and the desire for self-aggrandizement, sometimes to the total disregard of the feelings and needs of others. The existence of known and accepted moral rules following the creation of morality$_1$ is one thing; having the disposition and capacity to observe those rules in practice is quite another. Morality$_1$ does not automatically lead to morality$_2$. It is in connection with the latter that factors that motivate moral conduct come into play. And it is in that connection that sanctions – such a bugbear to those moral philosophers who want people to act autonomously, aided by their own moral light or "voice" – also come into play. If we look more closely, we might conclude that sanctions are perhaps not extrinsic, but are in some sense intrinsic to moral conduct. They are, to my mind, potent aids in countervailing the consequences of the "human predicament," in counteracting human weaknesses and temptations to do wrong or to refrain from doing the right thing. The fear or thought of shame, of disgrace, of loss of social esteem and opportunity, and so on, constitutes a real influence on moral conduct, and as such can be regarded as a kind of sanction, if an obscure one.

Some sanctions are so subtle that they may not be felt as such. What seems to have happened is that, as a result of the process of habituation, thought or fear of sanctions in making moral decisions may have receded so far back in our moral psychology that we hardly think of sanctions in deciding to do the right or to avoid the wrong. The right moral choice thus appears to be spontaneous and motivated by no other consideration than the rightness of the action itself.

In short, sanctions, whether human (social) or nonhuman (supernatural), do play an important role in our moral conduct: in obeying moral rules and translating our moral decisions into action. The thought of sanctions of any sort may add to our willingness to perform our moral duties; it may make us see our duties in a fresh light; it may prop us up where we might have faltered; it may make more acute our sense of guilt. The thought or fear or influence of sanctions therefore cannot, in my opinion, be completely extruded from the domain of moral practice. Since some of these sanctions derive in the Akan system from religious beliefs, it follows that religion cannot be completely banished from the *practice* of morality. It appears, though, that in the Akan system the supernatural sanctions, which follow upon religious beliefs, are limited to what I have earlier characterized as "extraordinary evils" and taboos. My conclusion, then, is that in terms of behavior, of responses to moral norms and rules, Akan morality$_2$ cannot be said to be wholly independent of religion. It may appear puzzling that the practical aspects of a morality$_1$ whose principles are not grounded in religion should be animated by religion; yet this position does not involve any logical inconsistency.

II. The Akan conceptual scheme

However, the clarification of the role of sanctions in the explanation of moral conduct provided above is not intended to imply that Akan moral thought recognizes sanctions as the *sole* reason for moral action, that the individual does that which is morally right in order *only* and always to avoid possible sanctions or undesirable consequences. That would be far from the truth. For the Akans have a conception of an inner urge conducing to moral practice: *tiboa*, translated by Christaller as "the inward voice, conscience."[35] Every human being "possesses" a sense of right and wrong – called *tiboa*, conscience or moral sense. It is not clear to me when and how a person comes to possess moral sense. Is *tiboa* something innate or acquired? And how is it acquired, if it is? No elaborate answers to these questions emerge from the Akan sources. Nevertheless, *tiboa* is held, among other things, as creating a sense of guilt in the individual, convicting him or her of bad actions. Thus, it is said of a guilty person who cleverly evades punishment or public censure, but who later confesses, that "His conscience has judged him guilty" (*ne tiboa abu no fo*). Similarly, a person who claims to be innocent but whose innocence is not accepted by others will always say, "My conscience does not trouble me" (*me tiboa nha me*). Since moral conduct, that is, response to a moral rule, is ultimately an individual or private affair, the notion of *tiboa* (conscience) is important. Bishop Sarpong was right when he wrote: "There appears to be no more *effective* measure against unethical behavior, whether detected or hidden, than conscience" (*tiboa*).[36] It is by virtue of *tiboa* that the notion of self-sanctioning in moral conduct becomes intelligible.

As a result of its power to induce a sense of guilt, *tiboa* is held to influence a person's moral choice, decision, response, and attitude. Thus, a person who often fails to act morally, frequently flouting the accepted moral rules of the community, is considered as one whose *tiboa* is "dead" (*ne tiboa awu*); that is, his or her moral sense (conscience) is dulled and has in consequence become inoperative. Although it may be said that the person who has frequently violated moral rules lacks conscience, we can, I think, also say that he or she lacks moral will. If this is correct, then *tiboa* can be rendered also as "moral will," as well as "conscience." But moral will and conscience are not identical. For, having a sense of right and wrong is not the same as having the capacity or strength of will (moral will) to do that which conscience prescribes as right or to refrain from that which conscience prescribes as wrong. There

142

must be some relation between the two concepts that is not easy to articulate; one can say that both of them bear on moral commitment. Presumably, moral will is the "executive" of conscience. When moral will falters, guilt sometimes results.

I said that the Akan sources appear to be silent on the origin of the notion of *tiboa* (conscience). But I maintain that *tiboa*, whether as moral sense (conscience) or as moral will, is not innate to man, but something acquired through socialization, through habituation, through moral experience. It is the cumulative result of the individual's responses to past moral situations. Thus, I interpret *tiboa* as nothing mysterious or supernatural in its origins. This interpretation appears consonant with the generally empirical orientation of Akan philosophy.

8.2. The social and humanistic basis of Akan morality$_1$

Arguments have been advanced in section 8.1 to show that, contrary to the views of a number of scholars, Akan morality$_1$ is not religiously grounded, even if religious beliefs may be said to have a bearing on moral practice (that is, morality$_2$). The question that naturally follows is this: Having removed Akan morality$_1$ from its alleged religious (supernaturalistic) moorings, where do we moor it? If religion is not the basis of Akan morality$_1$, what is?

Section 1.1 showed unmistakably the preoccupation of Akan moral thought with human welfare: The concern for human welfare constitutes the hub of the Akan axiological wheel. This orientation of Akan morality$_1$ takes its impulse undoubtedly from the humanistic outlook that characterizes Akan traditional life and thought. Humanism, the doctrine that sees human needs, interests, and dignity as fundamental, thus constitutes the foundation of Akan morality$_1$.

Unlike Western humanism, however, Akan humanism is not antisupernaturalistic. On the contrary, it maintains a rigid supernaturalistic metaphysics that is rejected by Western humanism. The rejection by Western humanist thinkers of supernaturalism stems, I think, from their supposition that such an outlook would divert the attention and concern required to promote human welfare in this world. In the words of Corliss Lamont, a leading exponent and protagonist of the philosophy of humanism in the West,

143

II. The Akan conceptual scheme

The philosophy of humanism, with its conscious limitation of the human enterprise to this existence, *sets us free to concentrate our entire energies, without distraction by either hopes or fears of individual immortality, on that building of the good society* that has been the dream of saints and sages since the dawn of history.[37]

The antisupernaturalistic metaphysics of Western humanism must be seen in relation to the theological context of Western humanist thought. The espousal of this kind of metaphysics was an attempt on the part of Western humanism to wriggle out of the Christian theological shell. The "fears or hopes of individual immortality" that Lamont refers to are but part of the doctrines of Christianity, the main religion of the West. It was the assumption of Western humanists that, unless our minds were rid of such hopes and fears, we would concentrate on the "other world," to the detriment of human interests in *this* world. The antisupernaturalistic stand of Western humanism is therefore the consequence of a strong determination to achieve human welfare, prosperity, and happiness by devoting all attention to this world and this life.

The position of Akan thinkers here is quite different. In their view, as I understand it, the pursuit of the welfare and interests of human beings in this world – which for them, as for every humanist, is the crucial meaning of humanism – need not lead to the rejection of supernaturalism. It is possible, they maintain, to believe in the existence of supernatural entities without necessarily allowing this to detract from the pursuit of human welfare in this world. Here, as in the case of Western humanism, the theological context is relevant, though it functions in importantly different ways. In Akan religious thought the Supreme Being is not conceived as a terrible being who ought to be feared because he can cast one into eternal hellfire. (The Supreme Being is believed to punish evildoers only in this world.) Again, in spite of Akan belief in immortality, their conception of the hereafter does not include hopes of a happier, more blessed life beyond the grave. Western humanism sees religion as impeding the concentration of human energies on building the good society. In Akan thought this tension between supernaturalism and humanism does not appear; for the Akan, religion is not seen as hindering the pursuit of one's interests in this world. On the contrary, the supernaturalistic outlook of Akan humanism is the consequence not only of a belief in the existence of a Supreme Being and other supernatural entities, but,

144

more importantly I think, of a desire to utilize the munificence and powers of such entities for the promotion of human welfare and happiness. The observation was made earlier (section 8.1.2) that the deities are censured on moral grounds if they fail to "deliver the goods." One implication of this, for our present purposes, is that the deities exist in order to supervise the well-being of human beings. Hence, supernaturalism was accommodated. Whether or not the supernatural entities actually fulfill their expectations is beside the point. The important point to note is that in Akan thinking about the foundations of morality₁ consideration is given solely to human well-being.

Although I see the point of Western humanism in its rejection of supernaturalism, I am not sure whether the mere rejection of supernaturalism (or the religious outlook) necessarily leads to the attainment of human well-being. (Lamont seems to assume that it does.) In the pursuit of human well-being – and that means the well-being of every individual human being – sufficient consideration must be given to the distribution of the material and social benefits of the society, the adequacy and fairness of its legal system, its system of class and social relationships, and so on. Legal and social justice, equality, equitable distribution of goods, and human rights are, to my mind, more essential to the achievement of human well-being than the mere banishing of religion. The banishing of religion in modern Marxist states has not led to the attainment of human well-being. But Akan humanism, which accommodates religion, will not necessarily conduce to the attainment of human well-being either, unless it is also underpinned by legal and social justice, equality, and the other benefits mentioned above. All this means that the acceptance or rejection of religion cannot – must not – be considered essential to humanist thought; to do so is to draw a red herring across the track.

A morality like that of the Akan, whose central focus is the concern for human well-being, would expectably be a social morality. This social character is intrinsic to the notion of morality, for unless human society existed, there would be no such a thing as morality. A society-oriented morality is necessarily grounded in human experiences in living together. Such is the nature of Akan morality. Akan proverbs are based upon the experiences of the people, which indicates the social or this-worldly origin of Akan moral values. It seems to me that the most adequate morality is one that is socially grounded.

II. The Akan conceptual scheme

Akan thought conceives the human being as a social animal and society as a necessary condition for human existence (see Chapter 10). This thought is expressed in the proverb

> When a man descends from heaven, he descends
> into human society.

But the person who descends into human society has desires, aims, interests, and will, and these have to be reconciled with those of others. An Akan proverb such as

> One man's curse is another man's fortune
> (lit.: What appears sour on one man's palate appears
> sweet on another man's palate),

indicates the view that the desires, interests, and passions of individual members of a society differ and may conflict with one another. One often hears the ordinary Akan say *obi mpē a obi pē*: "If one does not desire it, the other does"; that is, people have different desires, preferences, and choices. One Akan motif shows a "siamese" crocodile with two heads but a common stomach. The saying that goes with the symbol is that, although they have one stomach, the heads fight over the food that will eventually nourish both of them. The symbol, whose significance I discuss in detail in section 10.2, points to the conflicts that result from the existence of individual desires and needs. The problem is how to minimize such conflicts and at the same time allow room for the realization of individual desires and needs. The need for a system of rules to regulate the conduct of individuals and, consequently, for social harmony and cooperative living, thus becomes urgent. It is this social need that gives rise to morality₁, according to Akan ethics.

Thus considerations for human well-being and for an ideal type of social relationships – both of which are generated by the basic existential conditions of man – these, not divine pronouncements, constitute the crucible in which Akan morality₁ is fashioned. Whatever the moral virtues possessed by, or ascribed to, God and the other spiritual powers, it should now be clear that the compelling reason of the Akan for pursuing the good is not that it is pleasing to the supernatural beings or approved by them, but rather that it will lead to the attainment of human well-being. This *humanistic* moral outlook of the Akan is something that, I think, is worth being cherished, for its goal, from the moral point of view, is ultimate and, thus, self-justifying.

146

9

Ethics and character

9.1. The Akan word for "ethics"

It is difficult to say what the Akan equivalent of the word "ethics" is. The word ōbra has been used by Danquah to mean "the ethical life, conduct, behavior, moral life."[1] This rendition of ōbra is not wholly correct. Christaller's rendition of it as "life in this world, manner of life"[2] is better. Christaller, however, adds "conduct" and "behavior" as translations of ōbra, as does Danquah. Berry also renders ōbra as "behavior."[3] It must be conceded that the words "conduct" and "behavior" have ethical connotations and figure prominently in discussions on the nature of ethics, as when we say that moral rules are meant to guide the conduct and behavior of people in terms of what is right and wrong. Although the way one conducts oneself affects one's life, nevertheless it cannot be allowed that ōbra must therefore mean "ethics." Ōbra (life, manner of life) is certainly a much wider concept than ethics. Obviously not all aspects of life are ethical. In referring to the ethical aspects of life the Akans generally use the word suban, character.

The concept of character, suban, is so crucial and is given such a central place in Akan moral language and thought that it may be considered as summing up the whole of morality. Thus, when the Akans want to say, "He has no morals," they would say, "He has no character"(onni suban). Onni suban is much used to express moral disapprobation of all kinds. Sometimes the word pa or papa, meaning "good" (in the moral sense), is added: thus, onni suban pa ("He has no good character," "He has no morals," "His conduct is unethical"). An equivalent expression is *ōwō suban bōne* ("He has bad character"). The opposite of *onni suban pa* ("He has no morals") is *ōwō suban pa* ("He has morals," "He is ethical, moral"), said of a person whose actions are morally praiseworthy. Being a bad person (*onipa bōne*) and having a bad character (*suban bōne*) are considered identical; similarly, being a good person (*onipa pa*) and having a good character (*suban pa*) are considered identical. Thus, Berry was right in rendering *suban* (character) as "morals," though he was wrong in translating the word "character" as *ōbra*,[4] for the Akan word for character is *suban*. In the light of the place occupied by the concept of character in Akan moral life and thought, it may be more correct to use the word *suban* to translate "morals."

The Akans are not the only people to use a word that means "character" to refer to the general subject of moral phenomena. The word "ethics" itself comes from the Greek word *ethos*, which means character. Thus, a well-known Oxford classical scholar translates *he ethike* as "the science of character."[5] In Islamic moral philosophy the word used for "ethics," namely, *akhlāq,* means character. This Arabic word is more akin to the Akan word *suban* in that the word *khalaq*, from which *akhlāq* derives, means nature, creation, as does *su* (or *esu*), the first part of the word *suban*. In Yoruba language and thought the word *iwa* means both character (or morality) and being (nature).[6] The Akan word *suban*, as we have seen, sums up the whole concept of morality, and hence can correctly be used, sometimes with an additional word or words to reflect modern usage, as the Akan equivalent of the word "ethics." Thus, "ethics" may be translated as *suban ho nimdee* or *suban ho adwendwen*, "studies or reflections on character," a rendition which, in stressing the notion of character, agrees with the Akan conception of morality.

9.2. The centrality of character (*suban*) in Akan ethics

Morality is generally concerned with right and wrong conduct or behavior and good and bad character. We speak not only of a moral act but also of a moral person; we speak not only of an honest or generous or vicious act but also of an honest or generous or vicious person. When a person is generally honest or generous the Akans judge him or her to be a good person, by which they mean that he or she has a good character (*ōwō suban papa*), and when

148

the person is wicked or dishonest they judge him or her to be a bad person, that is, to have a bad character. It is on the basis of a person's conduct (deeds, *nneyēe*) that the Akans judge one to be good or bad, to have good character or bad character. According to them, the character of a person is basic. The performance of good or bad acts depends on the state of one's character; inasmuch as good deeds reflect good character, character (*suban*) appears as the focal point of the ethical life. It is, in Akan moral thought, the crucial element in morality, for it profits a society little if its moral system is well articulated intellectually and the individuals in that system nevertheless have bad character and so do the wrong things. A well-articulated moral system does not necessarily produce good character; neither does knowledge of moral rules make one a good person or produce good character.

For the Akans, and perhaps also for the Greeks and Arabs, ethics has to do principally with character. Ethics, according to Akan thinkers, deals essentially with the quality of the individual's character. This is a remarkable assertion, for after all the ethical response, that is, the response or attitude to a moral rule, is an individual, private affair. All that a society can do regarding morality is to provide or impart moral knowledge to its members, making them aware of the moral rules that are applicable to all living in it. But granted this, it does not follow that the individual members of the society will lead lives in conformity with the moral rules. A man may know and may even accept a moral rule such as, say, it is wrong to seduce someone's wife. But he may fail to apply this rule to a particular situation. He is not able to effect the transition from knowledge to action. According to the Akan thinkers, to be able to act in accord with the moral rules of the society requires the possession of a good character (*suban*).

What, then, is character? How do Akan thinkers define character? The root of *suban* is *su* or *esu*, meaning nature, which might imply that character is associated with a person's nature, that character develops from a set of inborn traits. Moreover, the earlier discussion of the Akan concept of the person may give a similar impression. There it was observed that *sunsum*, the active aspect of the soul, plays a role in character formation, that moral attributes are ascribed to the *sunsum*, and that like the superego of Freud it constitutes the moral dimension of personality. Overall, one might conclude that character is a state or condition of the soul which "causes" it to perform its actions spontaneously and easily. This implies that the moral habits are innate, that we are born virtuous and are not responsible for our character. That impression, however, is false. Despite its etymological link with nature, the *suban* of a person is not wholly innate. I shall in due course explain what it means to say that the *sunsum* plays a role in character formation.

Akan thinkers define character in terms of habits, which originate from a person's deeds or actions; character is the configuration of (individual) acts. Thus, several of my discussants opined that "Character is your deeds" (actions: *nneyēe*[7]); "Character comes from your deeds" (*suban firi wo nneyēe*). Moreover, sometimes the Akans use the sentence, "He has a bad character" (*ōwō suban bōne*) when they want to say "He does bad things" (*ōyē nneēma bōne*). The thought here is that moral virtues arise through habituation, which is consonant with the empirical orientation of Akan philosophy. This is, I think, the reason for the teaching of moral values embedded in proverbs and folktales to children in the process of their socialization; the moral instructions are meant to habituate them to moral virtues. If moral habits were thought to be acquired by nature or through birth it would be senseless to pursue moral instruction. But it is believed and expected that the narratives are one way by which children acquire and internalize moral virtues.

I hold the view that in general society presents us with a variety of modes of behavior. We see and are told what is good behavior and what is bad, what is praiseworthy and what is blameworthy. We are given a choice. To acquire virtue, a person must practice good deeds so that they become habitual. The newly acquired good habit must be strengthened by repetition. A single good deed may initiate further good deeds, and in this way virtue is acquired. Over time such an acquired virtue becomes a habit. This is the position of Akan philosophy, for this is what they mean by saying *aka ne hō*, "It is left (or has remained) with him," "It has become part of him," "It has become his habit."[8] Such practice and performance emphasize the relevance and importance of action in the acquisition of virtue. To be just, for instance, one must first behave in a just manner. The emphasis placed by Akan thinkers on the influence of actions on character illustrates their conviction that one is in some sense responsible for the sort of person one is; the person is responsible for the state of his or her character. The unjust man may be held responsible for becoming unjust, because his character is the result of repeated (*aka hō*) voluntary acts of injustice. He had the choice between committing acts of injustice and refraining from such acts.

The emphasis on the relevance of actions for states of character is reflected in the way that abstract terms for "goodness," "virtue," are formed. The usual words for "goodness" in Akan are *yieyē*[9] and *papayē*[10] (the latter also appears sometimes as *papa*). The last syllable of each word means to do or perform. Thus, the two words literally mean "good-doing" (that is, doing good).

This analysis of the Akan concept of character supports, as far as the Akan position goes, Mbiti's view that "the essence of African morality is that it is a morality of 'conduct' rather than a morality of 'being' . . . a person is what he is because of what he does, rather than that he does what he does because of what he is."[11] This view is repeated by Bishop Sarpong: "For it would appear that for the Akan what a man is is less important than what a man does. To put it more concretely, a person is what he is because of his deeds. He does not perform those deeds because of what he is."[12] The emphasis on deeds (*nneyēe*) is appropriate, for it agrees with the Akan belief that a person is not born virtuous or vicious. The previously quoted proverb

> One is not born with a bad "head," but one takes it
> on the earth,

implies, among other things, that a bad habit is not an inborn characteristic, but one that is acquired. The Akan position thus is that the original nature of human beings was morally neutral. If this were not the case, there would be no such thing as a moral person. The person's original moral neutrality later comes to be affected by actions, habits, responses to moral instruction, and so on. Consequently, what a person does or does not do is crucial to the formation of the character. A virtuous character is the result of the performance of virtuous *acts*.

There is one difficult question inherent in the Akan position, a question that has not been squarely faced or examined by scholars such as Mbiti and Bishop Sarpong. The question is this: How are we to perform virtuous acts if we are not already virtuous? The question places us on the horns of a dilemma, for if we are born virtuous, then we have nothing to acquire, for we are already virtuous. If on the other hand we are not already virtuous, how can we perform such acts as are virtuous?

As already noted, Akan moral thought assumes a person's original nature to be morally neutral, which is congruent with the assumption of the reality and meaningfulness of human free will and responsibility. Akan moral thought considers character (*suban*) to be dispositional, which implies that a person is not born with a settled tendency to be good or to be bad. Hence, Berry is reasonable in translating the word "disposition" as *suban*, character.[13] But then the question is: If a person is not born virtuous, how can he or she perform virtuous acts? The answer is through moral instruction, which in traditional Akan society was normally done by means of ethical proverbs and folktales. In this way the growing child and young adult become aware of what is a virtuous or vicious act and become virtuous by performing virtuous acts.

In dealing with the further question of how a person can perform such acts, the role of the *sunsum* in a person's psychological system must be recalled. It was observed earlier that a person's *sunsum* (spirit) plays a role in the formation and exercise of character (*suban*), which means that *sunsum*, considered as a capacity, enables a person to perform virtuous acts. One might regard the position of the Akan traditional thinker here as less than adequate on the grounds that capacity or power does not exist in the same degree in different individuals. In fact the idea of different degrees of capacity in individuals is reflected in such Akan locutions as "strong *sunsum*," "forceful *sunsum*," "weak *sunsum*," and so on. However, whatever a person's capacity, the Akans believe that the *sunsum* can be developed.[14] A weak *sunsum* can be strengthened by making an effort, and by making an effort a person can obey a moral rule, either by doing what is right or refraining from doing what is wrong. Thus, while none of the moral virtues is implanted in us by nature, nature gives us the capacity to acquire them. The developability of *sunsum* implies the possibility of moral reform and a change of character. All my discussants were unanimous in asserting that character can be changed (*suban wotumi sesa no*). For this reason people are to be held responsible for their characters (*suban*). It is on the possibility of change of character that the sensitivity to moral rules hinges. However, the Akan thinker's position here, if my interpretation is correct, cannot claim to be final and impregnable, for we can still pose the questions: Is it not the case that making an effort itself requires or presupposes antecedent factors? If so, what are these factors and how can they be acquired? The attempt to answer this set of questions will most probably involve us in a circle, and a vicious one.

One must conclude that the crucial place given to character in the Akan conception of morality is appropriate. If morality is concerned essentially with the right and the wrong in the way of conduct, then the quality of the individual's personal character lies at the heart of the moral life he or she will live. In a particular moral situation the individual must have the disposition to observe or obey a moral rule. Aristotle wrote: "We are inquiring not in order to know what virtue is, but in order to *become* virtuous."[15] Becoming virtuous certainly requires that one have a good or virtuous character. Erich Fromm, the social philosopher and psychoanalyst, wrote: "The subject matter of ethics is *character*, and only in reference to the character structure as a whole can value statements be made about single traits or actions. *The virtuous or the vicious character, rather than single virtues or vices, is the true subject matter of ethical inquiry.*"[16]

It is appropriate, of course, to bring within the compass and scrutiny of moral philosophy topics like duty, obligation, moral knowledge, moral judgment, and happiness. But after such matters have been thoroughly examined, the basic or ultimate aim of the ethical inquiry remains how to improve the quality of an individual's personal character. The carrying out of a person's moral duty depends on character. The way to happiness, whether of the society or of the individual, depends ultimately on the characters of the individual members of the society. Whatever may be the origin of moral rules, whether man or a divine being, the important thing is to obey them insofar as these rules have been accepted and approved by the society – and the state of a person's character is a crucial factor in obeying moral rules. The Akan thinkers therefore appear to be correct in attributing a pivotal place to character (*suban*) in their thinking about morality.

10

The individual and the social order

10.1. Communalism as a social theory

It is of course well known that the social order of any African community is communal. But I think it would be more correct to describe the African social order as amphibious, for it manifests features of both communality and individuality. To describe that order simply as communal is to prejudge the issue regarding the place given to individuality. The African social order is, strictly speaking, neither purely communalistic nor purely individualistic. But the concept of communalism in African social thought is often misunderstood, as is the place of the individual in the communal social order.

Scholars, usually from noncommunal social backgrounds, say about communalism (or communitarianism) that it offers no room for the expression of individuality, assuming that individuality is submerged by communalism, and that communalism is antithetical to individualism. The two cannot coexist, for, it is said, there cannot be a meaningful cooperative relationship between them. The burden of this chapter is to analyze the concepts of communality and individuality as they exist in Akan social thought, in order to articulate the Akan idea of the relationship between the individual and society.

Communalism, which is a doctrine about social organization and relations, is an offshoot of the Akan concept of humanism. It is perhaps indisputable that social institutions embody a philosophical perspective about human nature and social relationships. One way in which the Akan concept of humanism is made explicit is in its

154

social organization. Ensuring the welfare and interests of each member of society – the essential meaning of Akan humanism – can hardly be accomplished outside the communal system.

Communalism may be defined as the doctrine that the group (that is, the society) constitutes the focus of the activities of the individual members of the society. The doctrine places emphasis on the activity and success of the wider society rather than, though not necessarily at the expense of, or to the detriment of, the individual.

Aristotle proclaimed many centuries ago that man is by nature a social animal,[1] and that it is impossible for him to live outside society. Akan thinkers agree that society is not only a necessary condition for human existence, but it is natural to man. This idea is expressed in an already-quoted proverb:

> When a man descends from heaven, he descends
> into a human society.
> *(onipa firi soro besi a, obesi onipa kurom)*

[The idea of man descending from heaven stems from the belief that man is created by the Supreme Being, Onyame, in heaven (*soro*).]

This proverb rejects the concept of the state of nature, as explicated by those eighteenth-century European philosophers who asserted the existence of an original presocial character of man. In the state of nature, people lived solitary and uncooperative lives, with undesirable consequences that in time led to the formation of society. Akan thought, however, sees humans as originally born into a human society (*onipa kurom*), and therefore as social beings from the outset. In this conception, it would be impossible for people to live in isolation. For not only is the person not born to live a solitary life, but the individual's capacities are not sufficient to meet basic human requirements. For the person, as another proverb has it, is not a palm tree that he or she should be complete or self-sufficient. Consequently, the individual inevitably requires the succor and the relationships of others in order to realize or satisfy basic needs. As another proverb states it:

> The prosperity [or well-being] of man depends
> upon his fellow man.
> *(obi yiye firi obi)*

Human sociality, then, is seen as a consequence of basic human nature, but it is also seen as that which makes for personal well-being and worth. Because community life is natural to man, the kind of society that permits the full realization of human capacities, needs, and aspirations should be communal.

Communalism as conceived in Akan thought is not a negation of individualism; rather, it is the recognition of the limited character of the possibilities of the individual, which limited possibilities whittle away the individual's self-sufficiency. Thus, we have the following proverbs:

> One finger cannot lift up a thing.
> If one man scrapes the bark of a tree for medicine,
>   the pieces fall down.[2]
> The left arm washes the right arm and the right
>   arm washes the left arm.

The above proverbs, and many more similar to these in content, clearly underscore the rationale behind communalism. They indicate, on the one hand, the failures and frustrations of extreme individualism; that in spite of individual talents and capacities, the individual ought to be aware of his or her insufficiency to achieve his welfare through solitary effort. On the other hand, the proverbs also indicate the value of collective action, mutual aid, and interdependence as necessary conditions not only for an individual's welfare, but also for the successful achievement of even the most difficult undertakings. Communalism insists that the good of all determines the good of each or, put differently, the welfare of each is dependent on the welfare of all. This requires that the individual should work for the good of all, which of course includes his or her own good.

Thus, it is implicit in communalism that the success and meaning of the individual's life depend on identifying oneself with the group. This identification is the basis of the reciprocal relationship between the individual and the group. It is also the ground of the overriding emphasis on the individual's obligation to the members of the group; it enjoins upon him or her the obligation to think and act in terms of the survival of the group as a whole. In fact one's personal sense of responsibility is measured in terms of responsiveness and sensitivity to the needs and demands of the group. Since this sense of responsibility is enjoined equally upon each member of the group – for all the members are expected to enhance the welfare of the group as a whole – communalism maximizes the interests of all the individual members of the society.

If sociality is in fact fundamental to human nature, then the type of social order that ought to exist is that which would conduce to the full realization of that nature. One may therefore come down on the side of the communal social arrangement, as it would seem to be best able to express basic human nature. Thus, communalism could be regarded as the ideal social order even though, like other types of social arrangement, it also contains difficulties, to be mentioned in due course. For the moment one may say that in the communal social order material and other benefits are more likely to be available to all the members of the society than in any other social system. The reasons for this statement are that the communal social order is participatory, and that it is characterized by such social and ethical values as social well-being, solidarity, interdependence, cooperation, and reciprocal obligation – all of which conduce to equitable distribution of the resources and benefits of the society. It seems to me that the pattern of distribution of the resources and benefits of a society provides the litmus test for judging the fairness and worthwhileness of a particular social arrangement and its concomitant socioeconomic relations.

From another aspect – namely, that of psychological well-being – the communal social order is worthwhile. Its intricate web of social relationships tends to ensure the individual's social worth, thus making it almost impossible for an individual to feel socially insignificant. In a communal social order like that of the Akan, this assurance is already provided; the individual feels socially worthy and important because his or her role and activity in the community are appreciated. The system affords the individual the opportunity to make a meaningful life through his or her contribution to the general welfare. It is thus part of the doctrine of communalism that the individual can find the highest good – materially, morally and spiritually (psychologically) – in relationships with others and in working for the common good.

But inherent in the communal enterprise is the problem of contribution and distribution. The communal enterprise tends to maximize the common good because each individual is expected to contribute to it, but obviously individuals are not equal in their capacities and talents – a fact explicitly recognized in Akan thought (see section 9.2). It follows therefore that individual contributions to the common good will be unequal. Now, the question is: Should inequality in contribution lead to inequality in distribution? Akan social thought, with its social and humanistic thrust, answers this question in the negative. It may be objected that this leads to an unfair treatment of those who have contributed more, to which one may respond that those who have contributed more must have been endowed with greater talents and capacities – natural characteristics and assets for which they were not responsible. This counterargument is perhaps implicit in the proverbs, "The left arm washes the right arm and the right arm washes the left arm" and "The fingers of the hand are not equal in length." Even though the power or effort of one arm may not be as great as that of the other, nevertheless it is able to make *some* contribution. The natural assets of human beings are, as the two proverbs imply, different and should therefore not be made the basis of unequal distribution, even though the second proverb rejects the idea of absolute equality.

The Akan position is defensible for, irrespective of an individual's contribution to the common good, it is fair and reasonable that everyone's *basic* human needs be satisfied by the society: From each according to *whatever contribution* one can make to each according to one's *basic* needs will be the new slogan.

But having said all this, there remains the crucial question of the place of individuality in the theory of communalism. This question is an ultimate one, for, after all, the human being who "descends into human society" has personal will, identity, aspirations, and desires that can be said to be idiosyncratic. In discussing the Akan concept of destiny I observed that destiny is that which determines the uniqueness and individuality of a person, which means that Akan thought clearly recognizes the idea of individuality. But does it also recognize the possible tension between the two ideas of individuality and communality? The answer to this crucial question will occupy the remaining part of the chapter.

10.2. The tensions of individualism

A number of scholars, writing usually from noncommunalistic backgrounds and mentalities, consider communalism as absorbing the individual into the life of the group, with the consequent whittling away of individuality, personality, initiative, and responsibility. In charting the Akan response to this question, let us first turn to the ideas expressed in the following Akan proverb:

> The clan is like a cluster of trees which, when seen
>   from afar, appear huddled together, but which
>   would be seen to stand *individually* when closely
>   approached.

Annobil explains this proverb thus: "If one is far away from a cluster of trees, he sees all the trees as huddled or massed together. It is when he goes nearer that he recognizes that the trees in fact stand *individually*. The clan is just like the cluster of trees."[3] The proverb gives the impression that the clan or the community is a mere abstraction, not a reality. This is not so, however, for the cluster of trees is real. The proverb stresses the reality of the individual, which, the proverb implies, cannot be diminished or obliterated by the reality of the community. The proverb expresses the idea that the individual has a separate identity and that, like the tree, some of whose branches may touch other trees, the individual is separately rooted and is not completely absorbed by the cluster. That is, communality does not obliterate individuality. Thus, individuals have characters and wills of their own, an idea that comes out clearly also in Akan art.

I have already mentioned the Akan art motif of the "siamese" crocodile: a crocodile with two heads but a single stomach (section 8.2). The proverb connected with this symbol says that, although they have a common stomach, they always struggle over food. The symbol has implications for Akan social thought, particularly about the articulation of the uniqueness of the individual and his or her relationship to the society. First, the presence of two individual heads is important. In the Akan language the head (*ti*) is regarded "as the seat of intellect, thought, deliberation and determination, also of feeling ... that which perceives (and feels), thinks and remembers, reasons, wills and desires in man ... ."[4] The head in the symbol emphasizes individuality: It indicates the will, interests, tastes, and passions of the individual; it indicates the desire of the individual for self-expression. Conflicts in society, the symbol seems to imply, are the consequences of the clash of individuals expressing themselves and the desire to satisfy one's own needs, implying in turn that the aims, interests, passions, etc., of individuals differ. An Akan maxim says that "it is by *individual* effort that we can struggle for our heads" (*ti wopere no nkorokoro*). The proverb expresses the idea of individual effort as a necessary condition for protecting and, more particularly, struggling for our interests and needs. The notion of competition (*pere*) is also implicit here. Thus, individuality, which lies at the heart of social conflicts, is recognized in Akan social thought. Though social conflicts arise as the result of the implications of the individuality of members of the society, I do not think that Akan thought suggests that they are either inevitable or permanent, *if* individual members realize that, after all, their interests are identical or cannot be essentially different.

Second, the common stomach of the two crocodiles indicates that (1) at least the basic interests of all the members of the community are identical, and (2) the community of interests forms the basis for the maximization of their interests and welfare. Just as the common stomach becomes bigger as a result of each head's being fed, so the assets of the society increase with the contributions, great and small, of the individual members of the society. This means that a society cannot prosper without the full cooperation of its members. But if an individual made only a modest contribution, this would not prejudice his or her chances of getting a fair share of the material benefits of the society, a share that will at least satisfy basic needs.

I think therefore that the common stomach symbolizes the *common good*, that is, the good of all individuals embraced within a society. The common good, I take it, is not merely the sum of the various individual goods. The concept implies, I think, that there are certain needs that are *basic* to the enjoyment and fulfillment of the life of each individual. Such needs include shelter, food, health, equality of opportunity, and liberty. Thus conceived, the common good is predicated on a true or essential universal, the good of *all*, that which is essentially good for human beings as such. The common good, therefore, is not conceptually opposed to the individual good of any member of the society. It embraces his or her individual good as it embraces the goods of other members. If the common good is attained, then logically the individual good is also attained. Strictly speaking, there can or should be no conflict between the two, for the individual and the common goods are tied up together and overlap. Therefore, any conflict stems from a misconception either of the common good, of the individual good, or of the relationship between the two.

Thus, the symbol of the crossed crocodiles with two heads and a common stomach has great significance for Akan social thought. While it suggests the rational underpinnings of the concept of communalism, it does not do so to the detriment of individuality. The concept of communalism, as it is understood in Akan thought, therefore does not overlook individual rights, interests, desires, and responsibilities, nor does it imply the absorption of the individual will into the "communal will," or seek to eliminate individual responsibility and accountability. Akan social thought attempts to establish a delicate balance between the concepts of communality and individuality. Whether it succeeds in doing so in practice is of course another question.

The Akan acceptance of individualism is also indicated by their understanding of an important feature of the group. We see it expressed in the proverb,

> The clan (group) is (merely) a *multitude* (crowd).
> (*abusua yē dom*)

This proverb does not say that the group is amorphous or unreal, but that the individual cannot always and invariably depend on the group for everything. The proverb is thus intended to deepen the individual's sense of responsibility for oneself. The proverb suggests that the relevance and importance of the group (clan) are exaggerated even by the Akan people themselves. This gives the lie to the supposition that the individual in a communal social order is a parasite. The individual is supposed to have a dual responsibility: for oneself as an individual as well as to the group. This is not easy to do successfully, and the balance between individuality and communality is a precarious one indeed.

In striking the right balance between individualism and communalism, Akan social thought seeks to promote social arrangements that allow for the adequate expression of the individual's worth and self-fulfillment. If one is by nature a social being, and not merely an atomized entity, then the development of one's full personality and identity can best be achieved only within the framework of social relationships that are realizable within a communal social system. That is to say, the conception and development of an individual's full personality and identity cannot be separated from his or her role in the group. The interaction between the individual and the group is thus conceived in Akan social thought to be basic to the development and enhancement of the individual's personality.

Nevertheless, there is an enduring tension in the Akan philosophy of the individual. For while it offers a clear, unambiguous statement on the value of individuality, at the same time it makes an equally clear and unequivocal statement on the value of communality. Yet Akan social thought attempts to strike a balance between individualism and communalism. It therefore rejects the notion that claims of the individual and society are antithetical, while attempting to integrate individual desires and social ideals.

II. The Akan conceptual scheme

In Akan social philosophy, then, individualism and communalism are not seen as exclusive and opposing concepts, as they are in capitalist and Communist philosophies. There the two concepts are poles apart because both positions have, in my view, become unnecessarily exaggerated. On the one hand, the value attached to the idea of individual has been so exaggerated in the capitalist system as to detach the person from the natural communal social environment. On the other hand, the Communist system runs berserk, brandishing its sword indiscriminately against practically any trace of individuality. Neither system appears to offer the greatest opportunity for the full development of the human spirit. Akan social philosophy tries to steer clear of the Scylla of exaggerated individualism and the Charybdis of exaggerated communalism (= communism). It seeks to avoid the excesses of the two exaggerated systems, while allowing for a meaningful, albeit uneasy, interaction between the individual and the society.

I conclude by saying that if sociality is *basic* to human nature, then any philosophy that deemphasizes that nature and consciously overemphasizes individuality on the one hand, or overemphasizes that nature so as to suppress individuality on the other hand, could hardly be considered ideal. Due recognition must be given to the claims of both communality and individuality, for after all a society is a community of individuals, and individuals are individuals in society. In advocating a philosophy that would pay due attention to the roles of both, however, I am not oblivious of the practical problems involved in the attempt to balance the two concepts, rendering unto Caesar what is Caesar's and unto God what is God's.

11

Philosophy, logic, and the Akan language

Some philosophers, like Carnap[1] and Quine,[2] think that philosophical propositions are relative to language. They maintain that the plausibility or importance of a particular proposition can be grasped only within the context of the language in which it is formulated, and that it loses its plausibility when translated into another language. Other philosophers, like Ryle[3] and Cohen[4] think that such propositions are not relative to language but are language-neutral. As regards logic, Strawson[5] and Hahn[6] are among the proponents of the linguistic-conventionalist theory, which holds that logic is generated by language, that logical rules derive from conventions about the use of words such as "not," "or," "if," "some." Opposed to them are philosophers such as Pap[7] and Mitchell.[8] I believe that whether a particular statement or problem is language-dependent or language-neutral and whether logical rules derive from the grammatical rules of natural languages are not questions that can be determined on intuitive grounds, and that much might be achieved by actually examining statements formulated in one language on the basis of another language. Therefore I propose in this chapter to examine philosophical theses regarding the problem of the mind and body, time, existence and predication, and subject and predicate on the basis of the Akan language. I believe that such a discussion will be of interest to philosophers interested in the relation between philosophy and language on the one hand, and logic and language on the other hand.

11.1. The mind–body problem

It may be said that the mind–body problem is essentially a problem about the referent of the first-person pronoun "I." Thus, some English-speaking philosophers such as Pap,[9] Shaffer,[10] and

Lewy[11] have attempted to draw inferences regarding the nature of the referent of the "I" from sentences formulated in the English language with "I" as the grammatical subject. To explain their reasoning, let us examine the following groups of sentences in the English language:

Group A:
1. I am heavy.
2. I am thin.
3. I am tall.
4. I am ugly.
5. I am (or have grown) lean.

Group B:
1. I am happy (delighted).
2. I am patient.
3. I am hopeful.
4. I am jealous (or covetous).
5. I am humble.
6. I am in despair.
7. I am courageous.
8. I am generous.
9. I am arrogant.
10. I am aware.

The sentences of group *A* make sense when "my body" is substituted for the grammatical subject "I." It is obvious that in each sentence reference is being made to my body. Since such sentences present no difficulty to the mind–body problem, I merely mention them and am not concerned with them further.

However, if we substitute "my body" for the "I" in the sentences of group *B*, these sentences become nonsensical, for "I am humble" does not mean that my body is humble, nor does "I am patient" mean that my body is patient. From such cases dualist philosophers have concluded that the referent of the "I" in the sentences of group *B* must be something other than the body and that not everything that happens to a person happens to his or her body but that a great deal happens to a "part" or "something" in him or her that is nonphysical, immaterial – a thing variously called "mind," "soul," "spirit," "pure ego," or "consciousness." Thus, from the existence in the English language of such mentalistic or psychological expressions – as the predicate expressions in sentences of group

B are called – dualist philosophers have inferred the existence of the mental: Dualism in language, they argue, must be matched by, or correlated with, a dualism of entities or events. Thus, after having made some observations on the possible referents of the first-person pronoun, Pap remarked: "A little semantics, then, is sufficient to establish that not all that happens to a human being happens to his body, but that a great deal happens to his mind."[12]

Materialist philosophers, who hold that human beings are nothing but material objects and that human minds, actions, states, etc., are to be explained in terms of the same physical laws used to explain material (inanimate) objects, have, of course, controverted the dualists' inference from dualistic language to dualistic objects. For materialist philosophers the so-called mentalistic expressions in the English language denote the same objects denoted by physical-istic expressions, which objects, for them, are basically physical or material. Language, materialist philosophers would then say, is misleading as a guide to metaphysics. The English language, brimful of mentalistic expressions, has misled thinkers into an ontology of the mental. Now, let us turn to the Akan language and see to what conclusions translations of the mentalistic expressions of English lead.

We may begin by translating the sentences of group *B* into the Akan language, as shown in Table 11.1. These are the normal translations of the English sentences of group *B* into the Akan language, and there is nothing particularly interesting or revealing about them. But the point I wish to make is revealed in the etymologies of the Akan words. The etymological translations of these Akan sentences are also shown in Table 11.1.

It can be seen that the mentalistic expressions of group *B* translated into Akan actually become physicalistic expressions. In Akan, that is, the mentalistic expressions in English actually refer to the body or some organs of the body such as the eyes, chest, stomach, heart, ears, head, etc. (see Table 11.2), but the words of the original sentences in English made no reference to parts of the body.

Table 11.2 gives more examples of mentalistic expressions in English that become physicalistic in Akan. What conclusions can we draw from all this? First, it follows from these translations that the arguments of English-speaking dualist philosophers who infer the existence of the mental from the existence in English of mentalistic or psychological expressions cannot be sustained when

Table 11.1. *Group B mentalistic expressions translated into and out of Akan*

English . . .	into Akan . . .	and etymologically into English
1. I am happy	*M'ani agye*	My *eyes* are brightened
2. I am patient	*Me wõ abotare (boaseto).*	My *heart* subsides
3. I am hopeful	*M'ani da so*	My *eyes* are on it
4. I am jealous/ covetous	*M'ani abere*	My *eyes* are red
5. I am humble	*Me wõ ahobrease*	I have brought my *body* down/ low
6. I am in despair	*Mehome te me ho*	My *breath* is breaking/tearing apart
7. I am courageous	*Mewõ akokoduru*	I have a heavy/weighty *chest*
8. I am generous	*Me yẽm ye*	My *stomach* is good
9. I am arrogant	*Mema meho so*	I raise my *body*
10. I am aware	*M'ani da meho so*	My *eyes* are on/around my *body*

such expressions are translated into Akan. The mentalistic sentences of group *B* become physicalistic in Akan. In Akan the referent of the first-person pronoun "I" seems to be nothing mysterious or invisible; much that happens to the "I" happens to the body or parts of the body. Second, some kind of materialism is apparent in the Akan language, and if one were to reason like the English-speaking dualists, one would have to infer from this the *nonexistence* of the mental. An Akan thinker, ignorant of English, might thus come to hold a nonmental view of the person and of the world.

Yet the second inference is certainly not true of Akan ontology in general or of the Akan metaphysic of the person in particular. Akan ontology, as shown in Chapter 5, admits both visible (material, perceivable) and invisible (immaterial, unperceivable, spiritual) entities, although ontological primacy, in my view, is given to the invisible. In Akan conceptions what exists is primarily spiritual. There is a firm belief in the world of spirits (*asamando*), where all the dead live a kind of life that is patterned on the earthly one. The general belief of most Akan people in the existence of the world of spirits derives from their conception of the nature of a person. The discussion of the Akan concept of the person (Chapter 6) concluded that the Akans generally hold a dualistic conception of the person:

Table 11.2. *Further examples of expressions that are mentalistic in English but physicalistic in Akan*

English	Akan[a]	Etymological translation & comments
cunning, cleverness	*ani*teē	"one's *eyes* are open and clear"
ambition, determination, anxiety, jealousy, envy, covetousness, desperation	*ani*bere	"one's *eyes* are red/ reddened"
anger	*abo*fuw	"one's *chest* has sprouted/ burst out" The reference to the chest is actually a reference to the heart, which is covered by the chest.
awareness, consciousness, discretion	*ani*daho	"one's *eyes* are widely open"
shame	*ani*wuo	"one's *eyes* are dead," i.e., one cannot raise one's eyes to look
confusion, bewilderment	*ani*tan	reference is made here to the *eyes*
patience	*boa*setō	reference is made in both to the *chest*, i.e., the *heart*
satisfaction, contentment, composure	*abo*toyam	reference is made to both the *chest* (i.e., the *heart*) and the *stomach*
peace of mind	*aso*mdwee	"coolness/calmness of the *ears*"
disgrace, indignity	*anim*guase	"one's *face* has fallen down"
gentleness, meekness	ōdwo	"cool," not hot
grief, sorrow	*aweré*how	reference is made to the *heart*
pride, arrogance, haughtiness	*aho*maso	"raising one's own *body*"
tough-minded, strong-willed, resolute	*aniē*den	"one's *eyes* are hard"
courage, boldness, bravery	*ako*koduru *aboō*duru	"one's *chest* (*heart*) is heavy/ weighty"
confidence	*aweré*hyem	reference is made to the *heart*
dignity	*animu*onyam	"one's *face* brightens"

167

II. The Akan conceptual scheme

Table 11.2 (cont.)

English	Akan[a]	Etymological translation & comments
discouragement	*aba*paw *aba*buw	reference is made in both to the *arm*
fear, consternation, dismay	a*koma*tu	"the fleeing of the *heart*"
apprehension	a*yam*hyehye	"one's *stomach* burns"
disobedience	a*soŏ*den	"one's *ears* are hard"
impatience	a*ho*pere	restlessness of the *body*
cruelty	a*tirimoŏ*den *ayem*unwon	"one's *head* is hard" "one's *stomach* is bitter/sour"
envy	a*hoŏe*yaa	"*body* (or *skin*) pain"
to determine (resolve)	*bŏti*rim	reference is made to the *head*

[a]The italicized parts of the Akan expressions refer to the actual part of the body. It must be noted that the meanings of the Akan expressions are literal, though their English equivalents give the impression that they are or may be metaphorical. A word in any language that is used metaphorically must first have a literal meaning, and the Akan words here are literal in their meanings. The distinction made in modern linguistics between surface and deep structures of *sentences* is not in play here, as it generally affects sentences, not words. I am concerned here specifically with the etymology of *words* and what they seem to indicate.

A person is composed of two elements, a spiritual one, itself found to be complex, and a physical one, the body. The soul,[13] *ōkra*, which occupies the central place in this spiritual complex, is associated with the life principle in a person and is also considered to be immortal. The departure of the *ōkra* (soul) from the body means the death of the person. It is such departed souls that are believed to inhabit the world of spirits.

Thus, the Akan belief in disembodied survival in the form of spirit or soul presupposes a nonmaterial conception of a human being. The ontological pull of the Akan language toward materialism is consequently enfeebled. For in spite of the fact that sentences of group *B* are physicalistic in Akan, this does not lead to a materialist conception of man and the world.

168

I now turn to the question of whether logical rules are also language-dependent. Cohen, who believes in the language–neutral character of propositions, criticizes Carnap for saying that they are language-oriented. To Carnap's view that "From 'All *A* are *B*' and 'All *B* are *C*' you can logically infer 'All *A* are *C*' " was a transformation rule of the English language,[14] Cohen objected that this example is translatable into all natural languages. Thus Cohen: "You can find, for example, books about rules of Aristotelian logic written in many different natural languages and all using the same example for a syllogism. . . ."[15] Cohen's argument, however, may be sustained if we restrict ourselves to *formal* logic, for it is certainly plausible that a logical rule such as

$$[(p \rightarrow q) \land (q \rightarrow r)] \rightarrow (p \rightarrow r)$$

would be upheld in or by all natural languages. Thus, such a logical thesis is translatable, and one may therefore reasonably claim that it does not depend upon language.

In my view, both Cohen and Carnap err in drawing their examples only from formal logic and generalizing them for all *philosophical* theses. It seems to me that although the view of the language-neutrality and consequent translatability of philosophical theses may be generally true of formal logic, it would founder on questions in philosophical logic such as, say, the distinction between subject and predicate and the theory of meaning. A thinker using a language brimful of abstract expressions may be more likely to develop a Platonistic theory of meaning than one using a language character-ized by concreteness. The mistake of both Carnap and Cohen was that they overstated their case, in generalizing it. For me, whether a particular philosophical thesis or problem is language-oriented or language-neutral must be determined within the structure of a given natural language: It cannot be determined without examining the characteristics of other natural languages. It is not a logical or conceptual question but an empirical one.

11.2. Time ✓

The principal reason for including a discussion of the concept of time in Akan thought in a chapter on philosophy and language is Mbiti's assertion that his denial of the existence of the concept of distant or infinite future in African thought was arrived at through an analysis of the verb tenses of some East African languages.[16] The structures of those languages, according to Mbiti, do not generate a concept of an infinite future. Language, then, Mbiti precipitately concludes, is a sure guide to a general African conception of time. Since Mbiti draws his conclusions about the so-called African concept of time – particularly his denial to Africans of a concept of distant or infinite future – from the characteristics of two East African languages, Gikuyu and Kikamba, I deem it appropriate and necessary to rebut his generalized conclusions by examining the characteristics and vocabulary of the Akan language. First, however, I propose to comment on other aspects of the notion of time (*bere*) in Akan philosophy.

In Akan philosophy time is regarded as a concrete reality. But this does not imply that the abstract notion of time is lacking. The word *bere* (time) is used to express both the abstract and the concrete notion of time. Christaller was, thus, wrong when he wrote: "For the entirely abstract notion of time in general as in 'Time flies,' there is no proper word."[17] An Akan proverb says,

> Time is like a bird: If you do not catch it and *it
> flies*, you do not see it again.[18]

A well-known Akan maxim says,

> Time changes.
> (*bere di adannan*)

Both of these express an abstract notion of time. The fact that Akan thinkers generally put their thoughts in concrete terms should not be taken to mean that they lack abstract concepts.

The Akan thinkers consider time as a concrete reality, associated with change and growth. Time is associated with motion, as the notion of "flying" in the above proverb indicates, and hence with change and transformation. To experience time, then, is to experience concrete change, growth, generation, and passing away of specific things. Since such events are features of the phenomenal world, time is considered to belong essentially to the phenomenal world, although this does not imply a belief in the nonexistence of a future time. Thus, an Akan dirge runs as follows:

> This is for me a sad and memorable day;
> Be quick and let us depart;
> No place here [on earth] is safe;
> No one reigns forever on the throne of time.[19]
> (*bere akonnwa yenni nka so*)

The dirge speaks of the contingency, impermanency, and transitori-ness of the phenomenal world. Some lines of Akan poetry say:

170

Time has its boundary; we do not traverse it;
Man is but mortal: however hard he struggles,
he will depart (this world).
(*bere wō n'ehyeē; yennō ntra*
onipa de ōdasani, operepere a ōbēkō)[20]

The word translated as "boundary" is *ēhyeē*, which means the edge
or limit of one's farm or plot of land; the word *ɖo tra* translated
"traverse" actually means "to weed or plough beyond (the edge)."
The poetic language here is of course metaphorical. The Akan poet
is not saying that time as such is limited or finite, but that a person's
time, that is, life span (on earth) is finite, transitory, impermanent.
And when the dirge says that no one reigns or remains forever on
the throne of time, this means that time exists; it is real; it has an
objective existence that is continuous, but that everything that
exists in time is subject to change and decay. The metaphorical
expression, "the throne of time," is significant. It symbolizes, I
think, the idea that just as kings who sit on the throne of a clan or
nation come and go while the throne itself remains, so time exists
objectively and continuously, while the things that exist in time
change and decay.

Although it is not possible to provide a strict definition of the
concept of time in Akan philosophy, the foregoing discussion
should give us some idea of what, according to Akan thinkers, time
is. Time is to be associated with change, process, and events. But
this statement must not be taken to imply that it is these phenomena that generate our consciousness of time. On the contrary, these
phenomena occur within time; for time, as the dirge seems to
indicate, is held to have an objective metaphysical existence, so that
even if there were no changes, processes, and events time would
still be real. This is the reason why the Akans can, and do, have the
concept of a distant or infinite future. Mbiti's assertion that for
Africans "time is simply *a composition of events* which have occurred,
those which are taking place now and those which are immediately
to occur"[21] implies that time is composed or constituted by actual
events, and this implies in turn that since distant future events have
not yet occurred, Africans therefore do not consider such future or
potential events as constituting real time. This conclusion, which
derives from assumptions not made in Akan thought, is not
applicable to the Akan conception of time.

In Akan thought, it is not events that compose time; it is not events that generate the awareness of the existence of time. If that were the case, all talk about the future in Akan language and thought would be nonsense. Rather, it is time, conceived as objectively existing, within which such events and changes take place and which makes possible the dating of such events. Given a number of events, say festivals, f_1, f_2, f_3, etc., which occur at different times of the year, our ability to say that f_1 took place before (or earlier than: *ansa*) f_2 and that f_3 took place after (or later than: *akyi*) f_2 implies the presupposition of the existence of time. Mbiti may be right in saying that in African communities the reckoning of time is done in connection with events, but this fact cannot be taken to mean that time itself is composed of events. If the events were not taking place within time, they could not be reckoned temporally, nor could people in Akan communities speak of the Adai festival coming *before* or *after* the Ohum festival. But more on criticisms of Mbiti's views on "the African concept of time" anon.

Akan beliefs about the personal characteristics of people reveal their consciousness of time as an element in an individual's destiny. One's day of birth, *krada*, is held to be a factor in determining one's personal characteristics and aspects of one's behavior. People born on Monday are said to be suppliant, humble, calm (*okoto*); those born on Tuesday are said to be compassionate (*ogyam*); those born on Wednesday are said to be champions of the cause of others (*ntoni, atobi*); those born on Thursday are said to be courageous, aggressive, warlike (*preko*); those born on Friday are said to be wanderers (*okyin*), that is, bent on exploring, discovering; those born on Saturday are said to be great (*atoapem*)[22] and problem solvers (*oteanankaduro*; literally "he who knows the antidote for the serpent");[23] and, finally, those born on Sunday are said to be protectors (*bodua*; literally, tail of the animal). Now, the assumption that time is an influence on personality suggests that time has an objective metaphysical existence, and cannot, contrary to Mbiti's view, be held as "simply a composition of events." Indeed, the notion of time as a determinant of personal characteristics seems to invest it with some kind of cosmic power.

Mbiti maintains that African peoples conceive time to be a "two-dimensional phenomenon with a long past, a present and virtually no future."[24] The linear concept of time in Western thought, with an infinite past, a momentary present, and an infinite future, is practically foreign to African thinking. He says he reached this conclusion by his study of the verb tenses of some East African languages. According to Mbiti, the three verb tenses that refer to the future cover the period of about six months and in any case not beyond two years at most. Coming events have to fall within the range of those verb tenses, otherwise such events lie beyond the horizon of what constitutes actual time. The languages he examined, he says, lack words by which distant future events can be conceived or expressed.[25] It may well be that there is no expression for the distant future and hence the concept of a distant future does not exist in the thought of East African peoples. My objection is to Mbiti's generalization of a concept derived from just two local African languages to the whole of the African peoples. He admits that "languages are the key to the serious research and understanding of traditional religions and philosophy."[26] Languages, indeed, are vestibules to the conceptual world. But this indicates that a concept inferred from one language cannot necessarily be assumed for a people speaking another language. I am not denying that it is possible for an analysis of a concept made on the basis of different languages to produce identical or similar conclusions. Rather, I am asserting that the identity or similarity of such conclusions cannot be assumed without having investigated the other languages.

I now turn to an investigation of the characteristics and vocabulary of the Akan language in order to demonstrate the impossibility of attributing a "two-dimensional" conception of time to the Akan people. I have already pointed out that the concept of an infinite being in Akan thought logically involves the concept of an infinite future time, for the infinite being necessarily dwells in an infinite time, which, of course, extends to the future. I begin with a quotation from a well-known grammar book on the Akan language. Regarding the future tense the author wrote:

> The first future marks action in the time to come. The second future, or future proximate, marks action in the next future.[27]

Note that in the first future there is no specification of the period during which the action is to take place. Thus, a man observing the behavior of his younger son says to him:

1. wo bedi hen (*daakye*), that is, "You will be a king (*in the future*)."

2. wobeye onyansafo (*daakye*), that is "You will be a wise man (*in the future*)."

The ten-year-old boy will be made a king when he is twenty, thirty, or fifty years old; in any case, many years after his father's prediction. It was an expectation of the father that may not be fulfilled in his own lifetime. It is the second future that gives an indication of a period – a short period, that is, of time in the future, but it is not possible to say whether this short period is two or six months or within two years.

Second, the Akan language has definite expressions that are the equivalent of the English expression "future." These expressions are *daakye* and *da bi*. *Daakye* means "future" or "in the future"; *da bi* literally means "someday," that is, an unspecified day, a day as yet unknown, some time to come. The expression *da bi* is in fact translated by Christaller as "an *indefinite* time."[28] Expressions denoting infinite time are *daa, daapem, beresanten, afeboo*, all of which mean "eternally," "eternity." A brief disquisition on the word *beresanten* in particular is necessary for a reason that will be clear presently. The first component of the word, "*bere*," means time. The second, *santen*, means row or line of things or persons. *Beresanten* therefore literally means "time in a row," "the whole length of time." *Beresanten*, then, expresses the concept of linear time that Mbiti says is alien to African thinking. Christaller translates *mmeresanten* (*mmere* is the plural of *bere*) as "the times or days in succession, the whole length of times or days, eternity."[29]

In addition, there are Akan proverbs that refer to the future dimension of time. For example:

> The vulture says he is learning to walk in the royal
> manner for *someday* (*da bi*), a day unknown to
> him, he might be made a king.

> The rhinoceros beetle says he knew that famine
> would come, which is why he scraped the young
> raffia palm leaves to store.
> (*amankuo sē: onim sē ōkōm bēba nti na okuturuu ōkoro*)

These proverbs obviously refer to a future time, which, though unknown, is nevertheless thought to be real, actual; it is "there." Its reality is the basis of hope and anticipation. Other proverbs say:

> A child who burns his finger will be more careful
> in the future (*daakye*).

> If you see the hen destroy the corn of your
> neighbor, drive it away, for *someday* (*da bi*) it will
> destroy yours.

There is a saying among our elders, "In future God will inquire something of you" (*daakye Onyame bebisa wo asēm*), meaning that in

174

future God will ask each individual to give an account of his or her life on earth. This saying refers to a postmundane future time, life after death, as is indicated by the following lines from an Akan poem already mentioned:

> Time has its boundary: we do not traverse it;
> Everything will end in the hereafter (world of
>   spirits) *someday.*[30]
> (*bere wō n'ehyeē: yennō ntra;*
> *ne nyinaa besi assamando da bi!*)

In the Akan conception, then, the future exists as an actual time. Mbiti says: "People have little or no active interest in events that lie in the future beyond, at most, two years from now."[31] This statement is not true of the Akans. The proverb about the vulture and other proverbs falsify Mbiti's assertion that "the people neither plan for the distant future nor 'build castles in the air.' "[32] The vulture is planning or preparing for his kingship in the distant future. Similarly, the rhinoceros beetle has the forethought to provide for hard times in the future. That is to say, men have hopes for the future and prepare for the possible realization of those hopes. A line in an already-quoted poem says:

> Because there exists some future time, there exists
>   Hope.[33]
> (*bere bi wō hō nti na Anidaso wō hō*)

Furthermore, divination, a mystical activity that is much practiced in African communities, involves the notion of the distant future. Diviners are said to be people with special extrasensory abilities. There is no denying that their divining activities, which Mbiti discusses,[34] necessarily involve predicting future events or acts either in the life of an individual or in that of the community. Divination includes the attempt to discover future events by extraordinary or supernatural means. I do not believe that diviners in African communities restrict their divining activities to the present, merely giving "information concerning the cause, nature and treatment of disease (or other form of misfortune), and concerning thefts or loss of articles."[35] As "seers and fortune-tellers,"[36] these diviners must necessarily look into the future also, which cannot be limited to a period of not more than two years. Diviners and medicine men in Akan communities do give information about future events, particularly in the life of an individual. A diviner may tell a client in his twenties or even less, that the client will in future be a great person in his clan or tribe. Akan diviners do not limit this future to a specific period within which a prophecy will be fulfilled; it would be nonsense to specify that period when he is unable to do so, beyond the hope that it will be, *someday* (*da bi*). It is surprising that Mbiti does not see that divination is essentially or primarily about the future, and that whether this future is an immediate or a distant one depends on the nature of the event or act divined. Mbiti's mistake stems from his supposition that the African concept of time is anchored in the past (*Zamāni*) and the present (*Sasa*).

It is thus clear that the Akans do hold a three-dimensional conception of time: past, present, and future (both immediate and distant). Hence, it is not true for Mbiti to generalize that it is

> *modern change [that] has imported into Africa a future dimension of time.* This is perhaps the most dynamic and dangerous discovery of African peoples in the twentieth century. Their hopes are stirred up and set on the future. They work for progress, they wait for an immediate realization of their hopes, and they create new myths of the future. It is here that we find the key to understanding African political, economic and ecclesiastical *instability*. Africa wants desperately to be involved in this future dimension. Emphasis is shifting from the Zamani [that is, past] and Sasa [that is, present] to the Sasa and Future; and we are part of the historical moment when this great change-over is being wrought. . . .[37]

I quote this passage at length because it is a tissue of errors. It is one thing to have a conception of a future and quite another to act in a way that reflects that conception. It is, again, one thing to have a conception of a future and quite another to feel concerned about this future. It is certainly instructive that Jesus taught his followers not to worry about tomorrow, for "sufficient unto the day is the evil thereof"[38] (that is, there is no need to add to the troubles each day brings). Christians who have a conception of a future time are here being told not to be anxious about what they *will* (tomorrow, in future) eat, wear, etc. Yet the fact that they are to focus on the present does not obliterate their hopes of blessedness in the future. Thus, even if Africans may not have experienced "progress" in the past, this is not attributable to the absence of a conception of a future time. When we talk of progress, we have in mind opportunities, abilities, resources, and other similar factors, and these can hardly be said to be connected with such a metaphysical category as time. Nor is the "instability" in African political and economic affairs due to the alleged sudden emergence of a consciousness of future time.

I have controverted Mbiti's analysis of what he calls "the African concept of time" at length because he has given it a preeminent place in his book, calling it "the *key* to our under- standing of the basic religious and philosophical concepts. The concept of time may help to explain beliefs, attitude, practices and general way of life of African peoples not only in the traditional set-up but also in the modern situation."[39] Yet, despite the fact that East African peoples, according to Mbiti, hold a two-dimen- sional conception of time and the Akans (and possibly other peoples in Africa) hold a three-dimensional conception of time, there are certainly some philosophical doctrines common to all of them. Their doctrines of causality and fate and aspects of ethical philosophy and philosophical theology are similar in their essen- tials. This being so, "the African concept of time" cannot be the key or the basic category in the African religious and philosophi- cal orientation. For if it were in fact the key to the understanding of African religious and philosophical ideas, then the Akans and East African peoples, holding different conceptions of time as they do, logically must differ in most, if not all, of their religious and philosophical doctrines; yet this probably is not the case. Time, as a metaphysical category, is certainly a fundamental concept, but this does not warrant its being made the key to such other concepts as cause, soul, substance, etc. Thus, apart from the fact that Mbiti's analysis of "the African concept of time" is question- able, there is also no philosophical justification for making it more significant than other categories.

11.3. Existence, predication, and identity

Philosophers acquainted with ancient Greek philosophy are of course aware of the logical puzzles or confusions generated by the ambiguity inherent in the Greek verb *einai*, "to be." Often it is not clear whether the word was used to indicate existence, copula- tion (predication), identity, or some other relation. For instance, the opening sentence of Protagoras' (481–411 B.C.) work *On Truth* reads as follows: "Man is the measure of all things, of what is (*esti*), that it is (*esti*), of what is not, that it is not (*ouk esti*)." (*Esti* is the present tense third-person singular of *einai*.) It is possible to interpret the verb *einai* here as existential; it is equally possible, particularly since the subject is truth, to interpret the verb as "to be so," "to be the case," or "to be true," which is another meaning of *einai*.[40] In fact Kahn claims that this latter meaning is philosophically "the most fundamental value of *einai* when used alone (without predicates)."[41] Thus, the minds of scholars of Plato are much exercised about whether Plato in the *Sophist* intends *einai* existentially or predicatively. Owen, a foremost scholar of Aristotle, points out that Aristotle nowhere distinguishes the predicative and existential uses of *einai*.[42] Graham observes: "It is well known that Greek philosophy hardly ever distinguishes between the existential and copulative functions of *einai*, 'to be.'"[43]

In English and most other Indo-European languages the problem relating to existence and predication is not as acute as it is in Greek. In English, for instance, in addition to the word "exist," the expression "there is" also indicates simple existence. German *"es gibt"* and French *"il y a"* are equivalents of the English "there is" in terms of their functions. Although "exist" in

1. Lions exist

is a grammatical predicate, it is generally held not to be a logical predicate,[44] so that (1) is strictly not a predicate statement. It is an existential statement, asserting the existence of something – in this case, lions. Similarly,

2. There are lions

is also an existential statement.

In English, however, the same verb, "to be," is used to express existence, predication, and identity, as in

3. There are lions (existence)
4. Lions are fierce animals (predication: class membership)
5. Lions are the kings of the forest (identity).

Let us now turn to see how the Akan language handles existence, predication, and identity. Akan is more than adequate in meeting the logical difficulties inherent in the Greek *einai*. It may also have some advantages over English for these questions, for it has three separate verbs for expressing existential, predicative, and identity statements.

11.3.1. Existence

In Akan existence is expressed by the word *wǒ*: "to be somewhere," "to be or exist in a place,"[45] to which the deictic word *hǒ* ("there") is added. The complete existential expression is thus *wǒ hǒ*, "there is," "exists." [This is what is represented in modern logic by the formula $(\exists x)\ Fx$.] Thus,

God exists: Nyame *wǒ hǒ*.

The *hǒ* part of this existential expression is, in my view, not "semantically empty," as Boadi thought.[46] In Akan the existential verb involves location – and this is not peculiar to Akan[47] – and it is the *hǒ* that, it seems to me, contains the locative implication of the existential expression *wǒ hǒ*. Therefore, the *hǒ* cannot be semantically empty. And although *wǒ* and *hǒ* do not appear as a unitary lexical item – neither do "be" and "there" in English – nevertheless, insofar as it is the two together that adequately express the notion of existence, that is, existential locative, it would be a mistake to deny the *hǒ* a semantic function. In fact the two words constitute a semantic unit.

11.3.2. Predication

The predicative "be" in Akan is *yē*, which is used to indicate both class membership and class inclusion. As examples:

1. *anoma no* yē *patu.*
   (The bird *is* an owl.)
2. *bepow no* yē *tenten.*
   (The mountain *is* tall.)
3. *nnipa nyinaa* yē *Onyame mma.*
   (All men *are* children of God.)

Statements (1) and (2) indicate class membership, whereas (3) indicates class inclusion.

11.3.3. Identity

Identity statements in Akan are expressed by *ne*, "to be (identical with)."

1. *Onyame* ne *panyin.*
   (God *is the* elder.)
2. *Owusu* ne *sukuu no hwēfo.*
   (Owusu *is the* principal of the school.)
3. *sukuuhwēfo no* ne *Owusu.*
   (The principal of the school *is* (the same as) Owusu.)

Thus, *ne* necessarily involves and makes use of the concepts of definite description and proper name. The thought expressed in (1) and (2) would change if we substituted *yē* (the predicative "is") for *ne*. Thus,

> Onyame yē *panyin*
> (God *is an* elder.)

would not be an identity, but a predicative statement indicating class membership.

There is yet another word in the Akan language that expresses identity, but only in a limited or special sense. The verb *de* ("to be") is used in statements such as:

1. *ne din* de *Owusu*
   (His name *is* Owusu.)
2. *nsuo no din* de *Volta*
   (The river's name *is* Volta.)

In such cases the grammatical subject is generally the word "name" and the grammatical predicate must be a proper name. However, a proper name can be used as the grammatical subject, as in

> Owusu ne *ne*[48] *din*
> (Owusu *is* his name.)

In the latter case *de* becomes *ne*. (Christaller may be correct in saying that *de* is an old form of *ne*.[49]) Sometimes *ne* is used in place of *de* for emphasis, as in:

> *ne din* ne *Owusu*
> (His name certainly *is* Owusu.)

It is thus clear that the Akan language sharply separates the existential and copulative functions of the verb "to be" and that it has different words to express existence, predication, and identity. Consequently puzzles, confusions, or mistakes arising out of the use of such an ambiguous verb as the Greek *einai* cannot arise within Akan. So, if ancient philosophers such as Protagoras, Parmenides, Plato, and Aristotle had written in Akan, they would have been able to avoid the ambiguities of *einai*.

11.4. The ontological argument

In the ontological argument for the existence of God the claim is made that existence is an attribute (that is, predicate). This implies that the attribution of existence to an object adds something to its characterization: It provides new information apart from asserting the existence of the object.

Now let us consider this claim within the context of Akan. The Akan verb for "to exist" is *wō hō*. Thus, *Onyame wō hō* translates the English "God exists" or "There is God." There is, however, no direct equivalent of the noun "existence" in Akan; it would be rendered by "that something is there (exists)" (*sē biribi wō hō*). Thus, the question whether existence is an attribute becomes in Akan something like: "*Is that something is there* an attribute?" The bizarre nature of this question in Akan makes implausible the thesis about the reality of God that derives from the concept of existence. The ontological argument, then, loses its plausibility when considered within the context of the Akan language. Because of the qualities of the language, it is more than likely that a thinker using Akan would never have raised the ontological argument.

11.5. Subject and predicate

Here I wish to discuss, within the context of the Akan language, the logical criterion that P. F. Strawson, the distinguished Oxford philosopher, advances as a basis for a distinction between the subject and predicate of a sentence. The traditional view is that a predicate is an expression that provides an assertion about something, this something being referred to as the subject. Thus, in the sentence

Owusu walks

the predicate "walks" asserts something about Owusu, with Owusu, being that about which something is asserted, as the subject. Strawson rejects this characterization on the grounds that in the above sentence one might be talking about walking, and not necessarily about Owusu.[50] I think Strawson is right here. The traditional definition of the predicate as that which makes an assertion about something is not satisfactory.

In his arguments for the logical criterion for distinguishing between subject and predicate, Strawson uses the terms "complete" and "incomplete" to characterize the subject and predicate, respectively, terms which had been used by the German mathematician-philosopher Gottlob Frege (1848–1925) for practically the same purpose. Strawson's intention is to defend the Fregean characterizations of the subject and predicate. Subject expressions, he says, are complete, or better, are nearer completion, whereas predicate expressions are incomplete because they hardly ever occur alone. According to Strawson, the main difference between what are called subject expressions like "Socrates," "John," and "Owusu" and predicate expressions like "is wise," "smokes," and "walks," is that a subject expression "might be completed into any kind of remark (or clause), not necessarily a proposition, or it might stand by itself as designating an item in a list; but the expression 'is wise' demands a certain kind of completion, namely, completion into a proposition or propositional clause."[51] Thus, he explains that subject expressions "introduce their terms in a grammatical style (the substantival) which would be appropriate to *any kind of remark* (command, exhortation, undertaking, assertion) or to none,"[52] whereas predicate expressions "introduce their terms in a very distinctive grammatical style, viz., the assertive or propositional style."[53] The minimal claim Strawson makes is that "is wise" and "smokes" occur only in propositions; thus, they introduce their terms in the propositional style. A predicate expression, therefore, is an expression that can be completed *only* into a proposition or propositional clause, whereas a subject expression is an expression that can be completed into any kind of remark, not necessarily a proposition or propositional clause.

Strawson's thesis is based on the characteristics of English grammar, for in English the verb introducing the predicate expression is inflected to agree with the subject expression in number and in person. Verbs in Akan, however, are not inflected for person or for number. Strawson's theory may therefore produce problems when considered within the context of Akan. Let us consider the following sentence:

> *Owusu* nante
> (Owusu *walks.*)

In Strawson's theory the predicate expression, *nante*, is completable only into a proposition. But in Akan *nante* (unlike its equivalent "walks" in the above sentence) does not demand to be completed only into a proposition or propositional clause. It can be completed into other kinds of remark (or clause) that are not propositions. As examples:

1. *nante* can be used as a (grammatical) *subject*, as in:
   nante yē yaw
   (walking or to walk is painful) or

nante *yē ma honam*
(walking is good for the body).

2. *nante* can be used as *imperative*:
   nante! (walk!)
3. *nante* can be used in asking a *question*:
   nante? (walk?)

Thus, the predicate expression *nante* in Akan performs functions that "walks" cannot perform in English. Strawson's criterion collapses.

The picture, however, appears slightly different when the predicate expression is introduced by the verb "to be." Consider the Akan sentence

barima no yē kēse
(the man *is big*)

Although the predicate expression *yē kēse* cannot perform all the functions performed by *nante*, nevertheless it is not completable only into a proposition or propositional clause, for *yē kēse* can be used in a command, as in

yē kēse!
(Be big!)

Of course in English "is big" cannot be used for a command, but in Akan *yē kēse* can. In Akan the copulative (predicative) *yē* can be translated as "am," "are," "be," depending on the type of sentence. Thus,

Be big!: yē kēse
He *is* big: ōyē kēse
I *am* big: *me* yē kēse
They *are* big: wō yē kēse, etc.

The English sentence "Socrates is wise" can be rendered into Akan in three ways:

1. Socrates yē *onyansafo*
   (Socrates *is* a wise man)
2. Socrates wō *nyansa*
   (Socrates *possesses* wisdom)
3. Socrates nim *nyansa*
   (Socrates *perceives* wisdom; *nim* literally means "to know").

Expression (1) indicates a case where a part of the predicate expression, namely, *onyansafo* (wise man), itself designates a com-

183

plete symbol, for *onyansafo* can be, and is, used as a subject expression, as in the well-known Akan proverb *onyansafo wobu no bē na wõnka no asēm* ("The wise man is spoken to in proverbs, not in speeches or words").

Similarly, in (2) and (3) a part of the predicate expression, namely *nyansa* (wisdom), can be used as a subject, as in

> nyansa *yē ade papa*
> [*Wisdom* is a good thing (a virtue).]

It is obvious that Strawson's observation that the expression "is wise" or "smokes" ("walks" in my example) demands a certain kind of completion, namely, completion into a proposition or propositional clause, exploits some facts about English grammar: (a) the fact that the verb is inflected, as a result of which the expression "smokes," for instance, cannot perform any other function than being coupled with a subject expression like "Raleigh" to form a proposition;[54] (b) the fact that the verb must agree with the subject in person and number, as a result of which the expression "smokes," for instance, can be coupled only with a third-person singular subject expression. (As we have seen, neither of these applies to Akan.) Thus, it is clear that Strawson's observations were influenced by the characteristics of English. But Strawson seems to deny this: "It should be noticed that, in drawing this distinction between *A*-expressions [that is, subject expressions] and *B*-expressions [that is, predicate expressions], I am not merely exploiting the fact that English is a comparatively uninflected language, especially as regards its noun-forms . . ."[55] (But the English verb is inflected in the present tense.) The denial seems to imply that Strawson sees his criterion as applicable regardless of language. The facts he exploits, however, are not congruent with Akan grammar, for instance.

The idea behind the description of the subject expression as complete is that such an expression can occur alone and can be used in itself as salutation, command, and exclamation ("Owusu!"). Questions ("Owusu?") and assertions ("Owusu.") may also consist only of the proper name "Owusu." Predicate expressions behave differently in English; they can hardly occur alone – hence their incompleteness. In asking a question and in issuing a command in English, one says "walk" instead of "walks." But in Akan the case is different in respect of predicate expressions. The predicate expression *nante* (walk), like the subject expression, can occur alone and can be used in itself, as already noted, as command (*"nante!"*), as question (*"nante?"*), and as assertion (*"nante"*). If the predicate is "incomplete" because it cannot occur alone and also because it is completable only into a proposition, then it is difficult to see why predicate expressions in Akan should be depicted as "incomplete," for, after all, they can perform the functions that subject expressions are supposed to perform. Strawson's theory regarding the character and behavior of the predicate is therefore invalid with respect to the grammar of the Akan language.[56]

11.6. Conclusions

First, we may conclude that it is neither safe nor proper for philosophers or logicians to generalize for other natural languages a particular philosophical thesis or logical theory or principle that has been influenced or determined by the features of some particular language (or family of languages). Thus, the logical distinction based on the concepts of "completeness" and "incompleteness," respectively, is invalid not only in respect of Akan grammar but Chinese grammar as well, according to Tsu-Lin Mei.[57] Mbiti's analysis of the so-called African concept of time, which was based on a couple of East African languages, is incorrectly attributed to other African languages. Generalizations on such matters that are based on the characteristics of one or two natural languages ought to be made with circumspection. Thus Lemmon, after referring to the logical connectives, incautiously wrote: "This book is written in English, and so mentions *English* sentences and words; but the above account could be applied, by appropriate translation, to all languages I know of. *There is nothing parochial about logic*, despite this appearance to the contrary."[58] It is not clear how many and what kind of languages Lemmon knows. If one examines sentences and words in a number of languages, one would reject Lemmon's view that "there is nothing parochial about logic," at least as regards the aspects that are demonstrably language-oriented.

This is not to say, however, that the whole system of logic necessarily derives from the grammatical rules of language. I believe that there are logical rules or principles that can be said to be language-neutral and may operate in all natural languages. Such rules or principles that transcend the limits of languages, it seems to me, really belong to the realm of thought; that is, they can be known to be true by reflection. I suppose that the hypothetical syllogism $[(p \to q) \wedge (p \to r)] \to (p \to r)$ and the disjunctive syllogism $[(p \lor q) \land \sim p] \rightarrow q$ are among such logical principles whose validity can be ascertained by thought, and so can be said to be true in all languages.

Second, it is clear from our examination of the type of arguments used by Western dualist philosophers on the mind–body problem and from our remarks on the ontological argument that some philosophical theses formulated on the basis of one language lose their validity or plausibility or importance when translated into another language. Thus, despite the materialism apparent in the Akan language, the Akan philosophy of mind and body is nevertheless *not* materialistic, but thoroughly and undoubtedly dualistic.

Third, the discussions on existence, predication, and identity point up the fact that some logical or philosophical puzzles and confusions generated in ancient philosophy by the Greek verb "to be" (*einai*) evaporate when such matters are examined in, say, the Akan language. The Akan language is well equipped to handle logical matters relating to existence, predication, and identity. The implication here is that some philosophical or logical problems are relative to language. I use the word "some" here advisedly, for I do not believe that all philosophical problems relating to fatalism, bases (sources) of morality, civil disobedience, human rights, the existence of God, political legitimacy, moral obligation, among others, are relative to some natural language or other. Such philosophical problems, in my view, do in fact arise from common human experiences. This is why it is possible for thinkers from different cultural backgrounds and using different languages to arrive at similar conclusions.

Finally, because languages have different and peculiar structures, a philosophical or logical thesis that is *clearly* based on the characteristics of one language should not necessarily or precipitately be generalized to other languages, unless the evidence is extremely persuasive. Where such evidence is lacking, one should make circumspect statements and speak in terms of probabilities rather than certainties.

III

Toward an African philosophy

12

On the idea of African philosophy

I started this book with a discussion of the question of philosophy in African culture in which I argued that there *is* a philosophical dimension to African traditional thought. I end it with a discussion of thought systems as wholes, at the level at which we speak of Western or European or Oriental philosophy. The major question is: May we in similar vein talk also of *African* philosophy? Is the idea of African philosophy intelligible? One answering these questions in the negative would, I suspect, prefer to talk rather of Akan, Yoruba, Kikuyu, Bantu, or Mende philosophy. But it should be noted that in addition to Western philosophy, one can speak as well of American, British, French, and German philosophy, and similarly of Chinese, Japanese, Korean, and Indian philosophy in addition to Oriental (or Eastern) philosophy. (There is indeed a philosophical journal with the title *Philosophy East and West.*) If it makes sense to talk of Western or Eastern philosophy, would it not make sense to talk of African philosophy too?

In Part III I shall argue that the common features discernible in the cultures and thought systems of sub-Saharan African peoples justify the existence of an African philosophy. The intention here is not to argue that there is or ever will be either a unitary or a uniform African philosophical perspective, for such an argument will not hold water. It is to argue, rather, that a justification exists for talking of African philosophy or describing a body of ideas as African – not in the sense that these ideas are not to be found anywhere else in the world, but in the sense that this body of ideas is seen, interpreted, and analyzed by many African thinkers (and societies) in their own way. Thus, by "African" I do not mean to

189

imply that a particular body of philosophical ideas is uniquely or exclusively African. I am using "African" in the sense in which one might use "Western" or "European" or "Oriental." The task here is a formidable but a significant one.

12.1. The need not to generalize

In a critical discussion of Mbiti's *African Religions and Philosophy* I accused him of "generalizations, over-simplifications, premature judgments and sparse analysis."[1] In this well-known book Mbiti recognizes the diversity of religious beliefs and practices in Africa and so speaks of African "religions" in his title, whereas in his use of the singular "philosophy" he means perhaps to convey the impression that Africans have a common philosophical perspective, although he himself speaks of "philosophical *systems* of different African peoples."[2] Mbiti wrote: "But since there are no parallel philosophical systems which can be observed in similarly concrete terms we shall use the singular 'philosophy' to refer to the philosophical understanding of African peoples concerning different issues of life."[3] This statement invites two responses. The first is that even though the philosophical contours of the various African thinkers are yet to be seriously delineated, yet it is safe to say that it is impossible for the philosophical understanding of African peoples to be similar or uniform. Second, the view that "there are no parallel philosophical systems which can be observed" can hardly be advanced when one knows, as Mbiti does, that "the philosophical systems of different African peoples have not yet been formulated."[4]

As to Mbiti's generalizations, I shall cite only two examples, namely, his views on the so-called African concept of time and on the nature of moral evil in African thought. I have already criticized (in section 11.2) his views on the African concept of time, disagreeing especially with the way he generalizes his analysis from East Africa to the rest of African peoples. On the nature of moral evil Mbiti says that in African communities "something is considered to be evil not because of its intrinsic nature, but by virtue of who does it to whom and from which level of status."[5] Although this latter view is controversial, my difficulty with it here, as with his views on the African concept of time, concerns the basis for generalizing it for Africa as a whole even if it is true of his own ethnic group.

There is no need to generalize a particular philosophical position for all African peoples in order for that position to be African.

I wish to make it clear that in criticizing Mbiti some time ago, as now, my intention was not to deny the legitimacy of the idea of African philosophy (using "philosophy" in the singular), but to question the bases of some of his bald, generalized assertions about African thought, assertions that need not have been made and that can hardly be justified. I believe that in many areas of thought we can discern features of the traditional life and thought of African peoples sufficiently common to constitute a legitimate and reasonable basis for the construction (or reconstruction) of a philosophical system that may properly be called African – African not in the sense that every African adheres to it, but in the sense that that philosophical system arises from, and hence is essentially related to, African life and thought. Such a basis would justify a discourse in terms of "African philosophy," just as the similarity of the experiences, traditions, cultural systems, values, and mentalities justify the appropriateness of the labels European philosophy, Oriental philosophy, Western philosophy, and so on.

12.2. Common features in African cultures

The basis I have in mind is made up of the beliefs, customs, traditions, values, sociopolitical institutions, and historical experiences of African societies. This observation will doubtless evoke cynicism, even scandal, among many Africanists, who are given to harping on the diversities of the cultures of Africa. Such scholars see no affinities among the cultures of Africa, even though the fact of cultural pluralism, which they expend great intellectual effort in pointing out, is so obvious a consequence of ethnic pluralism in Africa. Yet cultural pluralism, I maintain, does not necessarily eliminate the possibility of horizontal relationships between individual cultures.

On the intellectual level the works of such eminent Western anthropologists as Rattray, Herskovits, Forde, Fortes, Evans-Pritchard, Radcliffe-Brown, Lienhardt, and Goody, which generally deal with specific ethnic groups in Africa, have produced the impression, which was not intended by their authors, that the institutions and practices of the ethnic groups in Africa are very different from one another. The reason is that none of these authors, through either lack of interest in other ethnic groups or consciousness of his own limitations, tried in any significant way to relate his own observations and conclusions to those of other scholars, where they were available. The few comparisons in their works are usually made in passing, as if tangential to the import and structure of the work. The valuable productions of such individual Africanists do not therefore provide an opportunity for a synoptic study of African cultures. Consequently, such works fail to convey the impression that African cultures can be examined from a continental perspective.

In this connection such works as *African Worlds*, edited by Forde (1954), *African Political Systems*, edited by Fortes and Evans-Pritchard (1940), and *African Systems of Kinship and Marriage*, edited by Radcliffe-Brown and Forde (1956) are of immeasurable value. Each of these books focuses on a specific theme as it may be found in a number of African societies: the first on cosmological ideas and social values, the second on traditional political systems, and the third on social institutions. The great value of such works is that they provide one with a horizontal conspectus of some of the cultural systems of a number of African peoples. Others, like Geoffrey Parrinder, cover the whole of Africa, or a big region of it, in one sweep, an approach that has didactic advantages, even though it may leave out important details and can lead to superficiality if not properly handled. The point is that anyone interested in offering a considered, not pedestrian, opinion on the general nature of African cultures must make comparative investigations. This approach is certainly arduous, for it requires that one delve into many publications on the various cultural systems of Africa. Yet it is the approach most likely to yield a fruitful result.

A painstaking comparative study of African cultures leaves one in no doubt that despite the undoubted cultural diversity arising from Africa's ethnic pluralism, threads of underlying affinity do run through the beliefs, customs, value systems, and sociopolitical institutions and practices of the various African societies.

This kinship among the cultural systems of Africa has been noted by a number of scholars, mostly non-African. Edwin Smith, an anthropologist and missionary in Central Africa during the first half of this century, believed that "there is an underlying identity in religion throughout sub-Saharan Africa which allows one to talk legitimately of a unified *African* Religion."[6] Gelfand was impressed by the similarities of African belief in different parts of the continent.[7] Forde wrote in the introduction to his collection of essays on social values and cosmological ideas of several ethic groups in Africa: "When these studies are considered *together* one is impressed not only by the great diversity of ritual forms, but also by *substantial underlying similarities* in religious outlook and moral injunction."[8] Later he spoke of "the religious ideas and social values which are *widespread* in Africa."[9] Elsewhere Forde asserted:

> Thus the linguistic distributions in West Africa suggest several important underlying features of cultural development ... Since ... all the languages of West Africa appear to be ultimately derived from a common stock, one would expect to find *significant elements of a common early tradition in the cultures of all West African peoples*. Little systematic enquiry has so far been given to this question but there are many indications that underlying the great regional and tribal differences in the elaboration of cult and cosmological ideas *there is a very widespread substratum of basic ideas* that persists in the rituals, myths and folktales of West African peoples.[10]

In an introduction to a collection of studies on the political systems of different African peoples Fortes and Evans-Pritchard opined that "the societies described are representative of *common types* of African political systems" and that "most of the forms described are variants of a *pattern* of political organization found among contiguous or neighboring societies ... we believe that all the major principles of African political organization are brought out in these essays."[11] Parrinder also observed that "there is much more kinship between the various peoples in Africa than might appear at first sight."[12] Hilda Kuper's view was that "the piling up of ethnographic detail produces an impression of chaos where there is in fact only variation on a few themes ... African tribal societies are relatively undifferentiated and homogenous."[13] Recently the eminent Ghanaian sociologist K. A. Busia observed that "from such studies as have already been done on the religious beliefs and rites of different communities, it is possible to discern *common* religious ideas and assumptions about the universe held *throughout* Africa, and which provide a world-view that may be described as African."[14] Earlier Busia had written: "I am not aware of an agreed Christian view of nature, but I submit that there is an *African* one which is that nature has power which may be revered as well as used for man's benefit."[15] Taylor observed that there is in Africa, south of the Sahara, "a basic world view which fundamentally is everywhere the same."[16] And according to Idowu,

> There is a *common Africanness* about the total culture and religious beliefs and practices of Africa. This common factor may be due either to the fact of diffusion or to the fact that most Africans share common origins with regard to race and customs and religious practices . . .; with regard to the concept of God, there is a *common* thread, however tenuous in places, running throughout the continent.[17]

Such views regarding the common features of the cultural systems of Africa justify, in my opinion, the assertion that ethnic pluralism does *not* necessarily or invariably produce absolute verticalism with respect to cultures, allowing no room for shoulder-rubbing of any kind, but producing windowless monads of cultural systems.

There are several ways in which the cultural systems of the various African societies may be said to be related. First, a number of Africa's ethnic groups are so small, and consequently their cultures have been so greatly influenced by those of neighboring large groups that they may now be said to a great extent to share the culture of the large groups. A foremost scholar of Akan culture, J. H. Kwabena Nketiah, said of the Akans: "Not only is their language the most widely spoken throughout the country but also their culture has influenced those of several ethnic groups within the borders of Ghana."[18] According to Kenneth Little, "The Mende . . . form the larger cultural group in Sierra Leone, and their culture is shared to a considerable extent by peoples living in a wide region around them."[19] The cultural influence of the Yoruba on the Fon of Dahomey has likewise been noted.[20] Second, it is a common feature of the cultural landscape of Africa that a seemingly distinct ethnic group may in fact turn out to be a subdivision or component of a larger ethnic group. In Ghana, for instance, the Nzema and the Ashanti are regarded by non-Ghanaian writers as separate ethnic entities, whereas in fact both of them are parts of the Akans, sharing common cultural experiences with other component Akan groups such as the Fantes, Akwamus, Akwapims, Akims, and others. The Shilluk of the Upper Nile are culturally related to the Nuer and the Dinka.[21] Third, there are ethnic groups in Africa that, following the arbitrary and unrealistic boundaries drawn a century ago by Africa's colonial masters, are found in two or more neighboring countries. Thus, there are Ewes in Ghana, Togo, and

Dahomey (Benin); there are Akans in Ghana, Togo, and Ivory Coast; there are Yorubas in western Nigeria and Dahomey. The Bantu are spread over central, eastern, and southern Africa: The Abaluyia, for instance, are Bantu tribes of the Nyanza province of Kenya.[22] Writing on "An African Morality," Godfrey Wilson stated: "The African people whose morality is here described are the Nyakusa of the Rungwe district of South Tanganyika; the same cultural group extends into Nyasaland under the name Ngonde."[23] "The Yoruba, Bini, and Dahomeans," wrote Fortes, "are closely related in culture . . . I have dwelt on their beliefs because they are characteristic of West Africa. . . ."[24]

A close look at the ethnic configuration of Africa shows a number of such dislocations or transplants resulting from the drawing of boundaries that placed peoples bound by ties of kinship, language, and culture in different states. As a result it is possible to see particular cultural patterns extending across states in Africa.

12.3. The community of cultural elements and ideas

I wish now to present, in a nutshell, the worldviews, sociopolitical ideas, values, and institutions that can with a high degree of certainty be said to pervade the cultural systems of different African peoples. What I have done is to extract the common or rather pervasive elements and ideas in the cultures of African peoples as may be found in as many of the existing publications as I have been able to look at. Such pervasive cultural elements and ideas are the elements which constitute the basis for constructing African philosophy (using "philosophy" in the singular). In some cases the attempt to bring out the philosophical implications of beliefs, ideas, attitudes or practices has led to brief philosophical discussions; so that this section is not just a catalog of facts about African cultures. We may start, then, with the African metaphysic.

12.3.1. Metaphysics
(a) Categories of being in African ontology
A critical examination of the scholarly literature[25] on traditional African religions shows that most African peoples do have a concept of God as the Supreme Being who created the whole universe out of nothing and who is the absolute ground of all

being. Thus, Busia wrote: "The postulate of God is universal throughout Africa; it is a concept which is handed down as part of the culture."[26] After studying the concept of God held by nearly three hundred peoples in Africa, Mbiti concluded thus: "In all these societies, without a single exception, people have a notion of God as the Supreme Being."[27] The Supreme Being is held to be omnipotent, omniscient, and omnipresent. He is considered uncreated and eternal, attributes implying his transcendence. But transcendence is also implicit in African beliefs about God removing himself far from the world of humankind as a result of our misconduct. "It appears to be a widespread notion in Africa that at the beginning God and man lived together on earth and talked one to another; but that owing to misconduct of some sort on the part of man – or more frequently of a woman – God deserted the earth and went to live in the sky."[28] But God is also held by African peoples to be immanent in that He is "manifested in natural objects and phenomena, and they can turn to Him in acts of worship, at any place and any time."[29]

African ontology, however, is a pluralistic ontology that recognizes, besides the Supreme Being, other categories of being as well. These are the lesser spirits (variously referred to as spirits, deities, gods, nature gods, divinities), ancestors (that is, ancestral spirits), man, and the physical world of natural objects and phenomena. Mbiti observed: "Myriads of spirits are reported from every African people,"[30] and "the class of the spirits is an essential and integral part of African ontology."[31] The reality of the ancestral spirits is the basis of the so-called ancestor worship that has been considered by some as an important feature of African religion. Thus, Fortes wrote: "It has long been recognized that ancestor worship is a conspicuous feature of African religious systems."[32] And Parrinder observed: "Thus there is no doubt that ancestral spirits play a very large part in African thought; they are [so] prominent in the spiritual world."[33] The physical world is also considered real in African ontology.

Mbiti thought that in addition to these four entities in African ontology – namely, God, qua the Absolute Being, lesser spirits (consisting of superhuman beings and ancestral spirits), man, and, finally, the world of natural objects – "there seems to be a force, power or energy permeating the whole universe"[34] which, in his opinion, is to be added as a separate ontological category.[35] But although African ontology distinguishes four or five categories of being, yet it must not be supposed that these entities are on the same level of reality. For God, as the Supreme Being and the ground of all existence, must be categorially distinguished from the lesser spirits and the other beings that were his creations. The Supreme Being is held as the ultimate reality, which is inferrable not only from the attributes ascribed to God,[36] but also from the religious attitude and behavior of African peoples, the majority of whose "prayers and invocations are addressed to God."[37] Moreover, in spontaneous religious outbursts references are made to the Supreme Being rather than to the lesser spirits.[38] The lesser spirits are thus on a lower level of reality. African ontology therefore is hierarchical,[39] with the Supreme Being at the apex and the world of natural objects and phenomena at the bottom.

African ontology appears to be essentially spiritualistic, although this does not imply a denial of the reality of the nonspiritual, empirical world. Conceptually, a distinction is made between the empirical and nonempirical (that is, spiritual) world. But this distinction is not projected onto the level of being, so that in terms of being both worlds are regarded as real. Thus, McVeigh stated: "Both the world of the seen and the unseen are realities."[40] And Mbiti observed that in African conceptions "the physical and spiritual are but two dimensions of one and the same universe."[41] Reality in African thought appears to be homogeneous. Thus, just as African ontology is neither wholly pluralistic nor wholly monistic but possesses attributes of both, so it is neither idealistic – maintaining that what is real is only spirit, nor materialistic (naturalistic) – maintaining that what is real is only matter, but possesses attributes of both.

(b)   Causation

African ontological structure constitutes the conceptual framework for explaining the notion of causality. Implicit in the hierarchical character of that structure is that a higher entity has the power to control a lower entity. Since man and the physical world are the lower entities of that hierarchy, occurrences in the physical world are causally explained by reference to supernatural powers, which are held to be the real or ultimate sources of action and change in the world. Wrote Mbiti:

> African peoples . . . feel and believe that all the various ills, misfortunes, accidents, tragedies . . . which they encounter or experience, are caused by the use of (this) mystical power. . . .

> It is here that we may understand, for example, that a bereaved mother whose child has died from malaria will not be satisfied with the scientific explanation. . . . She will wish to know why the mosquito stung her child and not somebody else's child. . . . Everything is caused by someone directly or through the use of mystical power.[42]

Elsewhere Mbiti wrote that "for many millions of African people" such phenomena, as the eclipse of the sun, "do not just happen without mystical, mythological, or spiritual causes. It is not enough for them to ask *why* or *how* this causes them to happen. In traditional life the *who questions and answers* are more important and meaningful than the *how questions and answers*."[43] McVeigh made reference to "the African concern with the deeper 'why' questions,"[44] and "the African tendency to seek immediately mystical answers."[45] In a book that deals specifically with eastern and southern African peoples, Monica Wilson referred to the dogmas regarding mystical power as "the explanation of good and evil fortune, the answer to 'Why did it happen to me?' "[46] She observed that in Africa scientific answers are regarded as incomplete, for science "cannot answer the question the Mpondo or Nyakyusa is primarily concerned with when his child dies: 'Why did it happen to me?' 'Who caused it?' "[47]

The evidence, then, is that causation is generally explained in terms of spirit, of mystical power. Scientific or empirical explanations, of which they are aware, are considered not profound enough to offer complete satisfaction. The notion of chance is the alternative to the African proclivity to the "why" and the "who" questions when the answers to the "how" and "what" questions are deemed unsatisfactory. But the Africans' conception of an orderly universe and their concern for ultimate causes lead them to reject the notion of chance. Consequently, in African causal explanations the notion or chance does not have a significant place.[48]

(c) Concept of the person

"Every culture produces a dogma of human personality, that is to say, an accepted formulation of the physical and psychical constitution of man." So wrote the renowned British anthropologist Meyer Fortes.[49] African systems of thought indeed teem with elaborate dogmas of the nature of the human being. The African philosophy of the person is, in my view, rigidly dualistic: The person consists of body and soul. However, the common conception of the soul varies widely in its details. In some cases the soul is conceived as having three or even more parts, as, for example, among the people of Dahomey;[50] others, such as the Dogon,[51] the Rwanda,[52] the Nupe and Gwari of northern Nigeria,[53] and the Yoruba,[54] conceive it as bipartite. Still others, like the Mende and the Shilluk,[55] have simpler conceptions of the soul.

The soul is understood as the immaterial part of a person that survives after death. The African belief in the soul – and hence in the dualistic nature of the person – leads directly to their conception of an ancestral world inhabited by departed souls. Thus the logical relation between the belief in the soul and the belief in the ancestral world is one of dependence: The latter belief depends on the former. It is the immaterial, undying part of a person, namely, the soul, that continues to live in the world of the ancestral spirits. Thus, McVeigh was right when he wrote: ". . . it is impossible to deny that African thought affirms the survival of the human personality (that is, soul) after death."[56] For this reason, "the Christian missionary," in McVeigh's view, "does not go to Africa to inform the people that there is a spiritual world or that the personality survives the grave. Africans know this from their own experience."[57] The psychophysical conception of a person common to African thought systems and the commonly observable phenomena of psychophysical therapeutics practiced in all African communities presuppose a belief in psychophysical causal interaction.

(d) Concept of fate (destiny)

As the absolute being and the ultimate ground of being in the African metaphysic, the Supreme Being constitutes the controlling principle in the world. This fact, together with others to be mentioned presently, is the basis of the belief in fate (or destiny) common in African thought systems. "Running through the African conception of God," observed McVeigh, "is a clear sense of fate or destiny."[58] Dickson also noted that "The concept of Destiny is quite widespread in Africa; certainly the literature on West Africa suggests that many of its peoples have some ideas which may be put down under the heading of Destiny."[59] Writing on the African ideas about the works of God, Mbiti said: "God not only continues to create physically, but He also *ordains the destiny* of His creatures, especially that of man."[60] Fortes, however, thought that the concept of fate is held only in the religions of West African people: "Indeed one of the characteristic marks of West African religions, as compared with other African religions (for example: East and South African Bantu religions) in which ancestor worship also plays a part, is the occurrence of the notion of Fate in them."[61] It is not true, however, that eastern and southern African religions lack the notion of fate. Mbiti, for instance, noted that "Similar notions of predestination are found among peoples like the Ila, Tswana, Bacongo, Barundi, Yao and others."[62] (These are peoples in eastern and southern Africa.)

The concept of fate must be implicit, in my view, in systems of thought, like the African, which postulate a creator who not only fashioned man and the world but also established the order of the world in which man lives. It makes sense logically to assume that if human beings were fashioned, then they were fashioned in such a way that would determine a number of things about them. This assumption therefore must have been a basis for the African belief in fate. Further, the repudiation of the notion of chance in African thought would seem to lead to the idea of fate. Thus, some other assumptions in African thought involve a general belief in fate.

What is not clear is whether fate is self-determined, that is, chosen or decided upon by the individual soul or divinely imposed. Some African peoples think that destiny is chosen by the individual whereas others think that it is conferred by the Supreme Being. Among the Yoruba the manner in which destiny comes to the individual is ambiguously conceived: In one way the individual "*chooses* his destiny"; in another he "*receives* his destiny," that is, from Olodumare (God): in yet another way "his destiny is *affixed* to him."[63] In the conceptions of the Rwandas, the Fon of Dahomey, the Lele of Kasai (southwestern Congo Kinshasa), and others, God decides the destiny of the individual.[64] However, whatever the source of the individual's destiny, the fact remains – as I pointed out in discussing the concept among the Akan (section 7.2.2) – that the individual enters the world with a predetermined destiny. The concept of fate in African thought appears to be quite complex and, like other concepts, stands in need of thorough analysis and explication.

(e) The problem of evil

Busia, to whose views I have already referred in my discussion of the problem of evil, claimed that the African concept of deity does not generate the problem of evil, for the sources of evil in the world are the lesser spirits and other supernatural forces.

That is to say, God is not the source of evil. Mbiti asserted that "many [African] societies say categorically that God did not create what is evil, nor does He do any evil whatsoever ... In nearly all African societies, it is thought that spirits are either the origin of evil, or agents of evil."[65] A few African peoples hold, however, that, in the words of McVeigh, God is "the explanation for what is good and evil in man's life."[66] Among such peoples are the Shilluk, Dinka, Nupe, Bacongo, and Vashona. The assumption of God as the source of evil in the world stems from the conception of God as the first principle and the ultimate ground of explanation for all existence. This of course raises the problem of evil, since God is also considered in African thought to be good[67] and omnipotent.

Most African peoples, however, deny that God is the source of evil. Does their view succeed in eliminating the problem of evil, as Busia and others claimed? Maquet, writing about the Rwanda, said: "The century-old problem of evil in the world, particularly acute where there is a belief in the existence of a being who is omnipotent and infinitely good, has been solved by putting the responsibility for all evil and all suffering on agents other than *Imana* ... *Imana* (God) himself does not cause any evil but he allows the causes of evil to act."[68] These agents or causes of evil, according to Maquet, are the "malevolent agencies of the invisible world,"[69] that is, evil spirits. Maquet is surely mistaken in maintaining that the fact that evil is traceable to evil spirits eliminates the problem of evil. For the questions I raised in discussing the problem of evil as it occurs in Akan thought (in section 7.4) are relevant here too. Thus even if it is the lesser spirits and not God which are held as the sources of evil, evil still remains a genuine problem for African philosophy and theology.

12.3.2. Epistemology: paranormal cognition – an important mode of knowing in African thought

Historically, Western epistemology has acknowledged two main sources of knowledge: reason (mind) and sense experience. The theories associated with these sources are known as rationalism and empiricism. Despite the activities of the Society for Psychical Research (founded in England in 1882) and despite much-publicized experiences in clairvoyance and telepathy – which are forms of extrasensory perception (ESP) – ESP has not been formally accepted as a form of knowing in the Western philosophy of knowledge. There are, to be sure, some individuals in Western societies who believe in ESP as a source of knowledge, but this is far from implying the recognition of ESP.

The case is different in African ways of knowing. Reason and sense experience are, to be sure, not unknown to African epistemology, even though, as in other areas, epistemological concepts in African thought have not been extensively investigated. In Akan thought, for instance, the well-known proverb

No one teaches a child God,
(*obi nkyerē abofra Nyame*)

implies that knowledge of God is intuitive and immediate,[70] rather than acquired through experience. Other proverbs indicate the Akan belief in innate ideas, such as

No one teaches blacksmithing to the son of a
blacksmith.
No one teaches the leopard's child how to spring.[71]
(that is, it is born with that knowledge even though
that knowledge is developed through experience).

Sense experience as a source of knowledge is also recognized in African thought. The Akan proverb

All things depend on experience,
(*nneēma nyinaa dan sua*)[72]

indicates the high regard the Akan thinkers have for knowledge based on experience.

But I wish to point out an important feature of African epistemology that makes it distinct from Western epistemology, namely, spirit mediumship, divination, and witchcraft. These modes of cognition are of course occasioned by means that differ from, but work alongside (*para*), the normal. Divination, witchcraft, and spirit mediumship are psychical phenomena common in all African communities. Middleton and Winter said: "Beliefs about witches and sorcerers have a worldwide distribution; *in Africa their occurrence is almost universal*."[73] Evans-Pritchard wrote: ". . . most, perhaps all, African peoples have witchcraft or sorcery beliefs or both – in some degree."[74] Debrunner also noted that "Witchcraft beliefs are prominent all over Africa."[75] "With a few exceptions," writes Mbiti, "African systems of divination have not been carefully studied, though diviners and divinations are found in almost every community."[76] Spirit medium and spirit possession are just as widespread.[77] Parrinder observed that "Divination . . . is very popular in Africa."[78]

202

In African communities it is commonly believed that some individuals are born with certain abilities that are not acquired through experience. Diviners, traditional healers, and witches are believed to possess ESP with which they can perceive and communicate with supernatural entities. African thought maintains that perception does not wholly or exclusively occur through the physical senses, and that human beings are not entirely subject to the limitations of space and time. Telepathy, a form of ESP in which information originating in the mind of one person is sent to that of another; clairvoyance, in which people can see objects that are far away or otherwise hidden from sight; and precognition, in which people acquire information about the future – all these forms of Western parapsychology are, in the African context, aspects of divination and spirit mediumship, for the African diviner claims knowledge of the thoughts of other persons and of certain facts that has been acquired without the use of the normal senses. In Africa, this information is thought to be the result of the activities of discarnate minds, that is, spirits. Divination thus links the physical and the spiritual worlds, and in Africa (as perhaps elsewhere) there are numerous stories about individuals communicating with the dead, which, if true, would attest to survival after death.

Divination and spiritual mediumship are parapsychological phenomena and should, if possible, be investigated scientifically, for if they are found to be genuine, they might establish that the human mind is *not* material but a spiritual entity – a conclusion with obvious implications for epistemology and the philosophy of mind. In Africa, however, judging from the popularity of diviners and mediums and from the assiduity with which people in an African community seek certain kinds of knowledge from them, it can legitimately be claimed that paranormal cognition is recognized by and large as a mode of knowing.

12.3.3. African morality: religious or nonreligious?

A number of scholars have made the observation that African peoples are very religious, and that religion permeates their lives. Mbiti asserted that "Africans are notoriously religious, and each people has its own religious system with a set of beliefs and practices. Religion permeates into all the departments of life so fully that it is not easy or possible always to isolate it."[79] According to him "in traditional life there are no atheists."[80] Busia observed that Africa's cultural heritage "is intensely and pervasively religious,"[81] and that "in traditional African communities, it was not possible to distinguish between religious and nonreligious areas of life. All life was religious."[82] Writing specifically on the Yoruba, Idowu said: "The keynote of their life is their religion. In all things, they are religious ... The religion of the Yoruba permeates their lives so much that it expresses itself in multifarious ways."[83] Elsewhere he refers to Africans generally as people "who in all things are religious."[84] Father Onuoha's view was that "Religion permeated the life of the African through and through,"[85] and McVeigh wrote that "The African is deeply religious."[86] Many colonial administrators in Africa used to refer to Africans as "this incurably religious people."[87]

The claim about the religiosity of African peoples has led some scholars to assert a link between religion and morality in African moral philosophy. At the end of Monica Wilson's chapter on "Moralities" she remarks: "To conclude, in the traditional societies in Africa there was a direct *connection* between religion and morality, though the concepts of sin varied and the sources of retribution were diverse."[88] Dickson opined that ". . . in Africa religion and life go together: life is to a very great extent believed to be permeated by religious values. I happen to subscribe to the view that in African thought there is some *link* between religion and morality."[89] Busia maintained that "religion defined moral duties for the members of the group or tribe,"[90] and again, that "The standards and loyalties, the obligations and reciprocities of social life in Africa are rooted in religion."[91] That some connection may exist between religion and morality in African thought is definitely conceivable in the allegedly religious environment of the African. It seems to me, however, that the nature of the connection is yet to be fully clarified.

The connection has been taken by some scholars to mean that the African moral system derives from, or is founded upon, religion, and that African morality is a religious morality. Busia's first statement quoted above implies such a view. Parrinder observed: "Morality is bound up with religion and receives its sanction from the Creator who gives the order of the world. What is ethically good must be ontologically good also."[92] Parrinder means, I think, that religion is the basis of morality, for elsewhere he wrote: ". . . the past has been (so) thoroughly impregnated with religion and *its* ethics . . ."[93] Thus, he sees African morality as an offshoot of African religion. Idowu also thought that "With the Yoruba morality is certainly the fruit of religion."[94]

Some scholars writing on the morality of specific African ethnic groups, however, deny the religious basis of the moral systems of those peoples. Godfrey Wilson wrote of the Nyakyusa: "Among the Nyakyusa the ideas of social behavior are not connected with religion, nonetheless they exist . . ."; after mentioning the moral virtues of the Nyakyusa, he added: "But the positive, ideal statement of these virtues is not made in religious terms."[95] Referring to African morality generally, Monica Wilson observed: "The basis of morality was fulfillment of obligation to kinsmen and neighbors, and living in amity with them."[96] On the morality of the Rwanda, Maquet wrote: "Thus the ethics of the Banyarwanda are not integrated on a religious basis such as the will of God . . . That is good (or evil) which tradition has defined as good (or evil)."[97] Among the Mende, "Wrong behavior is regarded as a breaking of some specific rule of conduct, not as the flouting of some divine or absolute law of the universe."[98] These are unambiguous statements of the nonreligious foundation of morality of at least some African peoples.

In order to ascertain the real basis of African morality and thus to clarify the link between religion and morality in African thought, two distinctions must be made. First, one must distinguish between morality as a system of moral rules or principles – and the question here is whether or not moral rules originate from divine prescriptions – and morality as the moral life or conduct of the individual person. Second, as I noted in section 8.1, the relation between religion and morality in African ethical thought must be examined from two angles: from the angle of religion or spiritual beings as the source of moral rules or values, and from the angle of religion as playing some active role in the moral behavior of the individual. The nature of the link between religion and morality that has been alleged by some observers becomes clearer when these distinctions are made. If they mean that the Supreme Being (God) and the other spirits play a significant role in the moral behavior of African peoples, this is a plausible view. If, on the other hand, they mean that religious or divine pronouncements constitute the bases of moral rules in African societies, this, in my opinion, is implausible.

A number of scholars have noted the significant roles played by the Supreme Being and other supernatural beings in the moral behavior of African peoples. Writing on religion and society in Africa, Parrinder observed that "religion provides the sanctions that society cannot fully supply of itself . . ."[99] Busia's view was that

"African religions support the idea that religion *regulates* conduct."[100] While supposing that "God rarely intervenes in the moral life of men on earth," Ray noted that "for the most part, it is the ancestors who act as the official guardians of the social and moral order."[101] According to McVeigh, "To speak of religious sanctions in African ethics is to recognize that the ancestors are the trustees of tribal morality."[102] In an allegedly religious environment it is conceivable that the objects of religious awe, the beings to which worshipful obeisance is made, may be said in some sense to affect the moral behavior of the people.

The interpretation of the link between religion and morality in terms that would make religion, that is, divine commands, the source of moral values appears to be conceptually impossible. The principal reason is that African traditional religion is essentially not a revealed religion.[103] The doctrinal system of a religion *revealed* by God to a single person, the founder, invariably includes elaborate prescriptions to guide the ethical life of the people who accept and practice that religion. A coherent system of ethics can be founded upon such divinely revealed commands. African religious experience has certainly included mystical encounters between human beings (that is, priests and priestesses, diviners, etc.) and spiritual beings. Such encounters occur in divinations, spirit mediums, communications with the dead, and other forms of the religious experience. Such contacts, however, take place in a religious atmosphere; they are some of the manifestations of African religion. The encounters therefore are the results, rather than the causes (or sources), of religion in Africa in the traditional setting. Thus, religious "truths" that people in an African community may claim to possess could not have originated in such events. The origins of African traditional religion appear to be more complex than those of religions like Christianity and Islam. It is clear, however, that African traditional religion cannot be said to be a religion whose doctrines were embodied in a revelation.

To say this, however, is not to deny that "messages" may be received by the practitioners or followers of African traditional religion and that part of the message may concern the moral life of its followers. Nevertheless, such messages carrying moral prescriptions appear to be too few and far between to constitute an adequate basis for a coherent ethical system. In any case the moral character of such prescriptions would have to be judged by the people themselves, using their own moral insight. After stating that

"With the Yoruba, morality is certainly the fruit of religion,"
Idowu added: "What have been named *tabu* took their origin from
the fact that people *discerned* that there were certain things which
were morally approved or disapproved by the Deity."[104] By "morality" Idowu, I take it, means a set of moral rules or moral values. If
this is the case, then there is a tension inherent in the above
statements. If moral rules are derived from religion or divine
commands, then they would immediately compel obedience irrespective of the moral views of the people. On the other hand, if
popular moral sentiment was relevant to the origin of taboos
("things not done"), as Idowu's second statement implies, then the
people were the final arbiters of what was morally right or wrong.
The logic of Idowu's statements, in the context of a nonrevealed
religion, suggests indeed that moral rules or moral values do not
derive from religion. I conclude therefore that the most plausible
way of interpreting the link between African religion and morality
is to see it in terms of the supernatural beings playing an important
role in the moral behavior of the people rather than in terms of such
beings constituting the sources of moral values.

This conclusion immediately raises this important question:
What constitutes the basis of African moral belief, values, and
principles, if not religion? I believe that in African conceptions
moral values originate from the basic existential conditions in
which people conduct their lives. McVeigh observed:

> Therefore, it is important to inquire concerning the African
> standard of judgment, what makes some things good and
> others bad. [Edwin] Smith replies that the norm of right and
> wrong is custom; that is, the good is that which receives the
> community's approval, the bad is that which is disapproved.
> The right builds up society; the wrong tears it down. One is
> social; the other anti-social.[105]

Regarding the basis of Bantu morality, Molema remarked:

> The greatest happiness and good of the tribe was the end and
> aim of each member of the tribe. Now, utility forms part of
> the basis of perhaps all moral codes. With the Bantu, it
> formed the basis of morality ... it was utilitarianism. This
> was the standard of goodness, and in harmony with, and
> conformity to, this end must the moral conduct be moulded.
> The effect of this, of course, was an altruism.[106]

Thus, it is clear that the guiding principles of African morality originate not from divine pronouncements as such, but from considerations of human welfare and interests. Reverence for non-human entities is not necessarily considered to lessen one's devotion to the welfare and interests of human beings in this life. The (alleged) religiosity of African peoples, even if true, is therefore not at variance with the pursuit of human welfare on earth. Indeed, African prayers are brimful of requests to the supernatural beings for material comforts and the things necessary for building a good life. Mbiti observed that "the prayers are chiefly requests for material welfare, such as health, protection from danger, prosperity and even riches."[107] Shorter also noted that African prayers are devoted to "the transmission and continuity of life and fertility. . . . Life and the sharing of life and [such] well-known, fundamental values in Africa . . ."[108] He continued: "Health and healing are most important values in African traditional religion, connected as they are with the fundamental theme of life. Sickness, for the African, is a diminution of life; and petition for healing is probably the most common subject of prayer."[109] In Monica Wilson's view, "What men continually sought in traditional African society – what they worshipped – was life, vitality, fertility."[110] The African love of life is a feature of their concern for human well-being, which constitutes the warp and woof of their moral life and thought.

12.3.4. Communalism in African social thought and practice

Communalism[111] is the doctrine that the group constitutes the main focus of the lives of the individual members of that group, and that the extent of the individual's involvement in the interests, aspirations, and welfare of the group is the measure of that individual's worth. This philosophy is given institutional expression in the social structures of African societies.

The communal social structures of African societies have been noted by many a writer on African social life. The sense of community and social solidarity that characterizes the social relations of African peoples stems from such communal social structures. This sense of community, observed Dickson, is a "*characteristic of African life to which attention has been drawn again and again* by both African and non-African writers on Africa. Indeed, to many *this characteristic defines Africanness.*"[112] Edwin Smith observed more than half a century ago:

The Africans have hitherto lived in the collectivist stage: the community has been the unit, every individual interest has been subordinate to the general welfare. In many respects this excites our admiration – even envy. There is a solidarity that civilized communities find it hard to attain. The corporate sentiment that trade unions create among their members is but a faint reflection of the brotherhood found within the African's clan.[113]

Writing on the Bantu, Molema observed: "Individualism, as understood in the Western World, could not thrive. Collectivism was the civic law, communism and a true form of socialism the dominating principle and ruling spirit."[114] According to Senghor, "Negro-African society puts more stress on the group than on the individual, more on solidarity than on the activity and needs of the individual, more on the *communion* of persons than on their autonomy. Ours is a *community* society."[115] Sékou Touré wrote: "Africa is fundamentally communocratic. The collective life and social solidarity give it a basis of humanism which many peoples might envy. These human qualities also mean that an individual cannot imagine organizing his life outside that of his family, village or clan."[116] Referring specifically to traditional life in Kenya, Kenyatta wrote: "According to Gikuyu ways of thinking, nobody is an isolated individual. Or rather, his uniqueness is a secondary fact about him; first and foremost he is several people's relative and several people's contemporary . . . this fact is the basis of his sense of moral responsibility and social obligation."[117] Elsewhere he observed that "Individualism and self-seeking were ruled out . . . The personal pronoun "I" was used very rarely in public assemblies. The spirit of collectivism was [so] much ingrained in the mind of the people . . ."[118]

Communalism is echoed in the works of some African novelists. Camara Laye's *The African Child* evokes a sense of community. Chinua Achebe's *No Longer at Ease* refers to the fellow feeling and neighborliness in African societies. The hero of William Conton's *The African* rages against "the European's exaggerated individualism, his constant exalting of the single human being . . ."[119]

Plainly, communalism holds a most significant place in African social thought, though this does not imply that individualism as such is smothered or ignored, as has been alleged by some scholars, such as Burke, who opined that communal values "tend to submerge the individual personality within the collectivity."[120] Much earlier Adolphe Louis Cureau had written of the Congo: "The village as an extension of the family, compels its citizens to strict communism, to dependence upon one another, and a fusion which reduces everyone to the same level and submerges personality and originality."[121] I have already argued against such a view in Chapter 10. Senghor, immediately after the statements referred to above, added: "This does not mean that it [that is, the community society] ignores the individual."[122] And contrasting the African conception of the social nature of the individual with that of the European, he said:

> The individual is, in Europe, the man who distinguishes himself from the others and claims his autonomy to affirm himself in his basic originality. *The member of the community society also claims his autonomy to affirm himself as a being.* But he feels, he thinks that he can develop his potential, his originality, only in and by society, in union with all other men. . . .[123]

In African social thought human beings are regarded not as individuals but as groups of created beings inevitably and naturally interrelated and interdependent. This does not necessarily lead to the submerging of the initiative or personality of the individual, for after all the well-being and success of the group depend on the unique qualities of its individual members – but individuals whose consciousness of their responsibility to the group is ever present because they identify themselves with the group. Some writers on African social thought and practice have failed to comprehend the nature of the relation between communalism and individualism as these concepts really operate in African societies. In African philosophy, as in African life, these concepts are not considered antithetical, as they are in European (both capitalist and communist) philosophies.

12.4. Conclusion: the legitimacy of talking of African philosophy

The main purpose of Part III is to point out one thing: namely, that it is legitimate and intelligible to talk of "African philosophy," the basis of which is the common or pervasive features in African cultural and thought systems. I do not claim that the features of the African life and thought I have presented are peculiarly African, for they are in fact found in non-African traditional settings as well. But this observation is harmless in itself, and does not detract from the need to explore ideas from the African perspective. African philosophical systems will not be unique. The important thing is to see how the ideas of being, causation, the nature of a person, destiny, evil, morality, the nature of human society and social relationships, etc., are comprehended and analyzed by African thinkers on the basis of African cultural and intellectual experience. African perspectives on these ideas may be similar to those of others; nevertheless, they are worth examining within the African conceptual crucible. After all, the fact that Indians, Chinese, and Japanese have concepts of communalism or destiny, for instance, does not mean that those concepts are necessarily the same as those of African thinkers.

I have already argued that a given culture forms the basis of a philosophy and creates the controlling and organizing categories and principles for philosophizing. For me, then, a philosophical discourse that critically interacts or communes with African cultural and intellectual experiences, with African mentalities and traditions, will be African. That thesis does not have to be accepted by all Africans in order for it to be African, nor does it have to be generalized for all Africans. *It only needs to be the results of the reflective exertions of an African thinker, aimed at giving analytical attention to the intellectual foundations of African culture and experience. That is all.* When modern African philosophers discuss ideas produced by African traditional thinkers, or when they philosophize with the contemporary African situation in mind, diverse, even incompatible, analyses will undoubtedly emerge. Yet they will all come under the umbrella of African philosophy. So that even though what will emerge as African philosophy will in reality be a philosophical mosaic, this fact will not detract from the Africanness of those philosophies. They will, after all, be the product of the "African mind," just as Western culture – Western mind – constitutes the ground for Western philosophy, which also consists of numerous philosophies. There is indeed no single philosophical idea or doctrine shared or adhered to by all Europeans or Westerners; yet such an idea or doctrine does not, on that account, cease to be European or Western. As noted recently by a Western philosopher, "There is no such thing as contemporary philosophy, of course, at least if this is construed as some sum total of commonly held tenets of the day. There are contemporary *philosophies, philosophies as numerous, one sometimes thinks, as philosophers.*"[124] But it must be noted that despite the numerousness of these philosophies (produced by Western philosophers), they all come, nevertheless, under the umbrella of Western philosophy. The reason for this is that they are all grounded in the Western cultural experience. This, then, provides the justification for the main title of this book.

I conclude, then, by saying that modern African philosophers should turn their philosophical gaze on the *intellectual foundations of African culture and experience* (in addition to contributions to Western philosophy, which some of them are in a hurry to pursue). It is never too late in human history to start from where one should start (or should have started). As part of the people of Africa and speaking their languages – which fact is essential for investigating the philosophy of a people – modern African philosophers are in a unique position to elucidate, analyze, and interpret the philosophy of African peoples and to sharpen its contours on the global philosophical map.

Notes

I. The question of philosophy in African culture

1. On the denial of traditional thought as philosophy

1. I use the term "traditional" in the sense of indigenous and aboriginal, something handed down from generation to generation.
2. Robin Horton, "Traditional Thought and the Emerging African Philosophy Department: A Comment on the current Debate," *Second Order, An African Journal of Philosophy*, Vol. VI, No. 1, January 1977, pp. 64–80.
3. Ibid., p. 66; my italics.
4. Robin Horton, "African Traditional Thought and Western Science," *Africa*, Vol. 37, Nos. 1 and 2, 1967; rpt. in Bryan R. Wilson (ed.), *Rationality* (Basil Blackwell, Oxford, 1974). The reference is to *Rationality*, p. 160.
5. Reuben Abel, *Man Is the Measure: A Cordial Invitation to the Central Problems of Philosophy* (Free Press, New York, 1976), p. xxiv; my italics.
6. Frederick Sontag, *Problems of Philosophy* (Chandler, Scranton, Penn., 1970), p. 1; italics in original.
7. Ibid., p. 2.
8. Richard Taylor, *Metaphysics* (Prentice-Hall, Englewood Cliffs, N.J., 1974), p. 2.
9. Sontag, pp. 1, 22; Taylor, pp. 1–2.

213

10. "Willard Van Orman Quine on Philosophy Minus the Mind." BBC interview with Bryan Magee, *The Listener*, 23 March 1978, p. 367; rpt. in Bryan Magee, *Men of Ideas, Some Creators of Contemporary Philosophy* (Oxford University Press, Oxford, 1982), p. 144.
11. A. C. Ewing, "Philosophy in India," *Philosophy*, Vol. XXVI, July 1951, p. 263.
12. K. A. Agyakwa, "Akan Epistemology and Western Tradition: A Philosophical Approach to the Problem of Educational Modernization in Ghana," Ph.D. diss., Columbia University, New York, 1975.
13. K. A. Busia, "The African World-View," in Jacob Drachler (ed.), *African heritage* (Crowell Collier & Macmillan, New York, 1963), p. 149; my italics.
14. D. W. Hamlyn, "Epistemology, History of," in Paul Edwards (ed.), *The Encyclopedia of Philosophy* (Macmillan, New York, 1967), III, 9.
15. Horton in Wilson (ed.), *Rationality*, p. 160.
16. Ibid., pp. 159-60. Horton, "Traditional Thought," p. 65.
17. Horton in Wilson (ed.) *Rationality*, pp. 159-60.
18. Kwasi Wiredu, "On an African Orientation in Philosophy," *Second Order*, Vol. 1, No. 2, July 1972, p. 13; rpt. in his *Philosophy and an African Culture* (Cambridge University Press, Cambridge, 1980), p. 36. The word "needful" in the original text is omitted in the reprint.
19. P. O. Bodunrin, "The Question of African Philosophy," *Philosophy*, Vol. LVI, 1981, p. 169.
20. Ibid.
21. Paulin J. Hountondji, *African Philosophy, Myth and Reality*, trans. Henri Evans (Indiana University Press, Bloomington, 1983), p. 53; my italics.
22. Ibid., p. 55-65.
23. Of course thinkers belonging to the same cultural milieu also may have different answers to philosophical problems. But I am concerned here with statements in which we use such terms as "Greek philosophy," "Western philosophy," "Indian philosophy" and "Islamic philosophy."
24. With the exception of Ethiopian philosophy, which has written sources. See Claude Sumner, *Ethiopian Philosophy*, 4 vols. (Commercial Printing Press, Addis Ababa, 1974-8).
25. E. G. Parrinder, *Religion in Africa* (Penguin, Harmondsworth, 1969), p. 25.
26. S. Dasgupta, *A History of Indian Philosophy* (Cambridge University Press, Cambridge, 1963), I, 10.
27. P. T. Raju, *Philosophical Traditions of India* (Allen and Unwin, London, 1971), p. 15.
28. Ibid., p. 114.

2. Philosophy and culture

1. Melville J. Herskovits, *Dahomey, An Ancient West African Kingdom* (J. J. August, New York, 1938), p. 296.
2. E. G. Parrinder, *Religion in Africa* (Penguin, Harmondsworth, 1969), p. 25.
3. W. E. Abraham, *The Mind of Africa* (University of Chicago Press, Chicago, 1962), p. 111.
4. William Fagg, "The Study of African Art," in Simon Ottenberg and Phoebe Ottenberg (eds.), *Cultures and Societies of Africa* (Random House, New York, 1960), pp. 466–7.
5. E. Bolaji Idowu, *Olodumare, God in Yoruba Belief* (Longmans, London, 1962), pp. 5–6. Cf. Dasgupta's observation about the philosophical tradition in India in Chapter 1.
6. John S. Mbiti, *African Religions and Philosophy* (Doubleday, New York, 1970), p. 87.
7. K. A. Busia, *The Challenge of Africa* (Praeger, New York, 1962), p. 11.
8. Ibid., p. 26.
9. Idowu, p. 45.
10. R. S. Rattray, *Akan–Ashanti Folk Tales* (Oxford University Press, Oxford, 1930), p. ix.
11. J. A. Stewart, *The Myths of Plato*, G. R. Levy (ed.) (Centaur Press, London, 1960), p. 26.
12. Mbiti, p. 86.
13. J. G. Christaller, *A Collection of 3,600 Tshi (Twi) Proverbs* (Basel, Evangelical Missionary Society, 1879).
14. R. S. Rattray, *Ashanti Proverbs* (Oxford University Press, Oxford, 1916), pp. 11–12; my italics.
15. See, for example, Ruth Finnegan, *Oral Literature in Africa* (Oxford University Press, Oxford, 1970); L. A. Boadi, "The Language of the Proverb," in Richard M. Dorson (ed.), *African Folklore* (Doubleday, New York, 1972), pp. 183–91.
16. For example, Abraham, Chap. 2; William Bascom, "Folklore and Literature in the African World," in Robert A. Lystad (ed.), *A Survey of Social Research* (Praeger, New York, 1965).
17. J. B. Danquah, *The Akan Doctrine of God* (Lutterworth Press, London, 1944), passim.
18. Abraham, *The Mind of Africa*, passim.
19. It is interesting to note that in Nzema, another prominent language in Ghana, the word for proverb is *erele* and the word for palm tree is *arele*. I owe this observation to Dr. I Chinebuah of the Institute of African Studies, University of Ghana, Legon.
20. Mbiti, p. 2; my italics.

21. Bascom, p. 483; my italics.
22. Finnegan, p. 399; my italics.
23. Abraham, p. 106.
24. *A Source Book in Chinese Philosophy*, comp. and trans. Wing Tsit Chen (Princeton University Press, Princeton, 1963), Chap. 2.
25. I have learned, however, that a few of the proverbs, particularly those of recent creation, have ascertainable individual origins. Such proverbs start thus: *"Nana Osei Bonsu a ofi Dwaben na obuu ne bē sē . . ."* (that is, "Nana Osei Bonsu of Dwaben created or uttered the following proverb . . .").
26. For example, some of the works of the Greek–Alexandrian philosophers edited in the series *Commentaria in Aristotelem Graeca*, Typis et impensis Georgii Reimeri, Berlin, 1882–1909. See Kwame Gyekye, *Arabic Logic: Ibn al-Tayyib's Commentary on Porphyry's Eisagoge* (State University of New York Press, Albany, 1979), p. 220, nn. 32 and 33.
27. Where authorship is in doubt, the word "pseudo" is sometimes placed before the name of the supposed author, as in pseudo-Plutarch, pseudo-Elias, etc.
28. G. S. Kirk, *Heraclitus: The Cosmic Fragments* (Cambridge University Press, Cambridge, 1954), p. 30; Philip E. Wheelwright, *Heraclitus* (Princeton University Press, Princeton, 1959), pp. 17, 30.
29. E. Duprée, "L'Aristote et la Traité des Catégories," *Archiv für Geschichte der Philosphie*, 1909, Vol. 22, pp. 230–51.; S. Mansion, "La doctrine Aristotéliciènne de la Substance et la Traité des Catégories," *Proceedings of the Tenth International Congress of Philosophy* (North-Holland Amsterdam 1949), Vol. 1, pp. 1099–100.
30. I have worked with Arabic MSS. myself. See Kwame Gyekye, *Ibn al-Tayyib's Commentary on Porphyry's Eisogoge*, Arabic text (Dar al-Mashreq, Beirut, 1975), pp. xxvi–xxxi.
31. Khalil Georr, "Fārābī est-il l'auteur, des Fuṣūṣ al-Ḥikma?" *Revue des études islamiques*, 1941–6, pp. 31–9.
32. S. Pines, "Ibn sīnā et l'auteur de la Risālāt al-Fusús fi'l-ḥikma," *Revue des études islamiques*, 1951, pp. 122–4.
33. E. Gilson, *History of Christian Philosophy in the Middle Ages* (Random House, New York, 1954), p. 185.
34. P. T. Raju, *Philosophical Traditions of India*, p. 35; also p. 45.
35. Ibid., p. 36.
36. Kirk, p. ix.
37. Ibid., p. 7; my italics.
38. W. K. C. Guthrie, *A History of Greek Philosophy* (Cambridge University Press, Cambridge, 1962), Vol. I, p. 407.
39. Wheelwright, p. 12; my italics.
40. Ibid., pp. 19, 29.

41. Paulin J. Hountondji, *African Philosophy, Myth and Reality*, trans. Henri Evans (Indiana University Press, Bloomington, 1983), pp. 51, 55.
42. Ibid., p. 60.
43. Ibid., p. 49.
44. Ibid., p. 59.
45. Ibid., p. 61.
46. Aristotle, *Metaphysics*, 983^{b}20 – 984^{a}4.
47. W. K. C. Guthrie, *In the Beginning* (London, 1957), pp. 61–2; F. M. Cornford, *From Religion to Philosophy* (Harper & Row, New York, 1957), p. 4.
48. F. M. Cornford, *The Unwritten Philosophy and Other Essays* (Cambridge University Press, Cambridge, 1950), pp. 10–18.
49. Ibid., p. 12.
50. Quoted by W. K. C. Guthrie, *The Greek Philosophers: From Thales to Aristotle* (Methuen, London, 1967), p. 11; my italics.
51. Bertrand Russell, *A History of Western Philosophy* (Allen and Unwin, London, 1961), p. 7; my italics.
52. Ibid., 11th paperback printing, (Simon & Schuster, New York, 1965), p. ix; my italics.
53. Ibid., p. 174.
54. Aristotle, *Nicomachean Ethics*, 1095^{a}28–9.
55. Aristotle, *De Anima*, Book 3, 430^{a}10–18.
56. W. F. R. Hardie, *Aristotle's Ethical Theory* (Oxford University Press, Oxford, 1968), p. 123.
57. T. Okere, "The Relation between Culture and Philosophy," *UCHE, Journal of the Department of Philosophy*, University of Nigeria, Nsukka, Vol. 2, 1976, p. 8.
58. See, for example, G. E. R. Lloyd, *Aristotle: The Growth and Structure of His Thought* (Cambridge University Press, Cambridge, 1968), p. 114; Russell, p. 202; William Kneale and Martha Kneale, *The Development of Logic* (Oxford University Press, Oxford, 1962), p. 27.
59. Mauthner, *Kritik der Sprache*, quoted in Stephen Ullman, *The Principles of Semantics* (Jackson, Son & Co., Glasgow, 1951), p. 21, and C. K. Ogden and I. A. Richards, *The Meaning of Meaning* (Routledge and Kegan Paul, London, 1949), p. 35, n. 1.
60. Manfred Sandman, *Subject and Predicate: A Contribution to the Theory of Syntax* (Edinburgh University Press, Edinburgh, 1954), pp. 13–14.
61. Aristotle, *Metaphysics*, 1028^{a}20–8; see Kwame Gyekye, "Aristotle and a Modern Notion of Predication," *Notre Dame Journal of Formal Logic*, Vol. XV, No. 4, Oct. 1974, pp. 615–18.
62. G. C. Field, *Moral Theory: An Introduction to Ethics* (Methuen, London, 1921), p. 68.
63. Ibid.

64. J. L. Austin, *Philosophical Papers* (Oxford University Press, Oxford, 1961), p. 130; my italics.
65. Alexis Kagame, *La philosophie Bantu-Rwandaise de l'être* (Brussels, 1956).
66. Mbiti, Chap. 3.
67. See Muhsin Mahdi, "Language and Logic in Classical Islam," in G. E. von Grunebaum (ed.), *Logic in Classical Islamic Culture* (Wiesbaden, 1970) and my review in the *Journal of the American Oriental Society*, Vol. 92, no. 1, pp. 100–2.
68. *Second International Conference of Negro Writers and Artists*, Rome, March 25–April 1, 1959 (Présence Africaine, Paris, 1954), p. 441; my italics.
69. W. E. Abraham, "The Life and Times of Anton Wilhelm Amo," *Transactions of the Historical Society of Ghana*, Vol. VII, 1964, pp. 60–81.
70. Kwasi Wiredu, "How Not to Compare African Thought with Western Thought," in Richard A. Wright (ed.), *African Philosophy: An Introduction* (University Press of America, Washington, D.C., 1977), pp. 166–82; rpt. in Kwasi Wiredu, *Philosophy and an African Culture* (Cambridge University Press, Cambridge, England, 1980), Chap. 3.
71. Ibid., Wright, p. 179; Wiredu, *Philosophy and an African Culture*, p. 48.
72. Ibid., Wright, p. 180; Wiredu, pp. 48–9; my italics.
73. Ibid., Wright, p. 181; Wiredu, p. 49.
74. P. O. Bodunrin, "The Question of African Philosophy," *Philosophy*, Vol. LVI, 1981, p. 162.
75. The members of that school, according to Bodunrin, p. 163, are notably Wiredu of Ghana, Oruka of Kenya, Hountondji of the Republic of Benin (Dahomey), and himself.
76. Ibid., p. 162.
77. Ibid., p. 169; my italics.
78. Hountondji, p. 62.
79. Ibid., p. 65.
80. Ibid., pp. 53–4.
81. Ibid., p. 66.
82. Modern African philosophers who want to tether the nature and content of African philosophy to Western philosophical categories would gleefully cite the alleged beginnings of philosophy in Islam to buttress their view and to salve their philosophical consciences.
83. Majid Fakhry, *A History of Islamic Philosophy* (Columbia University Press, New York, 1970), p. 40.
84. Gyekye, *Arabic Logic*, pp. 1–7.
85. David Sidorsky, "Shifts in the Pragmatic Scene: From the Real to the True to the Good," *Humanities*, Vol. V, No. 2, April 1984, p. 7; my italics.

86. Kwasi Wiredu, "On an African Orientation in Philosophy," *Second Order*, Vol. 1, No. 2, July 1972, p. 7.
87. Wiredu in Wright, p. 181.
88. Wiredu, *Philosophy and an African Culture*, p. 6.
89. Wiredu, "Philosophy and Our Culture," *Proceedings of the Ghana Academy of Arts and Sciences*, 1977, p. 52; my italics.
90. J. Raz, "Principles of Equality," *Mind*, Vol. LXXXVII, 1978, p. 321, writes: *"The starting point* [i.e., of his thesis] is the *existence within the western cultural heritage of an egalitarian tradition"*; my italics.
91. A. C. Ewing, "Philosophy in India," *Philosophy*, Vol. XXVI, July 1951, p. 263; my italics.

3. Methodological problems

1. Robin Horton, "Traditional Thought and the Emerging African Philosophy Department: A Comment on the Current Debate," *Second Order*, Vol. VI, No. 1, January 1977, p. 64; Robin Horton in Bryan R. Wilson (ed.), *Rationality* (Basil Blackwell, Oxford, 1974), pp. 153–5.
2. Horton, "Traditional Thought," p. 68.
3. Horton in Wilson (ed.), *Rationality*, p. 153. In his most recent article bearing on this question, Horton has revised some of his earlier views. In the face of better arguments and overwhelming evidence produced by others, he now abandons his characterizations of African thought as "closed" and Western thought as "open," acknowledging that "such a contrast *does not* do justice either to the African or to the Western subject–matter" [R. Horton, "Tradition and Modernity Revisited," in Martin Hollis and Steven Luked (eds.), *Rationality and Relativism* (MIT Press, Cambridge, Mass., 1984), p. 211; italics in original].
4. D. Gjertsen, "Closed and Open Belief Systems," *Second Order*, Vol. VII, Nos. 1 and 2, 1978, pp. 51–69.
5. Daryll Forde (ed.), *African Worlds* (Oxford University Press, Oxford, 1954), p. vii; my italics.
6. R. Horton, "Tradition and Modernity Revisited," p. 227.
7. Kwasi Wiredu, "The Akan Concept of Mind," *Ibadan Journal of Humanistic Studies*, in press.
8. R. S. Rattray, *Religion and Art in Ashanti* (Oxford University Press, Oxford, 1927), p. 155 et passim.
9. E. L. R. Meyerowitz, "Concepts of the Soul among the Akan of the Gold Coast," *Africa*, Vol. XXI, No. 1, January 1951.
10. I say "we" because on this occasion, 17 July 1976, my colleague Prof. Kwasi Wiredu accompanied me, and the two of us listened to Nana Boafo-Ansah of Akropong-Akuapem.

11. D. M. Warren and J. K. Andrews, *An Ethnoscientific Approach to Akan Arts and Aesthetics* (Institute for the Study of Human Issues, Philadelphia, 1937), p. 11; my italics.
12. Robert F. Thompson, "Yoruba Artistic Criticism," in Warren L. d'Azevedo (ed.), *The Traditional Artist in African Societies* (Indiana University Press, Bloomington, 1973), p. 19; my italics.
13. E. L. R. Meyerowitz, *The Sacred State of the Akan* (Faber and Faber, London, 1951), p. 85.
14. E. G. Parrinder, *West African Psychology* (Lutterworth Press, London, 1951), p. 207.
15. I refer to the traditional wise elders with whom I discussed Akan thought as discussants rather than as "informants."
16. A discussion of Quine's thesis of the radical indeterminacy of translation [W. V. O. Quine, *Word and Object* (MIT Press, Cambridge, Mass., 1960), Chap. 2] is not relevant here, as Quine believes the indeterminancy problem to be both translingual *and* intralingual, involving, that is, our understanding both of *our* own language as well as that of others.
17. P. T. Raju, *Philosophical Traditions of India*, p. 36.

II. The Akan conceptual scheme

4. The Akan conception of philosophy

1. J. G. Christaller, *Dictionary of the Asante and Fante Language Called Twi*, 2d ed. (Basel, 1933); Jack Berry, *English, Twi, Asante, Fante Dictionary* (London, 1960).
2. Interview with Oheneba Kwabena Bekoe, Akropong-Akuapem, 30 July 1976.
3. However, a person may seek to become *wiser* because the *sunsum* is thought to be developable; see section 9.2.
4. In Arabic, for instance, the original word for philosophy, *hikma*, means wisdom (in Persian, *hekmat*). The word *falsafa*, used in some philosophical works in Arabic and Persian, is an obvious transliteration of the Greek *philosophia*. For "philosophy" the Romance languages used variations on the Latin *philosophia* (itself from the Greek).
5. Interview with Oheneba Kwabena Bekoe.
6. Interview with Oheneba Kwabena Bekoe.
7. Christaller, *Dictionary*.
8. Liddell and Scott, *Greek–English Lexicon*, 9th ed. (Clarendon, Oxford, 1940).
9. Kwasi Wiredu, *Philosophy and an African Culture* (Cambridge University Press, Cambridge, 1980), p. 16.

5. Concepts of being and causality

1. R. S. Rattray, *Religion and Art in Ashanti* (Oxford University Press, Oxford, 1927), p. 70.

2. I think it better to call the *abosom* "lesser spirits" rather than "spirits" (as we have it in many books), since Onyame (God) too is a spirit, albeit the Absolute Spirit. I use "deity" synonymously with "lesser spirit" or "god." Asase Yaa, the Earth goddess invoked in the libation prayer is, I think, regarded as one of the *abosom*. I doubt whether she is considered as holding a special place in relation to Onyame. A reader of a draft of this book opined that "Asase Yaa's status in relation to Onyame is understood as modeled on the relation of a chief to his Queen-mother; just as Christ's relation to God is modeled on the relationship of son to father." The reader thought that Asase Yaa is not a "nature spirit" (lesser spirit). However, Asase Yaa does not appear to me to be a special daughter of Onyame.

3. There are a number of interpretations of the etymology of the word "Onyame," and I do not intend to add to them. Suffice it to say that it is the word used by the Akan people to refer to the highest being in their religious universe. On these etymologies of Onyame, see the analysis of Kwesi Dickson in his introduction to J. B. Danquah, *The Akan Doctrine of God*, 2d ed. (Frank Cass, London, 1968).

4. Danquah, p. 30.

5. This name of Onyame has been variously interpreted. The list of meanings here is Danquah's (pp. 56–69) which was confirmed during my own researches. See also J. G. Christaller, *Dictionary*, p. 90.

6. Danquah, p. 55. Thus, Nana Osei Bonsu (d. 1976), a famous Kumasi carver, said to me in a discourse on Onyame (10 January 1974): *obi nnim n'ahyēase ne n'awiei* (no one knows Onyame's beginning and his end).

7. Danquah, p. 55.

8. Interview with J. A. Annobil of Cape Coast, 2 September 1976.

9. This name of God (Onayme) is considered, wrongly, by Danquah, pp. 47 and 200, to mean "the ever-ready shooter." Danquah's misinterpretation follows from his reading the word as *atoapoma*. I accept Okyeame Akuffo Boafo of Akropong-Akuapem's interpretation (interview: 8 July 1974) that the word is *atoapem*, a word that cannot be rendered straightforwardly in English. Etymologically, the word consists of two parts, *ato* and *apem*. *Ato* means to come to, to reach; and *apem* means the end or cutoff point, the stop point of anything or any action. *Atoapem*, then, means "that which is reached finally," "that beyond which you cannot go," "an unsurpassable

Notes to p. 70
Notes to p. 70

point or thing." Christaller (*Dictionary*, p. 384) says *apem* means (among other things) to reach; he translates the sentence *asēm apem* as "it has come to an end." Thus the temporal word *daa-apem* (or *daapem*, as it is usually written) means "the end of the days." As applied to Onyame (God), the word *atoapem* may correctly be translated as Ultimate or Final; that beyond which nothing else is, perhaps implying that beyond which nothing greater is.

10. That the Akan people originally held this conception of God cannot seriously be doubted. Yet, because the Akan (or, for that matter, African) idea of God was comparable to, or had affinity with, that held by adherents of other (non-African) religions, European writers of the nineteenth century generally thought that the African idea of God was an importation, presumably from Europe. However, William Bossman, a traveler to West Africa about the end of the seventeenth century, observed that West Africans believed in a supreme God: "They have a faint idea of the true God, and ascribe to Him the attributes of Almighty and Omnipresent; they believe He created the universe, and therefore vastly prefer Him before their idol-gods; but they do not pray to Him, or offer sacrifices to Him" (William Bossman, *A New and Accurate Description of the Coasts of Guinea, Divided into the Gold, the Slave and the Ivory Coasts*, 1705, p. 348; quoted in E. G. Parrinder, *West African Religion*, p. 14).

Elaborate and painstaking research by contemporary scholars (including anthropologists, theologians, and missionaries) clearly indicate the autochthonous origin of the African idea of the Supreme Being. Smith noted that "It is the general testimony of pioneer missionaries that they have discovered some belief in the existence of God among the Africans" (Edwin W. Smith, ed., *African Ideas of God. A Symposium*, Edinburgh House Press, London, 1950, p. 33). Writing specifically on "The Akan Doctrine of God," Rev. H. St. John T. Evans, observed: "Evidence is now available to demonstrate that the roots of the belief in Nyame are buried in the remote past" (ibid., p. 245). See also Edwin W. Smith, *The Secret of the African*, United Society for Christian Literature, London, 1929, Chaps. 4–6 on "The African's Awareness of God." "Missionaries have found, often to their surprise," wrote Parrinder, "that they did not need to argue for the existence of God, or faith in a life after death, *for both these fundamentals of world religion are deeply rooted in Africa*" (E. G. Parrinder, *Religion in Africa*, Penguin Books, Harmondsworth, 1969, p. 39; my italics). Thus, "God was there [that is, in Africa] before the arrival of the gospel of Jesus Christ . . . The Africans had already identified Him," observed Malcolm J. McVeigh (in *God in Africa*, Claude Stark, Cape Cod, Mass., 1974, p. 24). The Akan, living in the deep forests of the hinterland, well knew of God prior to the arrival of Christian missionaries; thus the Akan proverb "No one teaches God to a child" (*Obi nkyerɛ abɔfra 'Nyame*). Symbols on the ancient gold-dust weights and on other forms of art, myths, proverbs, and the drum language make references to the Supreme Being (Onyame, in Akan), attesting the antiquity of the Akan conception of God.

11. Interview with Okyeame Akuffo of Akropong-Akuapem (8 July 1974): *biribiara fi Onyame na ewie 'Nyame.*
12. Here I am drawing on Kofi Asare Opoku's "Aspects of Akan Worship," in C. Eric Lincoln (ed.), *The Black Experience in Religion* (Doubleday, New York, 1974), pp. 297–8.
13. Kofi Antuban, *Ghana's Heritage of Culture* (Koehler and Amalang, Leipzig, 1963), pp. 159–60.
14. E. G. Parrinder, *West African Religion* (Epworth Press, London, 1961), p. 12.
15. John S. Mbiti, *African Religions and Philosophy* (Doubleday, New York, 1970) p. 257.
16. K. A. Busia, "The Ashanti of the Gold Coast," in Daryll Forde (ed.), *African Worlds* (Oxford University Press, Oxford, 1954), p. 191. The Ashantis are a subsection of the Akans. Busia's description of Onyame as "the Great Spirit" agrees with my own.
17. See Parrinder, *West African Religion*, p. 12.
18. R. S. Rattray, *Ashanti* (Oxford University Press, Oxford, 1923), p. 86.
19. Ibid., p. 212.
20. Rattray, *Religion and Art in Ashanti*, p. 23.
21. K. A. Opoku and K. A. Ampom-Darkwa, *Akom ho nkommobo (Kwaku Mframa)* (Institute of African Studies, Legon, Accra, 1969).
22. Helaine K. Minkus, "Causal Theory in Akwapim Akan Philosophy," in Richard A. Wright (ed.), *African Philosophy: An Introduction* (University Press of American, Washington, D.C., 1977), p. 136.
23. The concept of transcendence is implicit in a well-known Akan myth in which Onyame removes himself far from the world of human beings as the result of the ungenerous act of an old woman.
24. See Kwame Gyekye, "Al-Ghazālī on Causation," *Second Order*, Vol. II, No. 1, January 1973, pp. 31–9.
25. Parrinder, p. 12.
26. Another version of this proverb is "What Onyame has arranged (fixed), living man cannot alter."
27. Antubam, p. 165, proverb no.78.
28. C. A. Akrofi, *Twi Proverbs* (Waterville Publishing House, Accra, n.d.). This proverb was created as a result of events in the history of the Assin and Adanse people of the Akans.
29. The analysis of the Akan notion of causality presented here bears

close resemblance to Evans-Pritchard's discussion of the explanation of events among the Azande; see E. E. Evans-Pritchard, *Witchcraft, Oracles, and Magic Among the Azande* (Clarendon Press, Oxford, 1937), pp. 63–80.

30. K. A. Busia, *The Position of the Chief in the Modern Political System of Ashanti* (New Impression, London, 1968), p. 24; my italics.
31. I must say that why–questions are not unique to African thinking about causation. Western people, too, occasionally resort to them, even though they are supposed to be wedded to what are called scientific explanations. Occasionally, a Westerner may have difficulty in avoiding why–questions. A woman who believes she is on the brink of being raped, robbed by violence, or murdered may shout, "Oh God, *why me?*" A man who has been postponing his flight because of bad weather, but whose aircraft is about to crash on landing on the day he finally decides to travel, may shout, "*Why today?*" One hears or reads of such why–questions, and one wonders why, on such occasions, why$_1$-questions, to which Western people are said to be accustomed, give way to why$_2$-questions.
32. K. A. Busia, *The Challenge of Africa*, p. 20; my italics.
33. Among the translations of *kwa* (*ōkwa*) in J. G. Christaller's *Dictionary* are the following: without design, without cause, gratuitously, for nothing, to no purpose.
34. On the concepts of destiny (*nkrabea*) and accident (*asiane*), see Chapter 7.
35. Thus, the word *kra*, which forms part of the word *akrade* (luck, fortune), means "soul"; see Chapter 6.

6. The concept of a person

1. I say "a conception" because I believe there are other conceptions of the person held or discernible in that philosophy (see above, pp. 47, 55).
2. Kwasi Wiredu, "The Akan Concept of Mind," *Ibadan Journal of Humanistic Studies*, in press, p. 9. The page references are to the typescript.
3. Ibid., p. 10; my italics.
4. Wiredu, "The Akan Concept of Mind," p. 9.
5. Ibid.
6. Ibid., p. 19.
7. Bernard Williams, *Descartes: The Project of Pure Enquiry* (Pelican Books London, 1978), p. 78; also, *Descartes, Philosophical Writings*, trans. and ed. Elizabeth Anscombe and Peter T. Geach (Edinburgh University Press, Edinburgh, 1954), p. xxxvii, n. 2, and p. xvii.
8. Wiredu, "The Akan Concept of Mind," p. 19.

9. K. A. Busia, "The Ashanti of the Gold Coast," in Daryll Forde (ed.), *African Worlds*, p. 197; M. Fortes, *Kinship and the Social Order* (University of Chicago Press, Chicago, 1969), p. 199, n. 14; Robert A. Lystad, *The Ashanti, A Proud People* (Rutgers University Press, New Brunswick, N.J., 1958), p. 155; Peter K. Sarpong, *Ghana in Retrospect: Some Aspects of the Ghanaian Culture* (Ghana Publishing Corp., Accra, 1974), p. 37.

10. Busia, p. 197; Lystad, p. 155; E. L. R. Meyerowitz, *The Sacred State of the Akan* (Faber and Faber, London, 1951), p. 86; and "Concepts of the Soul among the Akan," *Africa*, p. 26.

11. Busia, p. 197; Lystad, p. 155; P. A. Twumasi, *Medical Systems in Ghana* (Ghana Publishing Corp., Accra, 1975), p. 22.

12. Here the views of W. E. Abraham are excepted, for he maintains, like I do, that the *sunsum* is not "inheritable" and that it "appears to have been a spiritual substance." W. E. Abraham, *The Mind of Africa* (University of Chicago Press, Chicago, 1962), p. 60.

13. J. B. Danquah, *The Akan Doctrine of God* (Lutterworth Press, London, 1944), p. 115.

14. Ibid., p. 116.

15. Busia, p. 197; also p. 200.

16. Danquah, p. 66.

17. Ibid., e.g., pp. 67, 75, 83, 205.

18. R. S. Rattray, *Ashanti*, p. 46.

19. E. L. R. Meyerowitz, *The Akan of Ghana, Their Ancient Beliefs* (Faber and Faber, London, 1958), pp. 98, 150, and 146; also her *Sacred State*, p. 86.

20. Busia, p. 197.

21. Corliss Lamont, *The Philosophy of Humanism* (Ungar, New York, 1974), pp. 81–95. Malcolm J. McVeigh, *God in Africa* (Calude Stark, Cape Cod, Massachusetts, 1974), pp. 26, 37.

22. E. G. Parrinder, *West African Psychology*, pp. 32, 46, 70.

23. Danquah, p. 67.

24. Ibid., p. 67.

25. Ibid., p. 112.

26. Ibid., pp. 66–7, 115.

27. Busia, p. 200.

28. Ibid., p. 197.

29. R. S. Rattray, *Religion and Art in Ashanti*, p. 154.

30. E. E. Evans-Pritchard, *Witchcraft, Oracles and Magic among the Azande*, p. 136; also E. G. Parrinder, *West African Religion*, p. 197.

31. Parrinder, *West African Religion*, p. 197.

32. Plato, *The Republic*, 571^c, beginning of Book IX.

33. James Adam (ed.), *The Republic of Plato*, 2d ed. (Cambridge University Press, Cambridge, 1975), Vol. 2, p. 320.

34. Plato, *The Republic*, ed. and trans. by Paul Shorey (Loeb Classical Library, Harvard University Press, Cambridge, Mass., 1935), p. 335.

35. Plato, *The Republic*, trans. by A.D. Lindsay (J. M. Dent, London, 1976), p. 346.

36. Thomas Gould, *Platonic Love* (Routledge and Kegan Paul, London, 1963), p. 108ff and p. 174ff.

37. Charles W. Valentine, *Dreams and the Unconscious* (Methuen, London, 1921), p. 93; also his *The New Psychology of the Unconscious* (Macmillan, New York, 1929), p. 95.

38. Wilfred Trotter, *Instincts of the Herd in Peace and War* (T. F. Unwin, London, 1916), p. 74.

39. H. Debrunner, *Witchcraft in Ghana* (Waterville Publishing House, Accra, 1959), p. 17.

40. Mbiti, *African Religions and Philosophy*, p. 102.

41. Busia, p. 197; also K. A. Busia, *The Position of the Chief in the Modern Political System of Ashanti*, p. 1.

42. Rattray, *Ashanti*, pp. 1, 45, 46, 48.

43. Rattray, *Religion and Art*, p. 319.

44. Interview with Opanin Twum Barimah, Kibi, 17 August 1974.

45. All three proverbs refer to the idea of giving birth (*awo*) and the belief that offsprings take on the characteristics of their parents. All the three seek to assert resemblance between parents and offsprings in respect of their characteristics. The first proverb means that the characteristics of the offspring of the crab will (have to) be those *of* the crab and not those of the bird, and the proverb is uttered when someone is utterly convinced of the character resemblances between a child and its parent(s). The other two proverbs must be understood in the same way. All such character resemblances are, according to Akan thinkers, attributable to the *ntoro*. The postulation of *ntoro* therefore is intended to answer questions about resemblances – particularly character resemblances (not so much physical resemblances) – between children and their parents.

46. Rattray, *Religion and Art* p. 154.

47. Ibid., p. 318, Soul-washing is a symbolic religious rite meant to cleanse and purify the soul from defilement. "This cult," wrote Mrs. Meyerowitz, "adjures the person to lead a good and decent life." *Sacred State*, p. 117; also p. 88.

48. Barima Aboagye-Agyeman, "God, Man and Destiny: Some Akan Metaphysical Ideas," 1976, undergraduate thesis, Department of Philosophy, University of Ghana, Legon, Ghana, p. 22; my italics.

49. Ibid., p. 25.

50. Incidentally, the "identity theory" immediately subverts any physical conception of the *sunsum*, since the *ɔkra* (soul), with which it is

being identified, is generally agreed to be a spiritual, not a physical, entity.

51. Rattray, *Religion and Art*, p. 154.
52. The dynamic and active character of the *sunsum* has given rise to metaphorical use as in the sentences, "there is 'spirit' in the game" (*agoro yi sunsum wɔ mu*), "the arrival of the chief brought 'spirit' into the festival celebration." Not long ago the dynamism, action and energy of a late Ghanaian army general earned him the by-name of "Sunsum!" among his soldiers.
53. Lystad, p. 158.
54. See Kwame Gyekye, "The Akan Concept of a Person," *International Philosophical Quarterly*, Vol. XVIII, No. 3, September 1978, p. 284.
55. This view was expressed also to Meyerowitz, *Sacred State*, p. 84.
56. See Kwame Gyekye, "An Examination of the Bundle Theory of Substance," *Philosophy and Phenomenological Research*, Vol. XXXIV, No. 1, September, 1973.
57. Busia, *The Challenge of Africa*, p. 19.
58. Sigmund Freud, *New Introductory Lectures on Psychoanalysis* (Penguin, Harmondsworth, 1973), pp. 101–2.
59. For example, Meyerowitz, *Sacred State*, p. 84, "Concepts of the Soul," p. 26; H. Debrunner, *Witchcraft in Ghana*, p. 15.
60. Freud, p. 92.

7. Destiny, free will, and responsibility

1. *Wɔabɔ wo dɛ ibenya adze a, wo 'kra nnkyir pɛtɛ.* J. A. Annobil (interview, 31 August 1976, Cape Coast) explained the proverb thus: the vulture is believed to be a sign of misfortune, and yet it cannot be an impediment to the person who is destined to be fortunate.
2. K. Wiredu, "Philosophy and Our Culture," *Proceedings of the Ghana Academy of Arts and Sciences*, Vol. XV, 1977, p. 48; my italics.
3. Interview with Nana Osei-Bonsu of Kumasi, 8–11 January, 1974.
4. The first use of "head" (*ti*) refers to the physical head, the second to the *soul*, the bearer of destiny.
5. Corliss Lamont, *The Philosophy of Humanism*, pp. 13, 109.
6. Interview with J. A. Annobil (*abrabɔ no mu na yehu sɛ nkrabea bi wɔ hɔ*).
7. Interview with Oheneba Kwabena Bekoe of Akropong-Akuapem, 30 July 1976: (*nkrabea no yi ne ho adi pefee wɔ abrabɔ mu*).
8. Interview with J. A. Annobil, 1 September 1976.
9. Akan proverbs are ultimately about mankind, its life, its conception of the universe, etc., although nonhumans such as animals, trees, rivers, also figure in the language of the proverb.
10. Peter K. Sarpong, *Ghana in Retrospect*, p. 38; my italics.

11. J. G. Christaller, *Dictionary of the Asante and Fante Language Called Shi (Twi)*, p. 262.
12. E. L. R. Meyerowitz, "Concepts of the Soul among the Akan," p. 24.
13. J. B. Danquah, *Akan Doctrine of God*, p. 202.
14. Christaller, *Dictionary*, p. 262.
15. For example, George P. Hagan, in conversation; see his "Some Aspects of Akan Philosophy." M.A. thesis, University of Ghana, Legon, 1964. Kwesi A. Dickson, *Aspects of Religion and Life in Africa* (Ghana Academy of Arts and Sciences, Accra, 1977), p. 7.
16. For all these expressions and their meanings, see Christaller, *Dictionary*.
17. George P. Hagan, M.A. thesis, see note 15 above.
18. Interview with Oheneba Kwabena Bekoe of Akropong-Akuaem, 30 July 1976.
19. Interview with A. A. Opoku, Aburi, 16 July 1975.
20. E. L. R. Meyerowitz, *The Sacred State of the Akan*, p. 87.
21. Meyerowitz, "Concepts of the Soul," pp. 26–7.
22. Danquah, p. 122.
23. Ibid., p. 112.
24. Ibid., p. 86.
25. Of course for one who believes that "*sunsum*" and "*ōkra*" refer to the same thing, this objection would not apply, but Danquah is not such a one.
26. Peter K. Sarpong, "Aspects of Akan Ethics," *Ghana Bulletin of Theology*, Vol. IV, No. 3, December 1972, p. 42.
27. Ibid.
28. Sarpong, *Ghana in Retrospect*, pp. 37–8.
29. Helaine Minkus, "Causal Theory in Akwapim Akan Philosophy," in Richard A. Wright (ed.), *African Philosophy: An Introduction*, 2d ed. (University Press of America, Washington, D.C., 1979), p. 118.
30. This myth is in K. A. Busia, "The Ashanti of the Gold Coast," p. 193; Rattray, *Ashanti Proverbs*, pp. 476–7; Rattray, *Ashanti*, p. 146.
31. Rattray, *Ashanti*, p. 146.
32. Interviews with Opanin Apenkwa, Keeper of the Shrine, Ghana National Cultural Centre, Kumasi, 6 September 1974, and Kronti-hene Boafo-Ansah of Akropong-Akuapem, 17 July 1976.
33. Sarpong, "Aspects," p. 42.
34. Kofi A. Opoku, "The Destiny of Man in Akan Traditional Religious Thought," in *Conch*, Vol. VII, Nos. 1 and 2, 1975, pp. 21 ff.
35. G. W. Leibniz, *Discourse on Metaphysics: Correspondence with Arnauld and Monadology*, trans. G. R. Montgomery (Open Court, La Salle, Ill., 1968), pp. 19–20.
36. K. Wiredu, "Philosophy and Our Culture," p. 46; my italics.
37. Ibid., p. 47.

38. K. A. Dickson, *Aspects of Religion and Life in Africa*, p. 9.
39. Kofi Antubam, *Ghana's Heritage of Culture*, p. 44; my italics.
40. Interview with J. A. Annobil of Cape Coast, 1 September 1976.
41. Akrofi comments: this proverb is "used in showing that every human being has a special talent." C. A. Akrofi, *Twi Proverbs*, proverb no. 791.
42. Interview with some elders in Pano, near Kibi, 12 August 1974.
43. Busia, "The African World-View," p. 148; my italics.
44. Interview with the Ankobeahene of Kibi, 15 August 1974.
45. Interview in Apapam, near Kibi, 16 August 1974.
46. Interview with Nana Dawson of Cape Coast, 4 September 1976.
47. Interview with Opanin Kofi Adu of Asikam, near Kibi, 13 August 1974.
48. Interview with Oheneba Kwabena Bekoe of Akropong-Akuapem, 6 August 1976.
49. Interview with J. A. Annobil, 3 September 1976: "Evil comes from man's will" (*bɔne fi onipa ne pɛ*).

8. Foundations of ethics

1. Kofi A. Opoku, "Aspects of Akan Worship," in C. Eric Lincoln (ed.), *The Black Experience in Religion* (Doubleday, New York, 1974), p. 286.
2. Kofi A. Opoku, *West African Traditional Religion* (FEP International Private Ltd., Singapore, 1978), p. 152; my italics.
3. Peter K. Sarpong, "Aspects of Akan Ethics," p. 41.
4. K. A. Busia, *Africa in Search of Democracy* (Praeger, New York, 1967), p. 10; my italics. See also p. 16.
5. J. B. Danquah, *Akan Doctrine of God*, p. 3. It must be pointed out, however, that Danquah presents ambivalent views about the basis of moral values in Akan thought, for four paragraphs before this statement he writes: "Tradition is the determinant of what is right and just, what is good and done."
6. Ibid., p. 27.
7. J. N. Kudadjie, "Does Religion Determine Morality in African Societies?–A Viewpoint," *Ghana Bulletin of Theology*, Vol. III, No. 5, December 1973, p. 47.
8. E. G. Parrinder, *Religion in Africa*, pp. 28–9.
9. Interview with Opanin Afoakwa of Aheneasi, near Kibi, 30 July 1974.
10. Interview at Apapan village, near Kibi, 15 August 1974.
11. Interview with J. A. Annobil of Cape Coast, 3 September 1976.
12. Ibid.; interview with Krotihene Boafo-Ansah of Akropong-Akuapem, 6 August 1976.

13. Interview with Oheneba Kwabena Bekoe of Akropong-Akuapem, 6 August 1976.

14. Interview with Opanin Kofi Adu of Asikam, near Kibi, 13 August 1974.

15. Interviews with Opanin Afoakwa, 18 August 1974; Opanin Apenkwa, Keeper of the Shrine, Ghana National Cultural Centre, Kumasi, 4 September 1974.

16. I find it puzzling that the word *musuo* never occurs in the writings of R. S. Rattray, whereas *akyiwade* (taboos) does occur in several places, taboos being 'things especially abhorred by the gods,' Rattray, *Ashanti*, pp. 146, 167, 171, etc.; *Religion and Art in Ashanti*, p. 52. I cannot find any good explanation for the complete absence of the word *musuo* in Rattray. It is not at all probable that he did not come across it during decades of his research. It is conjecturable, however, that he may have assimilated *musuo* to the taboos, and so used the word *akyiwade* to cover both *musuo* and *akyiwade* (taboos). Such an assimilation, however, would be an error.

17. There are indeed some taboos which are nonmoral. These include (1) religious taboos such as that "clients of certain deities may not eat certain food, twins may not eat certain food," etc., and (2) less serious, perhaps naive, ones such as the prohibition to sing when you are bathing or eating. Peter K. Sarpong, *Ghana in Retrospect*, p. 54.

18. Sarpong, *Ghana in Retrospect*, p. 58.

19. Ibid., p. 57.

20. J. B. Danquah, "Obligation in Akan Society," *West African Affairs*, No. 8, 1952, p. 3.

21. See, for example, Kai Nielsen, "Some Remarks on the Independence of Morality from Religion," in Ian T. Ramsey (ed.), *Christian Ethics and Contemporary Philosophy* (SCM Press, London, 1966); Peter T. Geach, *God and the Soul* (Routledge and Kegan Paul, London, 1969), Chap. 9.

22. Kofi Antubam, *Ghana's Heritage of Culture*, p. 46.

23. *Fufu* is a local meal. A one armed person cannot prepare it, for its preparation requires the use of two hands. The real meaning of this proverb, as of the next, is that God mercifully satisfies the needs of people, helping them in pursuits which may otherwise appear impossible.

24. J. B. Danquah, *Akan Doctrine of God*, p. 55.

25. K. A. Busia, "The Ashanti of the Gold Coast," p. 205; my italics.

26. W.E. Abraham, *The Mind of Africa*, pp. 56–57; my italics.

27. Busia, "The Ashanti of the Gold Coast," p. 207.

28. Sarpong, *Ghana in Retrospect*, p. 133.

29. Bernard Williams, *Morality: An Introduction to Ethics* (Harper & Row, New York, 1972), p. 70.

30. G. J. Warnock, *The Object of Morality* (Methuen, London, 1971), Chap. 2.
31. Ibid., p. 21.
32. Ibid.; also p. 27.
33. Ibid., p. 26.
34. J. L. Mackie, *Ethics: Inventing Right and Wrong* (Penguin, London, 1977), p. 108.
35. J. G. Christaller, *Dictionary*, p. 513.
36. Sarpong, "Aspects," p. 44; my italics.
37. Corliss Lamont, *The Philosophy of Humanism*, p. 115; my italics.

9. Ethics and character

1. J. B. Danquah, *Akan Doctrine of God*, p. 204.
2. J. G. Christaller, *Dictionary*, p. 46.
3. Jack Berry, *English, Twi, Asante, Fante Dictionary*, p. 24.
4. Ibid., pp. 23, 82.
5. W. D. Ross, *Aristotle* (Methuen, London, 1923), p. 187.
6. E. A. A. Adegbola, "The Theological Basis of Ethics," in K. A. Dickson and Paul Ellingworth (eds.), *Biblical Revelation and African Beliefs* (Orbis Books, Maryknoll, N.Y., 1969), pp. 119–20, 129–30.
7. The word *nneyẽe*, deeds, has also been used to translate "habits." *A Dictionary of English-Twi* (Basel Missionary Society, Basel, 1909), p. 89; "habitual" is rendered as *ayẽ ne su*, that is, "it has become his character."
8. Christaller, p. 214; *ka hõ*: to remain in an unchanged form or condition.
9. Ibid., p. 595.
10. Ibid., p. 376.
11. John S. Mbiti, *African Religions and Philosophy*, p. 279.
12. Sarpong, "Aspects," p. 40.
13. Berry, *Dictionary*, p. 42.
14. Thus, W. E. Abraham wrote that the "*sunsum* . . . is educable." *The Mind of Africa*, p. 60.
15. Aristotle, *Nicomachean Ethics*, 1103^{b}26.
16. Erich Fromm, *Man for Himself* (Greenwich Press, Conn., 1947), p. 42; italics in original.

10. The individual and the social order

1. Aristotle actually said "political" (Greek: *politikon*), by which he meant "social."
2. The idea here is that the person scraping the bark of a tree for

medicine needs some other person to collect the pieces so that they do not fall down or scatter about.

3. J. A. Annobil, translated from his book, *Mmebusem Nkyerɛkyerɛmu* (*Proverbs and Their Explanations*, Cape Coast, 1971), p. 29.
4. J. G. Christaller, *Dictionary*, p. 510 (*ti*).

11. Philosophy, logic, and the Akan language

1. R. Carnap, *Philosophy and Logical Syntax* (Kegan Paul, London, 1935), p. 78.
2. W. V. O. Quine, *From a Logical Point of View* (Harvard University Press, Cambridge, Mass., 1953), p. 61; *Word and Object* (MIT Press, Cambridge, Mass., 1960), p. 80.
3. G. Ryle, "Ordinary Language," *Philosophical Review*, Vol. LVII, 1953, pp. 167–86.
4. L. J. Cohen, "Are Philosophical Theses Relative to Language?" *Analysis*, Vol. IX, April 1949, pp. 72–7.
5. P. F. Strawson, *Introduction to Logical Theory* (Methuen, London, 1952), esp. Chap. 1, Pt. 1.
6. Hans Hahn, "Conventionalism" in Gary Iseminger (ed.), *Logic and Philosophy* (Appleton-Century-Crofts, New York, 1968), pp. 45ff.
7. Arthur Pap, "Laws of Logic," in ibid., pp. 52ff.
8. David Mitchell, *An Introduction to Logic* (Hutchinson, London, 1962), pp. 120ff.
9. Arthur Pap, *Elements of Analytic Philosophy* (Macmillan, New York, 1949), p. 254.
10. Jerome Shaffer, "Mind–Body Problem," in Paul Edwards (ed.), *Encyclopedia of Philosophy* (Macmillan, New York, 1967), Vol. V, p. 336.
11. C. Lewy, "Is the Notion of Disembodied Existence Self-Contradictory?" *Proceedings of the Aristotelian Society*, n.s. Vol. XLIII, pp. 59ff.
12. Pap, *Elements*, p. 254.
13. It is interesting to note that in Akan conceptualizations, the belief in the ɔkra (soul) is *not* inferred from certain expressions in the language. The concept of the ɔkra, thought to be a spiritual substance, could obviously not have been deduced from the abundance of physicalistic expressions in the Akan language.
14. Carnap, *Philosophy*, p. 43.
15. Cohen, p. 76.
16. John S. Mbiti, *African Religions and Philosophy*, pp. 22–3.
17. J. G. Christaller, *A Grammar of the Asante and Fante Language Called Twi* (Akan) (Basel, 1875), p. 83.
18. Ofei Ayisi, *Twi Proverbs* (Waterville Publishing House, Accra, 1966), proverb no. 100 (Twi is a dialect of Akan).

19. J. H. Kwabena Nketiah, *Akan Funeral Dirges* (Achimota, 1966), p. 120.
20. J. H. Kwabena Nketiah, *Anwonsēm* (Afram Publications [Ghana], Accra, 1975), p. 27.
21. Mbiti, p. 21; my italics.
22. *Atoapem* is one of the epithets of the Supreme Being.
23. J. B. Danquah, *Akan Doctrine of God*, p. 47. This book is the source of the information on the personal characteristics associated with birthdays. See ibid., pp. 47–8.
24. Mbiti, p. 21.
25. Ibid., p. 23.
26. Ibid.
27. Christaller, *A Grammar*, p. 59; also p. 161.
28. Ibid., p. 85.
29. J. G. Christaller, *Dictionary*, p. 428.
30. Nketiah, *Anwonsēm*, p. 28.
31. Mbiti, p. 23.
32. Ibid., p. 30.
33. Nketiah, *Anwonsēm*, p. 29.
34. Mbiti, pp. 224–33.
35. Ibid., p. 225.
36. Ibid., p. 232.
37. Ibid., p. 289.
38. Matthew, 6:34.
39. Mbiti, p. 21.
40. Aristotle, *Metaphysics*, 1017'33–5.
41. Charles H. Kahn, "The Greek Verb 'To Be' and the Concept of Being," *Foundations of Language*, Vol. II, 1966, p. 250.
42. G. E. L. Owen, "Aristotle on the Snares of Ontology," in R. Bambrough (ed.), *New Essays on Plato and Aristotle* (Routledge and Kegan Paul, London, 1965), pp. 84ff.
43. A. C. Graham, " 'Being' in Linguistics and Philosophy," *Foundations of Language*, Vol. 1, 1965, p. 224.
44. Of course, there is a dispute of long standing in Western philosophy as to whether existence is a logical predicate. The general view is that it is not. But see Kwame Gyekye, "A Note on Existence as a Predicate," *Second Order*, Vol. III, No. 2, July 1974, pp. 97–101.
45. J. G. Christaller, *Dictionary*, p. 560.
46. L. A. Boadi, "Existential Sentences in Akan," *Foundations of Language*, Vol. 7, 1971, p. 19.
47. Thus, Charles H. Kahn, "The Greek Verb 'To be' " p. 258, said that there is a "close connection between the ideas of existence and location in Greek philosophical thought." John Lyons also wrote: "In fact, the existential 'be' copula does not normally occur in

English without a locative or temporal complement; and it might appear reasonable to say that *all existential sentences are at least implicitly locative. . . .*" John Lyons, "A Note on Possessive, Existential and Locative Sentences," *Foundations of Language*, Vol. III, 1967, p. 390; my italics.

48. The second *ne* in "Owusu ne *ne* din" is genitive.
49. Christaller, *Grammar*, p. 110.
50. P. F. Strawson, "Proper Names," *Proceedings of the Aristotelian Society*, Suppl. Vol. XXXI, 1957, p. 193. The same doctrine appears in his *Individuals, An Essay in Descriptive Metaphysics* (Doubleday, New York, 1963), pp. 143–6.
51. Ibid., "Proper Names," p. 196; *Individuals*, p. 153.
52. Ibid., "Proper Names," pp. 193–4; my italics.
53. Ibid., p. 194.
54. It is strange indeed why Strawson fastens on the third person singular "walks." If he had chosen the first or second person (singular and plural), he might have arrived at different conclusions, for we can say "walk!" (imperative) or "walk?" (interrogative).
55. Strawson, "Proper Names," p. 195, n. 3.
56. This section on the subject and predicate was inspired by the two papers of Tsu-Lin Mei, "Subject and Predicate, A Grammatical Preliminary," *Philosophical Review*, Vol. LXX, April 1961, pp. 153–75, and "Chinese Grammar and the Linguistic Movement," *Review of Metaphysics*, Vol. XIV, No. 3, March 1961, pp. 487–92. In both papers, Tsu-Lin Mei rejects Strawson's conclusions as invalid in respect of Chinese grammar.
57. Tsu-Lin Mei's arguments are in the two papers of his referred to at the preceding note.
58. E. J. Lemmon, *Beginning Logic* (Nelson, London, 1971), p. 6; my italics, except for the word "English."

III. Toward an African philosophy

12. On the idea of African philosophy

1. In *Second Order*, Vol. IV, No. 1, January 1975, p. 86.
2. John S. Mbiti, *African Religions and Philosophy*, p. 2; my italics.
3. Ibid.
4. Ibid.
5. Ibid., p. 271.
6. Malcolm J. McVeigh, *God in Africa*, p. 5; also p. 142.
7. Michael Gelfand, *An African's Religion: The Spirit of Nyajena* (Juta, Capetown, 1966), pp. 110–17.

8. Daryll Forde (ed.), *African Worlds* (Oxford University Press, Oxford, 1954), p. x; my italics.
9. Ibid., p. xiii; my italics.
10. Daryll Forde, "The Cultural Map of West Africa," in Simon Ottenberg and Phoebe Ottenberg (eds.), *Cultures and Societies of Africa* (Random House, New York, 1960), p. 123; my italics.
11. M. Fortes and E. E. Evans-Pritchard (eds.), *African Political Systems* (Oxford University Press, Oxford, 1940), p. 1.
12. E. G. Parrinder, *African Traditional Religion* (Harper & Row, New York, 1962), p. 11.
13. Quoted in Parrinder, p. 11.
14. K. A. Busia, *Africa in Search of Democracy*, p. 4; my italics.
15. K. A. Busia, "The African World-View," p. 149; my italics.
16. John V. Taylor, *The Primal Vision* (SCM Press, London, 1963), p. 27.
17. E. Bolaji Idowu, *African Traditional Religion: A Definition* (SCM Press, London, 1973), p. 103.
18. J. H. Kwabena Nketiah, "Traditional Festivals in Ghana," in *Sankofa* (Accra), Vol. 1, 1977, p. 14.
19. Kenneth L. Little, *The Mende of Sierra Leone* (Routledge and Kegan Paul, London, 1967), p. 7.
20. Forde (ed.), *African Worlds*, p. 210.
21. Ibid., pp. 138, 140.
22. Ibid., p. 27, n. 1.
23. Godfrey Wilson, "An African Morality," in Ottenberg and Ottenberg (eds.), *Culutres and Societies*, p. 346; my italics.
24. M. Fortes, *Oedipus and Job in West African Religion* (Cambridge University Press, Cambridge, 1959), pp. 24–5; my italics.
25. Bibliographical citations will necessarily be limited by lack of space.
26. Busia, *Africa in Search of Democracy*, p. 5.
27. Mbiti, p. 37; also McVeigh, p. 16; Parrinder, pp. 32ff.
28. Edwin Smith (ed.), *African Ideas of God: A Symposium* (Edinburgh House Press, London, 1950), p. 7.
29. Mbiti, p. 43.
30. Ibid., p. 102; also Parrinder, pp. 23, 43ff; McVeigh, pp. 32ff; Forde (ed.), *African Worlds*; Monica Wilson, *Religion and the Transformation of Society* (Cambridge University Press, Cambridge, 1971), pp. 26–7.
31. Mbiti, p. 105.
32. M. Fortes, "Some Reflections on Ancestor Worship in Africa," in M. Fortes and G. Dieterlen (eds.), *African Systems of Thought* (Oxford University Press, Oxford, 1965), p. 122; also McVeigh, p. 34; Mbiti, p. 107ff.
33. Parrinder, p. 57. African scholars, however, argue that "ancestor worship" is a misnomer. Idowu, for instance, wrote that "ancestor worship" was not worship but only a veneration. E. Bolaji Idowu,

African Traditional Religion, A Definition (SCM Press, London, 1973), pp. 178–89.

34. Mbiti, p. 21.
35. Ibid., p. 257.
36. Ibid., pp. 37–49.
37. Ibid., p. 80.
38. Ibid., pp. 55, 84–6; also Parrinder, p. 33.
39. McVeigh, p. 139.
40. Ibid., p. 103.
41. Mbiti, p. 74; also p. 97.
42. Ibid., pp. 261–2; also p. 222. See also Forde (ed.), *African Worlds*, pp. 8, 173; Robin Horton in Bryan R. Wilson, *Rationality*, p. 133.
43. John S. Mbiti, "The Capture of the Sun," in *Modern Science and Moral Values* (International Cultural Foundation, New York, 1983), p. 191; my italics.
44. McVeigh, p. 164.
45. Ibid., p. 230, n. 57.
46. Monica Wilson, p. 38.
47. Ibid., p. 141.
48. Forde (ed.), *African Worlds*, p. 168; McVeigh, p. 163; Mbiti, p. 262; J. O. Sodipo, "Notes on the Concept of Cause and Chance in Yoruba Traditional Thought," *Second Order*, Vol. II, No. 2, July 1973.
49. M. Fortes, "Some Reflections," p. 126.
50. Forde (ed.), *African Worlds*, p. 227.
51. Marcel Griaule, "The Idea of Person among the Dogon," in Ottenberg and Ottenberg (eds.), *Cultures and Societies*, p. 366.
52. Forde (ed.), *African Worlds*, p. 174.
53. Ottenberg and Ottenberg (eds.), *Cultures and Societies*, p. 408.
54. E. Bolaji Idowu, *Olodumare*, pp. 169–70.
55. Forde (ed.), *African Worlds*, pp. 115, 155.
56. McVeigh, p. 26.
57. Ibid., p. 37.
58. Ibid., p. 130; also p. 144.
59. Kwesi A. Dickson, *Aspects of Religion and Life in Africa*, p. 3.
60. Mbiti, p. 52; my italics.
61. Fortes, *Job and Oedipus*, p. 19.
62. Mbiti, p. 52; also Forde (ed.), *African Worlds*, pp. 168ff.
63. Idowu, *Olodumare*, p. 173; italics in original.
64. Forde (ed.), *African Worlds*, pp. 9, 169, 228.
65. Mbiti, pp. 226–67; also Forde (ed.), *African Worlds*, pp. 43, 75.
66. McVeigh, pp. 128–9; also Forde (ed.), *African Worlds*, pp. 160–1.
67. Mbiti, p. 47; Forde (ed.), *African Worlds*, p. 169.
68. J. J. Maquet, "The Kingdom of Ruanda," in Forde (ed.), *African Worlds*, p. 172.

69. Ibid., p. 169.
70. W. E. Abraham, *The Mind of Africa*, p. 55; J. B. Danquah, *Akan Doctrine of God*, p. 153; C. A. Akrofi, *Twi Proverbs*, proverb no. 192.
71. Akrofi, *Twi Proverbs*, proverb No. 193; J. G. Christaller, *A Collection of 3,600 Twi Proverbs*, proverbs nos. 227–35; J. A. Annobil, *Proverbs and Their Explanations*, p. 88.
72. Christaller, *Proverbs*, proverb no. 2284; Akfrofi, *Twi Proverbs*, proverb no. 722.
73. John Middleton and E. H. Winter, *Witchcraft and Sorcery in East Africa* (Routledge and Kegan Paul, London, 1963), p. 1, et passim.
74. Ibid., p. vii.
75. H. Debrunner, *Witchcraft in Ghana*, p. 2.
76. Mbiti, p. 232.
77. Ibid., pp. 224ff; also J. H. M. Beattie and John Middleton (eds.), *Spirit Mediumship and Society in Africa* (Africana Publishing Corp., New York, 1969).
78. Parrinder, p. 119; also pp. 100–34.
79. Mbiti, p. 1.
80. Ibid., p. 38.
81. Busia, *Africa in Search of Democracy*, p. 1.
82. Ibid., p. 7.
83. Idowu, *Olodumare*, p. 5.
84. E. Bolaji Idowu, "The Study of Religion, with Special Reference to African Traditional Religion," *Orita, Ibadan Journal of Religion*, Vol. I, No. 1, June 1967, p. 11.
85. Bede Onuoha, *The Elements of African Socialism* (Andre Deutsch, London, 1965), p. 35.
86. McVeigh, p. 103.
87. Parrinder, p. 9.
88. Monica Wilson, p. 98; my italics.
89. K. A. Dickson, *Aspects of Religion and Life in Africa*, pp. 3–4; my italics.
90. Busia, *Africa in Search of Democracy*, p. 10.
91. Ibid., p. 16.
92. E. G. Parrinder, *Religion in Africa*, pp. 28–9.
93. Parrinder, *African Traditional Religion*, p. 146.
94. Idowu, *Olodumare*, p. 146.
95. Godfrey Wilson, "An African Morality," p. 348.
96. Monica Wilson, p. 98; also pp. 76–7.
97. J. J. Maquet, in Forde, p. 184.
98. Forde (ed.), *African Worlds*, p. 134.
99. Parrinder, p. 27.
100. Busia, *Africa in Search of Democracy*, p. 15; my italics.
101. Benjamin C. Ray, *African Religions* (Prentice-Hall, Englewood Cliffs,

N.J., 1976), p. 146; also Forde (ed.), *African Worlds*, pp. 62, 160–1, 183, 207.

102. McVeigh, p. 90.
103. For the definition of "revealed religion," see above p. 135.
104. Idowu, *Olodumare*, p. 146; my italics.
105. McVeigh, p. 84; also Forde (ed.), *African Worlds*, pp. 78–80, 134, 184; Monica Wilson, p. 98.
106. S. M. Molema, *The Bantu: Past and Present* (Edinburgh University Press, Edinburgh, 1920), p. 116.
107. Mbiti, p. 84; also Idowu, *Olodumare*, p. 116.
108. Aylward Shorter, *Prayers in the Religious Traditions of Africa* (Oxford University Press, Nairobi, 1975), p. 44.
109. Ibid., p. 60f.
110. Monica Wilson, p. 173.
111. Sometimes the word "communism" may be found particularly in older books, but this should not be given the connotation of modern communism as practiced in, say, the Soviet Union. The word "collectivism" is occasionally used by some writers in place of "communalism."
112. K. A. Dickson, *Aspects of Religion and Life in Africa*, p. 4; my italics.
113. Edwin Smith, *The Golden Stool: Some Aspects of the Conflicts of Cultures in Modern Africa* (CMS, London, 1927), p. 214.
114. Molema, p. 115.
115. Léopold S. Senghor, *On African Socialism*, trans. Mercer Cook (Praeger, New York, 1964), pp. 93–4, italics in original; see also Mbiti, p. 141.
116. Sékou Touré, in *Présence Africaine*, Nos. 24–5, February–May 1959, p. 118; quoted by Claude Wauthier, *The Literature and Thought of Modern Africa* (Heinemann, London, 1978), p. 173.
117. Jomo Kenyatta, *Facing Mount Kenya* (Vintage, New York, 1965), p. 297.
118. Ibid., p. 188.
119. William Conton, *The African* (Signet, New York, 1961), p. 95.
120. Fred G. Burke, "Tanganyika: The Search for Ujamaa," in William H. Friedland and Carl G. Rosberg (eds.), *African Socialism* (Stanford University Press, Stanford, 1964), p. 207.
121. Adolphe L. Cureau, *Savage Man in Central Africa: A Study of Primitive Races in the French Congo*, trans. E. Andrews (T. Fisher Unwin, London, 1915), p. 270.
122. Senghor, p. 94.
123. Ibid.; also Mbiti, p. 141.
124. Ralph M. McInerny, *Thomism in an Age of Renewal* (University of Notre Dame Press, Notre Dame, 1968), p. 17; my italics.

Name index

239

Name index

Danquah, J. B., 16, 19, 89, 90–1, 108, 111, 130, 135, 147
Dasgupta, S., 214n26, 215n5
Dawson, Nana, 229n46
Debrunner, H., 93, 202
Descartes, René, 10, 49, 87, 100
Dewey, John, 39
Dickson, K. A., 117, 199, 204, 208
Dieterlen, G., 235n32
Dorson, Richard M., 215n15
Drachler, Jacob, 214n13
Duprée, E., 216n29

Evans, Henri, 214n21
Evans-Pritchard, E. E., 191–3, 202
Ewing, A. C., 5, 43

Fagg, William, 13
Fakhry, Majid, 218n83
al-Fārābī, 11, 22
Field, G. C., 217n62
Finnegan, Ruth, 17
Forde, Daryll, 45, 191–3
Fortes, M., 191, 193, 195–6, 198–9
Frege, G., 181
Freud, Sigmund, 92, 98, 102
Friedland, William H., 238n120
Fromm, Erich, 153

Geach, Peter T., 224n7, 230n21
Gelfand, M., 192
Georr, Khalil, 22
al-Ghazālī, 223n24
Gilson, E., 22
Gjertsen, Derek, 44–5
Goody, Jack, 191
Gould, Thomas, 92
Graham, A. C., 198
Griaule, M., 236n51
Grunebaum, G. E. von, 218n67
Guthrie, W. K. C., 23, 217n50
Gyekye, Kwame, 216n30, 217n61, 223n24, 227n54

Hagan, George P., 109, 110
Hahn, Hans, 163
Hamlyn, D. W., 6
Hardie, W. F. R., 27
Hegel, G. W. F., 29, 39
Heraclitus, 23

Herskovits, Melville J., 13, 191
Homer, 27
Horton, Robin, 3–8, 44–6, 50
Hountondji, Paulin J., 8–9, 25, 35–6, 46
Hume, David, 25, 29, 100

Idowu, E. Bolaji, 14, 194, 204, 207
Iseminger, Gary, 232n6

Kagamé, Alexis, 31
Kahn, Charles E., 178
Kenyatta, Jomo, 209
Kirk, G. S., 23
Kneale, Martha, 217n58
Kneale, William, 217n58
Kudadjie, J. N., 131
Kuper, Hilda, 193

Lamont, Corliss, 143–5
Laye, Camara, 209
Leibniz, G., 19, 116
Lemmon, E. J., 185
Lewy, C., 164
Lienhardt, G., 191
Lincoln, C. Eric, 223n12
Lindsay, A. D., 226n35
Little, Kenneth, 194
Lloyd, G. E. R., 217n58
Locke, John, 25, 29
Lyons, John, 233n47
Lystad, Robert A., 98

McInerny, Ralph M., 238n124
Mackie, J. L., 140
McVeigh, Malcolm J., 197–9, 201, 204, 206–7
Magee, Bryan, 214n10
Mahdi, Muhsin, 218n67
Mansion, S., 216n29
Maquet, J. J., 201, 205
Marx, Karl, 36, 39
Mauthner, 217n59
Mbiti, John S., 14, 17, 31, 70, 73–4, 93, 151, 169, 170–7, 185, 190–1, 196–9, 200, 202–3
Mei, Tsu-Lin, 185, 234nn56,57
Meyerowitz, Eva L. R., 47, 50, 90, 108, 111
Mframa, Kwaku, 74

240

Name index

Middleton, John, 202
Minkus, Helaine, 74, 112
Mitchell, David, 163
Molema, S. M., 207, 209

Nielsen, Kai, 230n21
Nketiah, J. H. Kwabena, 194, 223n

Okere, T., 28
Onuoha, Bede, 204
Opoku, A. A., 228n19
Opoku, Kofi Asare, 115, 129
Oruka, H. Odera, 218n75
Ottenberg, Phoebe, 215n4, 236n51
Ottenberg, Simon, 215n4, 236n51
Owen, G. E. L., 178

Pap, Arthur, 163, 165
Parmenides, 15, 180
Parrinder, E. G., 13, 53, 73–5, 90, 92,
     192–3, 196, 202, 204, 205
Pines, S., 22
Plato, 10, 11, 15, 18, 25, 28, 30, 36,
     39, 49, 92, 138, 178, 180
Plotinus, 22
Porphyry, 216nn26,30
Pythagoras, 62, 177, 180

Quine, W. V. O., 5, 163

Radcliffe-Brown, A. R., 191–2
Raju, P. T., 22, 56
Ramsey, Ian T., 230n21
Rattray, R. S., 14–15, 47, 74, 90–1,
     94–6, 191
Ray, Benjamin C., 206
Raz, J., 219n90
Rosberg, Carl G., 238n120
Ross, W. D., 231n5
Russell, Bertrand, 26
Ryle, G., 163

Saint-Simon, C.-H., 39
Sandman, Manfred, 29

Sarpong, Peter K., 108, 111–12, 115,
     130, 134–5, 139, 142, 151
Senghor, Leopold S., 209–10
Shaffer, Jerome, 163
Shorey, Paul, 92
Shorter, Aylward, 208
Sidorsky, David, 218n85
Smith, Edwin, 192, 207–8
Socrates, 10, 25, 35, 49, 138
Sodipo, J. O., 236n48
Sontag, Frederick, 4
Steward, J. A., 15
Strawson, Peter, 163, 181–5
Sumner, Claude, 214n24

Taylor, John V., 193
Taylor, Richard, 4
al-Ṭayyib, Ibn, 216nn26,30
Thales, 26
Thompson, Robert F., 49
Touré, Sékou, 209
Trotter, Wilfred, 226n38
Twumasi, Patrick A., 225n11
Twum-Barima, Opanin, 226n44

Ullman, Stephen, 217n59

Valentine, Charles W., 92

Warnock, G. J., 140
Warren, D. M., 49
Wauthier, Claude, 238n116
Wheelwright, Philip E., 216nn28,39
Williams, Bernard, 87, 140
Wilson, Bryan R., 219n1
Wilson, Godfrey, 195, 205
Wilson, Monica, 204–5, 208
Winter, E. H., 202
Wiredu, Kwasi, 8, 32, 34–6, 41, 47,
     66, 86–7, 105, 117
Wittgenstein, Ludwig, 7
Wright, Richard A., 218n70

241

Subject index

242

Subject index

243

Subject index

innate faculty, 62
 ideas, 202
Islamic philosophy, *see* philosophy

language
 and metaphysics, 105
 and thought, 29, 32
laws of nature, 78–9, 83
life after death, 86, 99, 175, 199, 203
logic, 3, 5–7, 50
 and language, 32, 163, 185

magical powers, 73–4
materialism, 47, 165–6, 168, 186
matter as passive, 75
meaning of life, 8, 15
mental faculty, 61
metaphysics, 4–5, 7, 22, 44, 49, 68, 97,
 139, 143–4, 165, 195
 Akan, 86, 89, 100, 103
mind, concept of, 88, 203
mind–body problem, 163–8, 186
mogya (blood), 94, 99, 119
morality
 acquisition of moral virtues, 150–2
 definition of, 130
 humanistic basis of Akan, 132,
  143–4
 moral intuitions, 136, 138
 moral motivation, 139, 140–1
 moral practice, 138, 141–3
 moral psychology, 141
 moral sanctions, 138–9, 140–1
 moral sense, 126, 142
 moral will, 126–7, 142–3
 nonsupernaturalistic foundation of
  Akan, 41, 132, 134–5
 and religion, 129–30, 138, 204–5,
  207
mystical power (activity), 69, 72–4, 88,
 103, 175, 198
mysticism, 5
myth, 9, 13–16, 22, 33, 51, 113–14,
 193
musuo (great evil), 133–4

natural phenomena, 26, 68–9, 75, 79,
 83, 196–7
naturalistic explanation, 80
nipadua (body, human frame), 10, 85

nkrabea (destiny), 48, 104, 107–9,
 110–12, 117, 121, 127
nneyẽe (actions), 126, 150–1
nonsupernaturalistic foundation of
 Akan morality, 41, 132, 134–5
ntoro (semen-transmitted characteristic),
 94, 119
nyansa (wisdom), 61–2, 65–6

ōkra (soul), 10, 20, 47–8, 85–102, 104,
 110–11, 117, 168
ontic unity, 98
ontology, 5, 30–1, 69, 165–6
 African, 196–7
 hierarchical character of Akan, 69,
  70, 76, 83
 ontological argument, 180–1, 186
 ontological pluralism, 69, 76, 196
 ontological problems as basic in
  philosophy, 5
Onyame (God, Supreme Being),
 14–15, 48, 54, 68–9, 70–3, 75–8,
 85, 110, 118, 123, 131, 136, 155
oral literature, 13
 tradition, 10

panpsychism, 75
pantheism, 15, 74–5
paranormal cognition, 6, 41, 201, 203
parapsychology, 203
person, concept of, 8, 10, 47–8, 50, 85,
 89, 94, 100–1, 103, 119, 166,
 198–9
personality, 48, 89–90, 93, 97, 102,
 111, 149, 158, 161, 172, 198–9,
 210
philosophos, 62
philosophy
 African, 2, 8–11, 24–5, 32–6, 42–3,
  52–3, 57
 Akan conception of, 61–7
 British, 25
 Cartesian, 87
 definition of, 4, 7–9, 11, 51
 Greek, 6, 23–8, 35, 48, 177
 Indian, 5, 11, 22, 24, 28, 43
 as interpretation of human
  experience, 8, 10, 18, 21
 Islamic 5, 22, 24, 37–8, 42, 75
 and language, 163, 169

244

Subject index

Subject index